Camp free in B.C.

Volume One: British Columbia from Trans-Canada Hwy 1 to the U.S. Border, Vancouver Island to the Rocky Mountains.

Explored and written by Kathy & Craig Copeland

Voice in the Wilderness Press, Inc.
Riondel, British Columbia

Second Edition

First edition, March 1995
Updated, revised Second Edition, March 1997

Published by Voice in the Wilderness Press, Inc.
              P.O. Box 71, Riondel, British Columbia
              Canada V0B 2B0

Cover design by Kerry Reynolds

Typeset/Production by Shari Boucher, C.J. Chiarizia

Maps by C.J. Chiarizia

Photos by Kathy and Craig Copeland

Canadian Cataloguing in Publication Data

Copeland, Craig, 1955 -
   Camp free in B.C.

   Partial contents: v. 1, British Columbia from Trans-Canada
Hwy 1 to the U.S. border, Vancouver Island to the Rocky
Mountains.
   Includes index.
   ISBN 0-9698016-2-9 (v. 1)

   1. Camping—British Columbia—Guidebooks. 2. British
Columbia—Guidebooks. I. Copeland, Kathy, 1959- II. Title.
GV191.46.B7C66 1995   796.54'09711   C95-910165-9

Printed and Bound in Canada

ACKNOWLEDGEMENTS

First, we thank *you*. We appreciate anyone who's adventurous enough to buy this book and get out in the wilds and use it.

We also thank both our parents. They've always been understanding about our love of exploration, even though it's kept us from visiting them very often.

And we thank each other. To create *Camp Free*, we endured long drives on rough roads; days without exercise, showers or proper meals; arguments incited by discomfort and close quarters; the endless recording of niggling details, when we just wanted to cut loose; then months of sitting indoors, writing, while we ached to be outside. It took a lot of energy and determination to achieve this goal. Please excuse our chest-pounding, but each of us thinks the other deserves it.

So, here you go. Whether you're a fanatic explorer or a once-a-summer camper, we offer you the product of our passion and perseverance, in hope it will enrich your journeys.

CONTENTS

Philosophy, Strategies and Joys of Camping Free

Peering down at Khartoum Lake from the road, Sunshine Coast

The Antidote for Civilization

British Columbia has more than a thousand free campgrounds — tucked into immense forests, in the shadows of noble mountains, beside dancing rivers, snuggled up to lakes grand and petite.

Go. They're waiting. You'll savor a fresh perspective on the stunning geography of our glorious province. You'll be astonished at where B.C.'s seemingly endless network of backroads can take you. Just getting your tires off the pavement is fun. Though there's a lot to see from the highways, there's much more beyond. Even with our directions, you'll feel the excitement of discovery. It's a rush. Everyone should experience it.

You'll find some free campgrounds are as well-organized and maintained as any provincial park. Others are unknown, except to a few adventurous outdoorspeople and a handful of locals. Many are seldom visited and offer you what has become a rare treat: solitude. Most are hidden just a short distance off paved roads. And they're all free.

Free. Available to you whenever the urge strikes. Just show up, pick your spot, and camp. And because most of these campgrounds are away from towns and highways, you're likely to see an owl, a coyote, a bear, a salmon — sights that thrill and comfort, reminding you that despite the damage done, wilderness still exists and nature is alive and well.

That's the joy of free-camping. Not just what you keep in your wallet, but what you take away in your heart.

Free-camping is CPR for your senses. It opens your eyes to the night sky, with stars so thick they look like clouds. It opens your ears to the music of wind in the pines, water rushing over rocks, or maybe absolute silence. It reacquaints you with the simple, sweet pleasure of *not* feeling cement under foot, *not* being confined by fences or walls, *not* complying with rules, and, sometimes, *not* having to look at another human being. It's the antidote for civilization. It reminds you that free isn't just a word screaming at you from advertisements, it's a way to live.

Free-camping is *real* camping. It's an adventure — something sadly missing from most people's lives. And they certainly don't find it at private, pay campgrounds. Neon signs? Reception offices? Pop machines? Hook-ups? TV antennas? Where's the adventure in that? It's hard to tell many campgrounds from RV dealerships these days.

They're just parking lots. Even provincial park campgrounds are often within earshot of a roaring highway.

Yes, free-camping, real camping, requires you to forgo some modern conveniences. But you might be surprised to find a lot of what you thought were necessities, you can do without. And doing without somehow leaves you feeling more complete.

You'll also have to contend with the elements — wind, rain, bugs, cold — but if you're prepared, and can look beyond any minor discomfort, you'll feel more alive because of it.

With an open mind and an open heart, chances are you'll have a soul-stirring experience. You'll be revitalized, able to calmly slip back into the shackles of civilization with renewed vigor. Your memory, your mental gallery, will be filled with priceless, unforgettable images that will help sustain you until your next outing. If nothing else, you'll have an interesting story to tell your neighbors and co-workers who've never sought adventure beyond the nearest video store.

The view from Eagles Roost campground on the Chilliwack River

GET OUT WHILE YOU CAN

Free-camping is becoming more difficult. Twenty years ago it was easy. A short drive from any city would reward you with lots of beautiful places to park where nobody would bother you. But rampant development and population growth have overtaken those of us who would flee. Now you have to drive hours, and still you'll be contending with country homes, resorts, farms and ranches that make it almost impossible to free-camp — unless you know where to go.

That's why we wrote this book: to tell you about the wonderful, free campgrounds in British Columbia, explain exactly where they are and how to get there, and encourage you to enjoy and protect them.

We know there's a need for information like this, because we traveled throughout B.C. for years before accidentally stumbling on an official, free campground on the Nahatlatch River. Later we found more along the Chilliwack River. We gave thanks to the Camping God. Then it dawned on us. If we were unaware of these free campgrounds after all our explorations, other people were too. That was the beginning of our quest to create *Camp Free in B.C.* Until then, we'd free-camped in all kinds of weird, noisy, uncomfortable spots, many of which, we now realize, were only minutes from an established, free campground that would have made our night far more pleasant.

Too many people — perhaps you're among them — struggle to find places to pitch their tent or park their RV for a night without having to pay ten to twenty bucks for the privilege. We see it all the time. On our way to Sugar Lake, for example, we met a young European couple vacationing with their two kids, traveling across B.C. in a rented motorhome. They parked overnight at a pullout, only a few feet off the pavement, next to an ugly gravel pit. They settled for such a dismal spot because it was late, they were tired, and were uncertain where else to go. Too bad. Just across the highway, an unsigned, dirt road led to an official, free campground. Surrounded by trees, next to the Shuswap River, it was less than a mile away. Had they known, they would have been safer and enjoyed their stay infinitely more.

Now you have more choices. *Camp Free in B.C.* is your guide to official, free campgrounds, good overnight pullouts off quiet backroads, and other patches of public land claimed by the continuing, natural flow of free campers. The majority are Forest Service Recreation Sites. But who knows how long they'll remain free? Better get out there and take full advantage of them while you still can.

THE MAP IS NOT THE TERRITORY

Free campgrounds are rarely on paved roads. And you'll almost never see a sign on a paved road telling you there's a free campground in the area. It's only after you've driven onto a backroad that you'll encounter a sign, typically *way* after. Sometimes the only marker you'll see is a signpost at the campground. Occasionally campgrounds are unsigned. All of which makes *Camp Free* invaluable. There's no other resource like this.

A sign or signpost marks the entry to many Forest Service campgrounds.

Most Forest Service (FS) districts have yet to compile recreation atlases describing each campground and how to get there. A few, like Cranbrook and Kootenay, have. When available, these are worth consulting. You might also want to get the FS recreation maps. All districts offer these free of charge, and you'll find the addresses and phone numbers listed in the back of this book. But while helpful, these maps are crude and lack precise directions. Just figuring out where to turn off the main highway is a challenge, because the maps don't specify which FS road leads to each campground. And they give no indication of the numerous switchbacks and junctions you'll encounter.

Using FS maps, we were reminded: the map is not the territory. Even with maps, you need the skills of an explorer and the instincts of a detective to find the campgrounds. You're much better off with this book. It's all you really need.

While searching for campgrounds, we were often on edge. "How much longer is this gonna take?" "You *sure* this is the right road?" "Boy, I hope the car can make it." "I don't think there's any campground up here!" Sometimes we felt like rats in a maze. But you won't. Following our directions, you can relax and enjoy the drive knowing you *are* on the right road, your car *can* make it, and there *is* a campground up there.

Because one map was rarely adequate, we often used several, then relied on our intuition to unsnarl the discrepancies. Traveling the Interior Plateau, we worked with three maps, none of which agreed with each other. Whenever possible, we asked locals, hunters, fisherpeople, and gas station attendants for help. Sometimes we visited or called FS offices. All these people were generous with their time and knowledge. Still, we took lots of wrong turns and sometimes drove around like the Keystone Cops until we reached our goal. Fortunately, we have a strong sense of direction and a good feel for geography. Otherwise we might have quit and waited for someone else to pursue this onerous task.

NO PUNCHES PULLED

You can rely on *Camp Free* for detailed directions to many of B.C.'s best free campgrounds, as well as descriptions of what to expect when you get there. How's the scenery? What outdoor activities are possible? We'll tell you. We've even rated each campground. Is it a worthwhile **destination** for an extended stay? Good enough for a **weekend** visit? Or only useful as an **overnight** pullout on your way somewhere else? We'll give you our no-punches-pulled opinion.

Example of the excellent Forest Service campgrounds throughout B.C.

To help you confidently turn off the major highways and forge onto dirt backroads, we state the distance to each campground and the quality of the road. **Easy** means it's a short way and the road is good. **Moderate** means it's a bit farther and the road is fair. **Difficult** means it's a long way or the road is poor. Road surfaces, however, change over time — usually for the worse — so make your own assessment as you go. Keep in mind, we're conservative, cautious drivers, and we managed all these roads in a small, under-powered car. You'll probably be fine. **All the campgrounds listed are accessible by two-wheel drive, low-clearance vehicles.** Only occasionally do we warn motorhome pilots to reconsider.

TURN LEFT AT THE BOULDER

"Any chance I'll get lost?" you ask.

Very little. We've done our best to give explicit directions that should make sense to you now, and will become perfectly clear en route. "Turn left at the boulder" will be a no-brainer once you're out there, in the shadow of a looming boulder the size of a house.

But cut us a little slack. Occasionally we had a tough time. We'd turn around, backtrack and try again. We believe we calculated all our meanderings accurately. We certainly gave it a supreme effort. But it's possible we goofed without knowing. The forests of B.C. conceal a bird's nest of interlaced dirt roads — 32,000 kilometers in total. Without guidebooks or detailed maps, it drove us bonkers at times. So if you run into a discrepancy, bear with us. It's certainly a minor one, and we've probably given enough description to steer you to the campground regardless. Just use your logic and common sense. Poke your nose around the next corner. You'll find it. Remember, free-camping is an adventure. And when you get home, please send us your suggested corrections.

Find out what's happening. Do something about it.

YOU CAN MAKE A DIFFERENCE

The roads to most free campgrounds in B.C. are logging roads. Though logging practices have been irresponsible, keep in mind these campgrounds wouldn't be there, so you probably wouldn't either, if logging companies hadn't built the roads. Ideally, the great wild lands of B.C. would be unscarred, preserved in their original majesty forever. Now the best we can do is get out there and look after what's left. It's a lazy king who never leaves the castle to survey his domain. Just be prepared for disappointment: your forests have been logged rapaciously.

Environmental integrity. Scenic value. Future viability. When you see a clearcut, it's hard to believe any of these were considerations. The good news is that forest practices are supposed to be improving. Low-impact harvesting techniques, like selective logging, can sustain our forests and save forestry jobs. But they won't be implemented if you turn your back. We all need to stand guard. An informed public is an empowered public. If you don't know enough or care enough to hold logging companies and the Ministry of Forests responsible for their actions, who will?

Just by going free-camping, you can make a difference.

On your way, you'll probably drive past a devastated hillside, a cutblock. You might be horrified. But if you think about it, you'll realize the logging company didn't cut those trees to improve the view; they did it in response to public demand. We've all wasted wood and paper products. Now we all have to reduce, reuse and recycle. Paper plates, paper napkins and paper towels, for example, are luxuries we can no longer afford. To take paper plates on a camping trip, and still expect the campground to be surrounded by pristine forest, is an absurd contradiction.

If *Camp Free* encourages you to appreciate and conserve our forests, we'll be gratified. We also hope it spurs you to keep B.C.'s free recreation sites *free*. Considering all the taxes you shell out, all your raw lumber that's been shipped abroad, and all the profits multinational logging companies have pocketed, you shouldn't have to pay to stay at FS campgrounds. You've already paid enough. If the government ever tries to impose camping fees across the province, respond with letters and phone calls. Defend your right to camp free on land already designated for that purpose. Fees for passive recreation, like camping and hiking, are unjust and unnecessary.

HOW TO BE A BACKROADS JOCKEY

Unless you're an experienced backroads jockey, there are a few do's and don'ts to learn before you hit the dirt. The better prepared you are, the more confident and safer you'll be.

• Drive cautiously. You never know who's coming or what's up ahead. It's possible the road has been damaged recently by severe weather or other natural hazards.

• Be patient. Keep your speed down, unless the road is clearly flat and straight for a long way. Even then, there might be holes or rocks you can't see.

• On logging roads, always drive with your headlights on. Obey all posted restrictions. Some active logging roads are closed to the public from 5 a.m. Monday until 8 p.m. Friday. Don't be tempted to sneak in. The closure is for your own safety. Monster logging trucks are belting down those roads.

• Yield to logging trucks or other industrial vehicles. As soon as you see one, pull as far off the road as possible and let it proceed.

• Avoid towing on any but the widest backroads — most are too narrow and contorted for travel trailers.

• Never block the road. If you stop, pull far enough off to allow industrial vehicles to pass at high speed.

• Slow down on washboarded roads. Go too fast and your dash will clack like a player piano. Worse, you could lose traction and slide out of control as your vehicle hops from one ripple to the next.

• Remember to check your fuel supply and engine fluid levels before leaving the highway.

• Carry more food and water than you think you'll need for your camping trip, in case of emergency.

Don't let the logging companies' warning signs scare you off the roads. Except when the area is specifically closed to the public between certain hours, they're just telling you to be aware and drive safely. Sometimes you'll see lots of signs. It can be intimidating. But it doesn't mean you'll be fighting your way upstream against a constant flow of industrial traffic. We rarely saw logging trucks.

We admit, early in our explorations we weren't sure we should be on some of these roads. For instance, on our way to Glacier Creek, on Duncan Lake, a logging company employee in a pickup truck saw us reading a warning sign. He hollered, "You got a radio?" We answered "No." He thought about this and said, "Where ya goin'?" Worried he would force us to turn around, we responded, "Why do you want to know?" He said, "So I can radio ahead for you and see if any trucks are comin'." The road was clear. He smiled and waved us on. That incident proved to us the public is welcome on logging roads. You don't need a radio. His calling ahead was only a courtesy. You just have to know what you're getting into and drive accordingly.

Don't let the signs scare you away. Just drive safely.

TWO-WHEELING IT

These suggestions will be helpful when you're heading for a campground we've labeled *Difficult,* or whenever you run into a stretch of rough, challenging road. But don't be alarmed. Most backroads won't require you to negotiate serious obstacles.

• Before you go, look at your vehicle's underbelly. Get on your knees and really see what's down there. Make note of where you have the least clearance and where you have the most, so you'll know how to straddle rocks.

• When the road looks questionable, it's often the grit of the driver, not the vehicle itself, that determines whether you'll make it. That's not to say you should be bull-headed and plow through come what may. When you assess the road, just be aware of your level of confidence and your capacity for patience. More than once, Kathy's steadfastness pulled us through unscathed after Craig declared the road impassable.

• Faced with deeply worn tracks on the sides of the road, and a high ridge in the middle that might scrape your underbelly, drive with one tire on the ridge and the other outside the track.

• When there's a deep rut across the road, don't approach it straight on. You might bottom-out. Instead, slice across at an angle, from one side of the road toward the other. That way your tires drop into the rut one at a time, instead of both at once.

We didn't have to check this one with a stick.

• Before you splash through a big mud hole, get out and check how deep it is. Feel with a stick, or drop a large stone in and see what happens. That's a lot easier than getting stuck.

• In mud or sand, don't slow to a crawl. You need momentum. If you feel you're getting stuck, don't waste time trying to turn around or you might end up in a bigger mess. Reverse out immediately.

• Know what you're risking. Ask yourself: "How many vehicles have been on the road today? What's the likelihood of seeing another? How far back was the highway? The last possible telephone? The nearest lived-in-looking house?" Consider your worst-case options before you plunge in. It might sway your decision.

HELP IS ON THE WAY

Are you worried about having car trouble on a lonely road? Don't be. Help is probably on the way. Even on roads that seem desolate, someone usually comes along within an hour. There are more locals and outdoorspeople wandering the backcountry than we expected. You'll often cross paths with logging company employees in pickup trucks. Every time we signaled them to stop and asked for directions, they were friendly and glad to assist. If you have a breakdown, loggers all have radios in their vehicles and can call for help. So it's unlikely you'd be stranded long.

LOCAL COLOR

When asked where to turn off for Thalia Lakes, a long-time resident of Tulameen told us, "If you go too far, you'll know it. The valley gets narrow enough ya can chuck a rock acrost it." When we got there, we saw exactly what he meant, and we've never forgotten him or his quirky description.

You'll enrich your free-camping experiences by chatting with the locals along the way. We had to. Often they were our only source of information. But the value of the exchange was not in *what* they told us, but *how* they said it. Some were comical. Others shy. Most were proud to share their knowledge of the area and pleased to meet a visitor interested in more than just passing through as quickly as possible.

Once, we hailed a young man who couldn't have been older than 35. "Is there still a campground on this end of the lake?" we inquired. Wistfully, he slowly shook his head, then replied like an old man, "That's been long gone since I growed up."

Another time we stopped a woman in a tiny, beat-up Toyota, rattling along a backroad. We asked if there was a campground above Christina Lake and what the road was like. She said, "Oh yeah. I was driving this car over the mountains to Rossland when I was five months pregnant and I almost had the kid on the way! But you'll be fine. It doesn't get rough until after the campground."

You'll meet a lot of locals *at* the campgrounds too. Engaging them in conversation can be enlightening and entertaining. It will always give you a better feel for the land you're exploring.

MEN IN TRUCKS KNOW

With this book in hand, you shouldn't need to ask anyone for directions. But when you explore backroads we haven't described, you'll probably want to check your bearings with someone. Before you do, a word of caution: people have widely varying conceptions of what camping is.

Many people don't think FS sites are campgrounds. Even some residents of small towns, who you'd expect to have a more organic bias, believe *campground* means a reception office, manicured grass lawn, electrical hook-ups, indoor washroom with hot showers, and perhaps a playground and small store.

One especially vivid instance of this mindset was when we asked a woman for directions to the free campground at Trout Creek. She emphatically stated there was no free campground, no place at all to camp on the road to Santa Rosa, and nothing anywhere near there called the Old Cascade Highway.

She was so self-assured, we almost bought it. But skepticism kicked in: even if she'd lived there all her life, maybe she didn't know. Followed by logic: even if the sign said Santa Rosa, it had to be the Old Cascade Highway, because it connected major towns. So we started up the steep, narrow road and drove and drove and drove until, sure enough, we found it. Too bad it was so unappealing. We had to persist, though. We didn't want to miss a possible winner.

It was a good reminder to be very specific when asking for directions. You can't assume anything. State the names of roads, geographic features, or other landmarks. Be certain you're both talking about the same thing. Rely on your intuition as much as anyone else's opinion — even if they're locals and should know the area. It's surprising how many people are unaware of what's beyond their backyard.

Look for men in trucks. It sounds like a chauvinistic stereotype, we admit. But we've found men in trucks usually dispense reliable information. They tend to ply the backroads to earn their living, or at least to hunt and fish.

So if you're a man, you're in a truck, and you don't know, you better find out, because here they come.

Typical side road off a main logging road, Sunshine Coast

HOW'S THE ROAD?

Stop four drivers on the same road and you'll get four different impressions of what it's like. Ask "How's the road?" and you'll often hear "It's gravel." Unless you're driving a rugged truck, a 4WD vehicle, or an old beater you don't care about, that's too vague. If you want a detailed road report, ask specific questions. How rough is the road? How steep? How narrow? How muddy? How rocky?

Locals who frequent the backroads are generally quick and direct with their answers. But before you heed anyone's advice, consider the source. Do they seem sensible and mature? Inexperienced and timid? Wild and reckless?

Some four-wheelers are determined to uphold the macho mystique of their off-road rigs. They consider cars an inferior subspecies, little more than go-carts. They would eye ours with disdain and say, "I wouldn't try it in *that*." Then they'd leave us in a cloud of dust, and we'd slowly pick our way through the rocks and potholes until we reached our destination.

Others tried to be open-minded. After giving our car a thorough inspection, one fellow said, "Well, if you go slow, you'll probably make it. But there's a lot of sharp rocks. You better have a good set of spare tires." To us, that sounded like a pretty accurate summary of road conditions. We decided even if our car would survive, we'd hate it, and you would too. So we didn't continue to Chehalis Lake. We'd already had enough.

Even when the road looked questionable to us, people were usually encouraging. "Aw, you'll be fine," they said. "Just take 'er easy. Lots of people make it. There's big RVs in there." And they were right.

Listen to opinions, then decide for yourself. Our motto is, you won't know if you don't go. So after asking for information, we often test it. Sometimes the power you need to get past a rough spot is in your head, regardless of what's under your hood. Technique and determination will take you surprisingly far. And if the road gets too hairy, just turn around. There's always someplace else to explore.

BEYOND *CAMP FREE*

No, this is not a comprehensive guide. Beyond *Camp Free* there are hundreds of free campgrounds in B.C. We don't describe them all. Some are too far off main highways. Twenty-five kilometers (fifteen miles) of dusty, rocky, bouncy backroad is about the limit of most people's patience. And some roads leading to campgrounds are too rough. If you need 4WD and a kidney belt to get there, we didn't include it. Which leaves plenty of campgrounds for the locals to enjoy without competition. Besides, had we taken the time to record detailed directions to every free campground, you'd be waiting another two years for this book.

OFF-SEASON AT PROVINCIAL PARKS

Most provincial park campgrounds charge fees from May 1 or 15 through September 15 or October 1. But they're usually open for camping from April 1 through October 31. Some are open year-round. Each spring that gives you at least a month to camp free. The weather can be wonderful then, bugs aren't a problem, and the crowds have yet to arrive. Fall is also a great time to enjoy these otherwise busy, regimented campgrounds. Provincial parks are signed on major highways, so they're a cinch to find. For details get in touch with BC Parks. You'll find the addresses and phone numbers listed in the back of this book.

GUERILLA CAMPING

It's getting dark. You're nowhere near an official, free campground. You also don't know of any private campgrounds in the area, but you don't want to pay to camp anyway. And hotels aren't your thing.

You need to find your own free-camping spot.

We're in that situation all the time. We rarely know where we'll spend the night until sunset forces us to make a decision. Sometimes we're traveling, cruising late at night, and drowsiness finally compels us to stop. Or we've reached an official, free campground, but it's full or too noisy, and we want to camp alone, in peace.

Sniffing out places to free-camp is a skill you can develop. As you get more proficient, you'll only pay to camp when you're desperate for a shower. Even then, you can just pay for the shower and camp free elsewhere. Unless the land is all fenced off or way too steep, and you absolutely must stop now, you probably don't have to pay to camp.

The free-camp spots you find on your own, however, might not be great places to hang around the next morning. They're likely to be adequate only for a good night's sleep, nothing more. And it's much easier if you have a vehicle you can sleep in — at least the back of a truck or the bed of a station wagon. It's hard to find places you can safely, comfortably pitch a tent for free.

So what we're really talking about here is creative parking. We call it guerilla camping. It's the only way to cope with all the *No Camping* signs that have appeared on public land during the last few years.

It seems there's a conspiracy to make us all pay to sleep. We resent it. From what we've seen, it's unwarranted. Campers who pull off the road for a night, whether they sleep in their vehicle or are brave enough to pitch a tent, rarely harm the land or other people. They're just sleeping! If they're allowed to park there all day, why not at night? What's the harm?

There's so little land the public can use without paying for it, we should all ask, "Why?" Why isn't there more provincial and federal land where we can play during the day and, if we choose, spend the night?

Beat the system. Be a guerilla camper. The following questions will help you assess where and when. Just don't violate people's property rights. If you know it's private, don't camp without asking permission. And always respect the land. Never trash it. As a thank-you for a night's sleep, leave it cleaner than you found it.

What are the options? Be open-minded. Use your imagination. How far you have to stretch your thinking will, of course, depend on where you've free-camped before, what you consider safe, and how bold you are. Some people are audacious. They'll camp anywhere it's wide enough to pull their vehicle off the road. We're more cautious. We're stealth campers.

What's your general sense of the place? Does it feel inviting or creepy? Trust your instinct. If it looks clean, you know people don't park there to drink and party. If it makes you feel vulnerable, that feeling will only grow with every noise you hear. You'll lay awake in the dark, straining to detect anything suspicious. A passing car will slow down and you'll be on edge until it's gone. That's not a good night's sleep. That's miserable. Find another spot where you can relax.

Is it secluded enough? Before you decide to stay, consider what might awaken you later. Are bright lights shining nearby? What's the noise level? How many cars or pedestrians are passing by? If you've pulled off what you think is a little used, paved road, sit there for ten minutes to see how heavy the traffic is. After diving into our sleeping bags, we were surprised to hear cars whiz past us throughout the night on Highway 23, north of Revelstoke. We only got a few hours sleep.

Will you harm the land? Guerilla camping isn't crashing your way into places you shouldn't be. It's gliding in at night, then slipping out in the morning, without leaving a trace. Vegetation, even grass, should be left intact. Harm nothing, take nothing, leave nothing. If that's not possible, move on.

Have you tried residential areas? Sometimes we feel safer if we're parked in a town near homes, rather than on a road that's lonely but still close to civilization. Just outside a town, we're within range of malicious teenagers or other suspicious characters, and somewhat defenseless against them. In town, on a quiet, dark, residential street, we feel it's unlikely we'll be hassled, because help is just a horn-honk away.

If you do stay on a residential street, you'll be less obvious if you don't park directly in front of a house. We look for fields or vacant lots within residential areas. Parked there, we're not intruding on anyone's privacy. We've done it countless times and, apparently, never been noticed. Residents who peek out their windows probably assume we're guests of their neighbors.

Our impression is that people in small towns, compared to residents of big cities, aren't so jumpy about unfamiliar, parked cars. Live and let live seems to be the rural attitude. Plus, small towns have far fewer parking restrictions and fewer police to enforce them.

Are you arriving late enough so you won't be noticed?
Residential streets, university grounds, and hospital, hotel, resort or church parking lots are places where the later you arrive the better your chances of a comfortable night. You want to be situated so you're inconspicuous — where it's normal to see a few cars parked overnight, but not too many. If you're noticed, it shouldn't occur to anyone that you're sleeping in your vehicle. That means you have to finish cooking and arranging your bed elsewhere, before you park. You'll probably have to leave early in the morning, too, but at that point it hardly matters if anyone realizes what you've done.

If you're noticed, will anyone care? This is highly subjective. We figure if we're parked close to anything of obvious importance or value, near any potential object of theft or vandalism, people will care if they notice us. If they care, they'll wake us up and tell us to move, which is always a pain and can be downright scary. It's better to spend a little more time finding a spot where nobody could possibly care if you're sacked out.

RESPECT OTHER CAMPERS

Don't horn in on someone already at a small campground. Make sure there's room for one more. Most people live cheek-by-jowl with their neighbors back home. They want a little privacy when they go camping. If you can't leave a buffer between your camp and others, and there's still daylight left to look elsewhere, please go. If it's late and you decide to stay, do what we do: be as quiet as church mice. We can be in our sleeping bags within ten minutes of arriving at a campground.

If you're the captain of a fully-equipped motorhome, please consider the rest of us before you fire up your generator. Those damn things make a wicked racket and have, several times, forced us to crawl out of our sleeping bags and drive away to find a quiet pullout. Generators really shouldn't be used in campgrounds at all. How hard would it be to drive down the road, generate all you want, then come back and join the quiet? Everyone would appreciate that.

Too many people talk loudly, blast stereos, or let their unmuzzled kids go rampaging. It's rude and obnoxious — night or day. Then there's the couple who arrives late and doesn't know how to efficiently back their trailer into a campsite. The wife shouts directions for fifteen minutes while the husband rocks and rolls the rig. If any of these descriptions sounds like you, please be quieter and more considerate.

Because of problems with rowdy, disrespectful campers, a few Vancouver Island campgrounds now charge a "keep the peace" fee of $5 per campsite, to employ live-in FS patrolmen during summer. They make sure everyone's quiet after 10 p.m. It's happened on Cowichan Lake, at Pine Point and Maple Grove. That's two free campgrounds crossed off the list. Don't let it become a trend.

BE REVERENT

Reverence is achingly absent from the world today. And if there's anyplace we can and should feel reverent, it's out in nature. Reverence is simply being aware of and respecting life in all its manifestations, including our forests, meadows, rivers and lakes. What you revere, you care for.

All FS campgrounds are *User Maintained*. Obviously, so are all the unofficial, free campgrounds and overnight pullouts listed in this book. No garbage trucks. No cleaning crews. It's your responsibility to pick up after yourself. That's partly why they're free. If campers leave messy sites and mistreat the land, we'll eventually lose access to these campgrounds or we'll be slapped with camping fees to cover maintenance costs. The majority of us can't imagine leaving garbage at a campground. Please help spread that ethic.

Bring garbage bags.

Always carry a few extra garbage bags. Since it's likely a previous party will have left something behind, you can pick up for them. You'll feel good doing it. The campground will look better. And anyone who sees you will get a lesson in reverence.

Whenever trash is left, even in a fire pit, it encourages others to assume, "Guess it doesn't matter if I leave stuff too." So take a few minutes to fill up your garbage bag. Drop it in a dumpster on your way home. If you can, it's best to haul it to a city. Small towns have garbage pickups less frequently, and their limited dumpsters can get overstuffed.

Anything campers leave behind after camping is trash. Even cigarette butts. Smokers have been allowed to assume butts don't qualify as litter. It's time to change that. Butts take forever to break down. Meanwhile they give campgrounds a dirty, worn out, ravaged feeling that degrades the quality of the camping experience for everyone else. Never leave your cigarette butts at a campground. It's easy to haul them away with the rest of your trash.

In general, leave as little impact as possible. For example, you'll find more fire rings than are necessary at most campgrounds. If you light a campfire, don't scar the land. Please use an existing ring. Also, never wash dishes in or near a lake or stream. Use a plastic basin, then dump the water in thick brush, well away from campsites. Always use biodegradable soap.

Wouldn't it be refreshing to arrive at a campground and find no evidence anyone had camped there before you? If you do it for the next campers, maybe someone will do it for you.

PRACTICAL STUFF

Our intention isn't to teach you how to camp. It's to motivate you to camp free, in places you've never been. We figure you already know what to take camping. It's not like backpacking, where you can only haul so much and you're a long way from a road. This is *car* camping. You can take whatever you want — as much as your vehicle can hold. So, if you're not sure, just bring it. The more you camp, the better you'll get at keeping your load light and compact, without forgetting necessities. Until then, this list of practical stuff might be helpful.

• **Water.** Bring plenty. You'll almost never find a potable water source at a free campground.

• **Toilet paper, trowel, plastic bag.** FS campgrounds are basic, often referred to as primitive or rustic. Most have outhouses. They're usually stocked with toilet paper, but not always. Bring your own. The unofficial free campgrounds and overnight pullouts we list have no facilities whatsoever. There you'll need a trowel to bury your shit, and a plastic bag to carry away used toilet paper.

• **Garbage bags.** Bring one for all your trash, and another to pick up after other campers less considerate than you.

• **Matches.** Cold food and no campfires can get depressing. Keep extra matches or a lighter in your vehicle. There might not be other campers to mooch from.

• **Can Opener.** Ever try to open a can with a rock?

• **Flashlight and extra batteries.** There are no Tiki torches lining a cement walkway to the "comfort station" at free campgrounds. If you let your eyes adjust to the dark, it's surprising how well you can see without a flashlight. But there are times you'll need one. Like when you're rummaging through your gear to find something. Or even while you're driving and want to read the directions in this book.

B.C. STANDS FOR BEAR COUNTRY

We've seen black bears and grizzlies on many backroads, even on some highways. You don't have to be hiking to encounter one. That doesn't mean they're everywhere. Don't be paranoid. Just be practical and avoid inviting them into your camp. Never leave food out during the day. At night, don't even leave your cooler out. When walking, stay alert and always make noise so you won't surprise a bear. If you see one, don't run and don't look it in the eyes. Talk softly and back away in slow motion.

Rating System for Campgrounds and Backroads

Scenery and Recreation

You'll enjoy staying longer at campgrounds with better scenery and more recreation. So that's the basis for our ratings. Just keep higher-rated campgrounds in mind for short stays too, because they're not necessarily farther away.

DESTINATION
You could spend your vacation here. Even if it's a long drive, it's worth it. The scenery and the campground are wonderful. The recreation is excellent and varied.

WEEKEND
A couple days here might be pleasant, but any longer and you'd want a prettier campground or more impressive scenery. Recreation is available but limited.

OVERNIGHT
Stop here for a quiet, convenient place to sleep, but that's it. Don't expect anything special. Something's lacking: either the scenery or the site itself is poor to mediocre.

Note: All official, free campgrounds have tables, pit toilets, and fire rings, unless we mention their absence. The unofficial, free campgrounds and overnight pullouts we list have no facilities whatsoever.

Access

At a glance, these ratings tell you the distance to the campground, the quality of the road surfaces, and the patience needed to follow the directions.

EASY
Right under your nose. A greenhorn backroads jockey could find it. The road is smooth and the distance short.

MODERATE
Just around the corner. Probably 10 to 15 kilometers (6 to 9 miles) off the paved highway. There could be a few rough stretches.

DIFFICULT
Back of beyond. You'll need patience and a confirmed sense of adventure. The navigating is difficult, the roads challenging, the distances longer — up to 25 kilometers (15 miles).

Maps

You'll find a map at the beginning of each regional chapter. Maps are for general reference only. You don't need to see every road, creek and campground, because our directions give you all the details.

Tripometer

When you read *Set your tripometer to 0* in the directions, push the button to reset your trip odometer to zero at that point.

Odometer readings on different vehicles can vary. Mechanics say this might be the result of road jostling, or using tires that are not the manufacturer's specified size, or an imprecise odometer. So your distances might differ slightly from ours. Just be looking for the turns or landmarks near our stated distances. If you encounter a discrepancy of half a kilometer or more, we apologize. That might be an error, in which case we'd appreciate your writing us with suggested changes.

Recreation Site Numbers

The numbers after each of the Forest Service Recreation Sites (campgrounds) in our book are the numbers the FS uses on their recreation maps. So, if you have the FS maps, you can use them in conjunction with this book.

Map of
Camping Regions

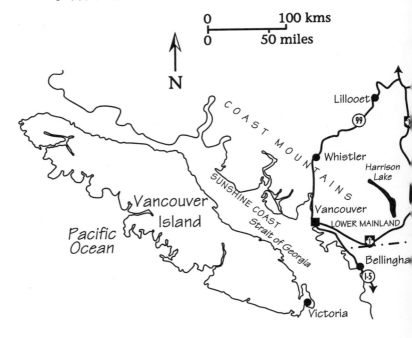

BRITISH COLUMBIA, CANADA

0   100 kms

0   50 miles

N

COAST MOUNTAINS

Lillooet

99

Whistler

Harrison
Lake

SUNSHINE COAST

Vancouver
Island

Pacific
Ocean

Strait of Georgia

Vancouver

LOWER MAINLAND

1

Bellingha

I-5

Victoria

This map shows the major geographical features and highways we've used to divide southern B.C. into eight camping regions. You'll find a more detailed map at the beginning of each regional chapter.

Got everything? Okay, lets go.

Directions to the Campgrounds

Confusing but enticing network of backroads, Sunshine Coast

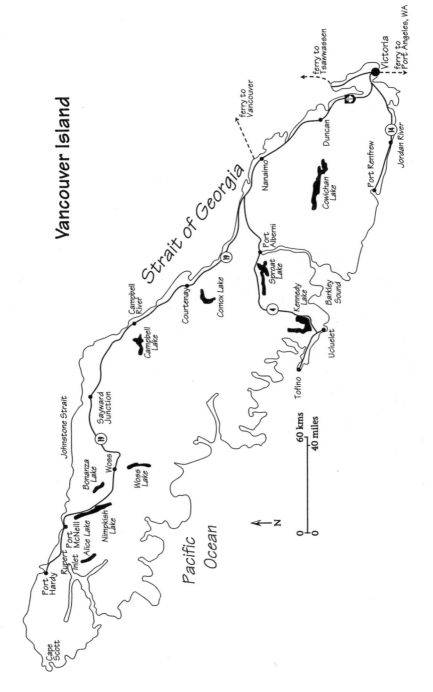

Vancouver Island

Strait of Georgia

Johnstone Strait

Pacific Ocean

Cape Scott

Port Hardy

Rupert Port Inlet McNeill

Bonanza Lake

Woss

Sayward Junction

Alice Lake

Nimpkish Lake

Woss Lake

Campbell River

Campbell Lake

Courtenay

Comox Lake

Port Alberni

Sproat Lake

Kennedy Lake

Barkley Sound

Ucluelet

Tofino

Nanaimo

ferry to Vancouver

Duncan

Cowichan Lake

Port Renfrew

Jordan River

Victoria

ferry to Tsawwassen

ferry to Port Angeles, WA

← N

60 kms
40 miles

0   0

Vancouver Island

The long, spectacular lakes here provide a wealth of recreation. It's definitely worth a special trip to visit the campgrounds we label Destination. The others don't justify a journey all the way from the Mainland, but they're fine if you're already traveling in the area. Brace yourself: the island has been clearcut mercilessly. Even without that detraction, the geography is less spectacular than that of the rest of B.C.

HWY 14: VICTORIA TO PORT RENFREW

From downtown Vancouver, including the ferry ride to Schwartz Bay, it's about six hours to Port Renfrew. Victoria to Port Renfrew is an easy two-and-a-half hours.

0 km / 0 mi
On Hwy 14, in Colwood — a town just west of Victoria.

26.1 km / 16.2 mi
Drive through Sooke, at the start of the West Coast Road. The road follows the shoreline, giving you ocean views.

36.7 km / 22.8 mi
Arrive at Gordon's Beach, a good place for sunbathing.

39.7 km / 24.7 mi
Turn left after crossing a bridge and arrive at a big, gravel parking lot. It might suffice as an **overnight pullout** if you need one.

48 km / 29.8 mi
Pass French Beach Provincial Park.

56 km / 34.8 mi
Pass Sandcut Beach Trail pullout, provided by Western Forest Products (WFP).

57.8 km / 35.9 mi
Come to Jordan River **overnight pullout** on your left, at a WFP sign. It's okay for a night's sleep if you're arriving late, but it's not pleasant enough for a longer stay.

58.4 km / 36.3 mi
Arrive at Jordan River official campground.

WFP JORDAN RIVER RECREATION AREA
Destination (if you love ocean campsites) / Easy
10 tables lined along a gravel lot, fire pits with grates,
6 tables in trees for tenters

This is a popular campground, for good reason: it offers you a front-row view across Juan De Fuca Strait, to the Olympic Mountains in Washington. Which explains why 15 RVs were settled in here on a weekday in July. There are water faucets, but you must purify the water for drinking. You'll find more campsites without tables beyond the stand of trees, in another big, gravel lot, along the river's mouth.

62.8 km / 39 mi
Pass China Beach Provincial Park.

64.7 km / 40.2 mi
Pass Mystic Beach Trail (logged in the 40's, planted in '46). After Jordan River, views of the ocean or the Olympics are limited until you reach Port Renfrew.

78.2 km / 48.6 mi
You get a sweeping view of coastal forest in various logging stages. The bouncy, serpentine, paved road winds higher onto the hillsides. There are lots of one-lane bridges, so drive cautiously. We averaged 50 kph.

84.5 km / 52.5 mi
Ascend a hairpin turn.

85.5 km / 53.1 mi
Come to an **overnight pullout** on your left. The immediate surroundings are not particularly nice, but you get great views of the Strait and the Olympics.

95.6 km / 59.4 mi
Descend a long hill.

96.6 km / 60 mi
Arrive at a sign: West Coast Trail Info straight ahead. Welcome to Port Renfrew.

98.8 km / 61.4 mi
There's a white sign beneath the West Coast Trail info sign: Lake Cowichan. That's where you'll head for the campgrounds northeast of Port Renfrew. The turn is on your right, just before the Orca whale and the information centre. In Port Renfrew the highway becomes Parkinson.

If you drive to the end of the road and turn right at the fork, you'll come to the Trailhead Store. You can buy ice, bait and tackle, or take a shower and do your laundry.

~

NORTHEAST OF PORT RENFREW

0 km / 0 mi
Set your tripometer to 0 in Port Renfrew, when you turn onto the road signed for Lake Cowichan. You'll be on Deering Road, and you'll cross a bridge in 300 meters.

.6 km / .4 mi
Continue on the main road for FS campgrounds not far away. Or stay here at the Native-owned **campground** on a sandy spit jutting into the bay of Port San Juan. Turn left by the yellow sign (if it's still there): Pacheenaht Band. The lovely beach is ideally situated for late afternoon sun. Everyone in town said we could camp free. But apparently someone does occasionally show up to collect a $7-per-night fee. The campers we spoke to, who were waiting to get on the West Coast Trail, hadn't paid for two nights.

1.6 km / 1 mi
At this fork, go right, heading northeast.

3.2 km / 2 mi
Go right again. See a Timber West sign: Public Route, Harris Crk Mainline, Fairy L campsite 3 km, Lizard L campsite 14 km, Mesachie L 52 km. Mesachie Lake is on the southeast end of Cowichan Lake, off a paved road. So you can drive the logging road all the way through to Hwy 18, if you don't mind the continuous jostling.

6.5 km / 4 mi
Arrive at Fairy Lake. Continue on the main road for San Juan River campground.

FAIRY LAKE RECREATION SITE #9
Weekend / Moderate
30 campsites, most with tables

Although heavily used, this large campground will usually have room for you. The lake is okay, but the overall scenery isn't great unless you enjoy seeing clearcuts. There's a warning sign: Campsite floods during heavy rains.

12 km / 7.4 mi
Go right at the fork, staying on pavement, which soon lapses into stoney, bumpy dirt.

16.3 km / 10.1 mi
Go right at this fork, for the San Juan Recreation Site. If you go left, you'll reach Lizard Lake, described below.

16.6 km / 10.3 mi
Pass Lens Creek Trailhead. The sign says: Return trip - 3.8 kms, 2 hrs.

18.8 km / 11.6 mi
Go right at the fork, staying on the main road. See a yellow sign: Dead End Road. Williams Creek Bridge has been dismantled. But don't worry, you're not going that far.

20.3 km / 12.6 mi
Descend the hill to the river.

20.8 km / 12.9 mi
Cross the bridge.

21 km / 13 mi
Arrive at San Juan River campground, on the left.

SAN JUAN RECREATION SITE #8
Weekend / Moderate
5 cozy, well-spaced campsites, no tables

This campground is just above a fine gravel beach on the San Juan River. It's a great spot for a family to stay a couple days. The shallow, slow water, and smooth, sandy riverbed are perfect for wading and splashing about. There's plenty of shade, with a mammoth Sitka Spruce enhancing the setting.

From the 16.3 km / 10.1 mile junction described above, turn left to go to Lizard Lake campground and Lake Cowichan, instead of turning right to the San Juan Recreation Site.

16.3 km / 10.1 mi
Turn left at the junction.

17.9 km / 11.1 mi
Arrive at Lizard Lake campground.

LIZARD LAKE RECREATION SITE #10
Weekend / Moderate
5 tables, 4 picnic tables, garbage cans

The sandy beach and the exceptionally deep, clear water will entice you to plunge in for a swim — if the tree carcasses on the bottom don't spook you. The lake is ringed by forest, but you'll see clearcut hillsides in the distance. All campsites were full when we visited mid-week in July.

It's possible to travel north past Lizard Lake all the way to the community of Mesachie Lake, near Hwy 18. To do that, follow the directions below.

22.7 km / 14.1 mi
Heading north, stay right at the fork. A creek will be on your right.

33.5 km / 20.8 mi
Come to a white sign: Lk Cowichan 24 km. There's also a blue Fletcher Challenge sign: Port Renfrew 33 km.

46.9 km / 29.1 mi
Go right at the fork.

56.3 km / 35 mi
Arrive at a stop sign in Mesachie Lake. Pavement resumes. Go right, to the town of Lake Cowichan.

If you're heading southwest from Lake Cowichan to Port Renfrew

Follow Hwy 18 to the 3-way intersection on the east side of the town of Lake Cowichan. Drive 1.1 km / 0.7 mile into town and set your tripometer to 0 across from Central Park where the South and North Shore roads join. You'll see a green highway sign MESACHIE LAKE, HONEYMOON BAY ^, YOUBOU >. Follow the signs straight (southwest) to Mesachie Lake.

0 km / 0 mi
Going southwest on South Shore Road.

6.5 km / 4.0 mi
Arrive at the community of Mesachie Lake.

7.0 km / 4.3 mi
A sign points left PUBLIC ACCESS TO PORT RENFREW 53. Turn left in 100 meters at the flashing yellow light.

Continue following the directions on pages 33 and 32 in reverse, starting at the 56.3-km / 35.0-mile point. So, in about 9 km / 5.5 miles from the flashing light in Mesachie Lake, go left at the fork. Arrive at **Lizard Lake Recreation Site #10** in about 38 km / 23.5 miles. About 1.6 km / 1.0 mile beyond Lizard Lake, stay right at a junction; then stay left at the next junction to reach Fairy Lake Site #9. At Fairy Lake, you're only 6.5 km / 4 miles from Port Renfrew.

Sunset view from Spring Beach tent site, Cowichan Lake, Vancouver Island

NEAR LAKE COWICHAN

Most people will get to these campgrounds by driving west on Hwy 18, from Duncan. Or you might arrive from Port Renfrew, as described previously. There's one special campground for tent-camping-only on Cowichan Lake. Two FS campgrounds on the north shore now charge a fee during summer. Just beyond the east side of town, there's a campground and many unofficial campsites along the Cowichan River.

SPRING BEACH RECREATION SITE #3
Destination / Easy
Tent-camping and day-use only, 1 table, garbage can

A lush hemlock-and-cedar forest at the northeast end of Cowichan Lake conceals a special spot for tents. Only a couple-minute walk from the roadside parking, the campground is right on the lakeshore, where lapping waves will lull you to sleep. The gravel beach allows for good swimming, too. You won't feel you're in the wilds, because private residences are nearby and jet skiers might shatter the silence. You also might hear logging trucks on the north-side road. But it's a beautiful spot, and we're lucky it's been preserved for public, non-fee use. Help preserve this excellent campground by using only the existing fire rings.

On Hwy 18 at the east side of Lake Cowichan (the town)

From the junction of Hwys 1 and 18, drive 26.2 km / 16.2 miles west to the 3-way intersection and large road-map on the east side of Lake Cowichan.

0 km / 0 mi
From the 3-way intersection, continue on Hwy 18 toward Youbou.

4.9 km / 3.0 mi
The highway crosses Meades Creek.

6.4 km / 4.0 mi
Turn left (south) onto Meades Creek Road. Then curve left past a NO THRU road.

6.9 km / 4.3 mi
Look for a layby on the right next to yellow posts. This is across from a tree farm. Park there and walk into Spring Beach.

Back at the Meades Creek Road junction with Hwy 18, you could continue west past Youbou and the lumber mill, to **Pine Point Recreation Site** in 12.8 km / 7.9 miles or **Maple Grove campground** 1.9 km / 1.2 miles farther. The FS now charges a $5 camping fee here, and the sites are only open from the long May weekend through Labor Day. The fee pays someone to supervise the camp and keep rowdies quiet after 10 p.m. Sleep insurance, in other words. These big campgrounds get awfully busy in summer, so if you don't like that atmosphere, go elsewhere.

~

COWICHAN RIVER AND RIVERBOTTOM ROAD CAMPGROUND
Weekend if you live on the island, Overnight for others / Easy
9 tables, some garbage cans

Lots of families camp here during summer. Cowichan River Provincial Park used to be a free-camping area beside Skutz Falls, but it's now day-use only. Just beyond it are several individual sites along the river where you could camp if you don't mind being next to the road. The large, free Riverbottom Campground is not particularly beautiful, but it's useful if you're in the area. The nearby Cowichan River Footpath provides pleasant hiking along the river through maples, firs, cedars, and ferns. The access point for this 19-kilometer maintained trail is described below.

If you're heading west on Hwy 18

Drive to Highway 18. It's 50 km / 31 miles southeast of the Nanaimo ferry terminal, or a couple kilometers north of Duncan. A stoplight marks the junction of Hwy 1 and 18.

Drive west 19.2 km / 11.9 miles on Hwy 18, heading toward Lake Cowichan. Turn left (south) at the sign SKUTZ FALLS RD. Set your tripometer to 0.

If you're heading east from Lake Cowichan

From the 3-way junction on the east side of town, by the large map-sign, drive east 7.0 km / 4.3 miles to the sign SKUTZ FALLS RD and turn right (south). Set your tripometer to 0.

For either approach above, now follow the directions below

0 km / 0 mi
At the turn south off Hwy 18. Cross Cowichan Lake Road and head downhill. Skutz Falls Road soon becomes gravel.

3.1 km / 1.9 mi
Turn left, pass Heger Road, then go slightly downhill. In 100 meters, arrive at Cowichan River Provincial Park (Skutz Falls) day-use area.

About 100 meters beyond begins a 300-meter stretch of **unofficial campsites** along the river. These spots are not desirable, but might be acceptable. Some have a steep access, others are muddy, or trashed, or tiny, but they're within sight and sound of the river. All were occupied on a June weekday morning, so good luck finding a vacancy.

3.7 km / 2.3 mi
Arrive at unsigned **Riverbottom Road Campground** on the left, in a large open area. Several sites might afford shade if you hunker close to the trees around the perimeter.

Just across from this campground, the Skutz FS Road crosses a bridge over the river. One kilometer in, on the left, you can start hiking at the sign COWICHAN RIVER FOOT PATH, MILE 12 / KM 20. Head downstream.

Driving back, return to Hwy 18 the way you came.

~

HWY 4: PORT ALBERNI
TO THE TOFINO - UCLUELET JUNCTION

ARDEN CREEK RECREATION SITE #8
Weekend / Difficult
4 tables in trees, on the edge of Alberni Inlet

This is a small, idyllic spot on Alberni Inlet, south of Port Alberni. To get here you must travel through some awful landscape. The hillsides were never impressive, but now that they're logged the area just looks abused. You'll be relieved to reach the haven of Arden Creek, after enduring the jittery road through depressing country. Don't get discouraged. This spot is worthwhile, but probably not for a special trip from Vancouver or farther east — only if you live on the island.

Across from China Creek Provincial Park, where more than 15 RVs were jammed together without shade on a summer weekday, Arden Creek offers great shade for relaxing, and access for boating. You can launch a cartop boat here. The inlet often gets strong winds — ideal for board-sailing. Half a dozen were sailing off China Creek in mid-July. Mosquitoes can be bothersome here when it's not windy. The camp-ground is far enough off the road so there's no annoyance from truck traffic.

If you're heading west

0 km / 0 mi
Turning off Hwy 19 southeast of Parksville, onto Hwy 4, heading toward Tofino.

47.0 km / 29.2 mi
Pass this first turn to Port Alberni. Continue west.

51.1 km / 31.8 mi
Turn into Port Alberni city center and head generally west through the city. When you're on Hwy 4 on the western edge of town, just past a marina on your left, you'll come to a cement bridge. Drive 2.7 km / 1.7 miles farther and cross a grey-painted, metal bridge over the Somass River. Just 200 meters beyond it, turn left (south) onto paved Mission Road.

If you're heading east

When approaching the western side of Port Alberni, turn right (south) onto paved Mission Road. This turn is 200 meters before the highway crosses the metal bridge over the Somass River. If you miss the turn and cross the bridge, you might have to drive 2.8 km / 1.75 miles east before you can safely turn around at the marina on the right.

For either approach above, now follow the directions below

0 km / 0 mi
At the turn onto Mission Road. Immediately bear left.

0.5 km / 0.3 mi
Stay left on pavement. Don't take the fork right where there's a sign: Sproat L Woodlands Division. At 2.1 km / 1.3 mi the road becomes gravel.

2.4 km / 1.5 mi
Go right at the fork, heading uphill. Follow the sign to Maktush and Nahmint Lakes.

2.9 km / 1.8 mi
Go left at the fork. Maktush is marked again on the red-and-white signs, above the Sproat Lake - Woodlands sign.

6.0 km / 3.7 mi
Go left. Summit Road is on the right. The road surface is better after this fork — fewer large, sharp rocks.

10.3 km / 6.4 mi
Go left at the junction. Bear left again, on the other side of the bridge.

16.9 km / 10.5 mi
Now the road is beside the inlet.

20.8 km / 12.9 mi
The road veers left and comes to a signpost in the 'V'. You've arrived at the turn-in to Arden Creek campground.

View of Alberni Inlet from Arden Creek

We didn't go to **Nahmint Lake**, which is about 35 kms / 22 miles farther south, then northwest from Arden Creek. Like many lakes on Vancouver Island, it gets good boardsailing winds. If that's your passion, you're sure to find Nahmint Lake. It's too far for the purposes of this book.

Generally, continue south to Nahmint Bay, where the road turns inland going west. You'll be traveling on Nahmint Main FS Road.

There's a FS campground at the north end of the lake, where the river flows in. Stop by the FS office in Port Alberni, or write MacMillan Bloedel, to get a map of the network of logging roads you'll have to pick your way through.

~

TAYLOR RIVER & SPROAT LAKE

If you're heading northeast from Tofino

Skip ahead past the directions for *heading west,* to find directions for heading northeast.

If you're heading west from Port Alberni

0 km / 0 mi
On the western edge of Port Alberni, on the low cement bridge, just past the marina. Follow the highway signs to Sproat Lake.

31.9 km / 19.8 mi
Arrive at turnoffs to **unofficial Sproat Lake campsites.** Go down 300 meters. A short road takes you to a secluded campsite in the trees, with your own beach on the lake. You can launch a cartop boat here. The steep drop from shore makes the blue water especially beautiful. If you continue another kilometer, on the main dirt road along the lake, you'll find other campsites. They seem to be well known, so don't be surprised if they're occupied on a sunny, summer day. But if you search, you might find one open.

34.8 km / 21.6 mi
Entrance to an **unofficial campsite** with a great swimming hole.

35.7 km / 22.2 mi
See a big, Mac Blo sign: The Working Forest. This pullout is for day use only, but if you're camped nearby and want to sample more of the good swimming holes on the Taylor River, you might enjoy this spot. It's not far enough off the road for you to be comfortable here overnight.

36.4 km / 22.6 mi
Arrive at the turnoff (near a highway sign) to **unofficial campsites on a sidestream of the Taylor River**. Be looking across from rocky ledges on the right, then turn down toward the river. There's room for two vehicles. Access is easy, but there's little shade. Despite the wall of trees between you and the highway, you'll definitely hear traffic.

37.7 km / 23.4 mi
Arrive at the turnoff for a large area of unofficial campsites along the Taylor River. It's a little beyond the western end of Sproat Lake, just

after a highway sign: Pt. Alberni 40 km. If you miss the turn and get to the Taylor River Bridge, you only have to drive back 2.9 kms / 1.8 miles.

TAYLOR RIVER UNOFFICIAL CAMPSITES
Weekend / Easy
Room for 7 or 8 vehicles, well spaced, some shade trees

This is a full, gorgeous river, at the west end of long Sproat Lake. There are several areas where people pull off the highway to camp. In summer, it's easy to find the pullouts as you drive along Hwy 4, because you'll see people parked along the Taylor, splashing and sunbathing on sunny days. It's fun wading in the clear water.

Continuing on Hwy 4

40.6 km / 25.2 mi
Just after the bridge, turn left onto the South Taylor Main logging road, to reach the unofficial campsites on the south side of the Taylor River and the official Snow Creek Recreation Site. Set your tripometer to 0. For a shortcut to these campsites, skip past the Snow Creek description.

Or continue west on Hwy 4, toward Tofino and campgrounds at Toquart Bay and Clayoquot Arm.

SNOW CREEK RECREATION SITE #10
Weekend / Easy
7 campsites, 2 with tables, rocky boat launch

Snow Creek campground is on the southwest end of vast Sproat Lake. If you love boating, or just want to rest your bones and gaze at the water, this is a great place to spend a weekend. There's a level, rocky beach where you can plunk your lounge chair in the water, or where children can horseplay. Some campsites are in the open. Those in trees, off the lake, are less appealing — they've been trashed, and the regrown forest is scrubby and forlorn.

This is the easy-to-see turnoff, at the 40.6 km / 25.2 mile point described above, where you set your tripometer to 0.

0 km / 0 mi
Turning off Hwy 4, just south of the bridge over the Taylor River. Go east onto the South Taylor Main FS Road. When we drove here, we had to rumble over crushed rock left from highway construction. It's possible the entrance will have changed. The FS road has large, loose rocks at the beginning.

.6 km / .4 mi
Bear left at the junction.

2.1 km / 1.3 mi
Come to an **overnight pullout** on your left, on the creek.

3.4 km / 2.1 mi
The road calms down, because the rocks are smaller.

5 km / 3.1 mi
Come to a junction. Turn east before the bridge and continue on the main dirt road, if you're heading to Snow Creek on Sproat Lake. Drive 4.7 kms / 2.9 miles farther, to the turn-in on your left.

Snow Creek site on Sproat Lake, Vancouver Island

The **unofficial campsite** is on the other side of the river, below the bridge. Go left and cross the bridge to get to it. Drive .3 km / .2 mile farther to a left turn. Take the left fork. It's rough, but short: .5 km / .3 mile. You'll find room for two vehicles. This is a great spot during hot weather. There's a beautiful, deep, natural swimming pool, and a bit of shade from scrubby foliage. Otherwise the scenery's not great.

If you stay at this swimming-hole site, you can take a short-cut out. When you drive back to the main dirt-and-rock road, turn left, which you'll probably sense is toward the highway. Just 150 meters / .3 mile, and a short, steep run will pop you out onto the highway.

The shorter, easier approach to Snow Creek campground and unofficial campsites

We found this access upon returning to Hwy 4. It saves 4.2 kms / 2.6 miles of really slow, rough, bouncy driving. It's difficult to spot, so pay attention when you're near the western end of Sproat Lake, whether you're heading west or east on Hwy 4. Look for numbers on the telephone poles. There's one marked 14/14 near this entrance. There's also a huge rock outcropping next to the highway, right across from the pole. Just west of it, a dirt road slants down. If you miss the approach we're referring to, you might end up 150 meters farther west and confront a route that's a bit steep for low-clearance cars. Though we made it, you don't have to. The 14/14-pole approach is less extreme. To reach the swimming-hole camping spot, drive in 150 meters / 100 yards, then take the side road to your right. The campsite is just ahead.

If you're heading northeast from Tofino

The following areas are described in the Heading West section above.

0 km / 0 mi
On Hwy 4, at the junction of the road south to Ucluelet and the road northwest to Tofino.

1.6 km / 1 mi
West Main FS Road, on the left, goes to **Clayoquot Arm Recreation Site** (described two sections below).

10.5 km / 6.5 mi
Arrive at a pullout on your right, just after a bridge. You can park here and walk to the **unofficial tent camping** down on a rocky beach, where a point juts into Kennedy Lake.

12.5 km / 7.8 mi
Arrive at a large pullout on the right. This is the turnoff for **Toquart Bay Recreation Site** (described below).

Continuing on serpentine Hwy 4, through the McKenzie Range

51.6 km / 32.1 mi
Turn right, just before the bridge, onto the South Taylor Main logging road, to reach **unofficial Taylor River campsites and Snow Creek Recreation Site** on Sproat Lake.

54.5 km / 33.9 mi
Turn right for **unofficial Taylor River campsites**. This is just before a highway sign: Port Alberni 40 km.

55.9 km / 34.7 mi
You'll see the green back of a highway sign near here. Be looking across from rocky ledges on the left, for a right turn down to **unofficial campsites on a sidestream of the Taylor River.**

56.6 km / 35.1 mi
Pass the day-use parking area, by a Mac Blo sign. There are good swimming holes on the Taylor River.

57.5 km / 35.7 mi
Arrive at the turnoff to an **unofficial campsite** with a great swimming hole. It's about .5 km / .3 mile after a lily pond, below on the right.

60.4 km / 37.5 mi
Arrive at turnoffs to **unofficial Sproat Lake campsites**.

92.2 km / 57.3 mi
Arrive in Port Alberni, near the marina.

~

TOQUART BAY RECREATION SITE #11
Destination / Moderate
28 tables, garbage cans, boat launch, log pier

This is the departure point for kayak trips into Barclay Sound and the Broken Group Islands. It's also popular for fishing the Pacific waters. The campground is a huge, flat area, so there's always room for more, but zero privacy in summer. People jam into this well-known site. Mid-week in July, we counted 40 rigs parked to camp, 25 cars left by kayakers, and 20 boat trailers. There's space for about 15 vehicles on the oceanfront. Some campsites are in stands of trees, but most are in the open, just above the waterline. It's often foggy, damp, and drizzly here, even in summer.

If you're heading west

Drive through Port Alberni. After you pass the marina, on the western edge of town, set your tripometer to 0 on the low cement bridge. Continue toward Tofino.

0 km / 0 mi
On the bridge in Port Alberni.

32 km / 20 mi
Pass the west end of Sproat Lake. You'll soon drive the serpentine road through the MacKenzie Range.

79.7 km / 49.5 mi
Turn left, off Hwy 4, for the Toquart Bay campground. Set your tripometer to 0.

If you're heading to Clayoquot Sound, continue on the highway. Skip below for directions to Clayoquot Arm.

If you're heading east

From the Tofino - Ucluelet junction, drive 12.5 kms / 7.8 miles to the Toquart Bay turnoff.

For either approach above, now follow the directions below

0 km / 0 mi
Turning onto the logging road to Toquart Bay. The road is level and generally smooth, except for a few potholes.

4.2 km / 2.6 mi
You'll see a brown signpost: Toquart Bay straight ahead.

6.3 km / 3.9 mi
At a rough section, stay straight, passing a road veering off right.

8 km / 5 mi
Pass Maggie Lake on the right.

16.1 km / 10 mi
Come to an **overnight pullout** on the right, for secluded camping in trees. There's a boat launch, a log wharf, and room for two or three vehicles. Just beyond this, the road crosses a bridge.

16.3 km /10.1 mi
Arrive at the official Toquart Bay campground.

Toquart Bay, near the Broken Islands, Vancouver Island

~

CLAYOQUOT ARM BEACH RECREATION SITE #12
Weekend / Moderate
12+ campsites in a line, no tables

The picturesque image of Clayoquot Arm on Kennedy Lake will probably linger long in your memory. If you feel the souls of chopped-down ancient trees calling to you, listen. Remember how important it is to preserve the special beauty of the world's great forests. This one has been marred forever by clearcutting. Maybe it will inspire you to think of ways to reduce your family's paper-product consumption, and to demand responsible, sustainable logging practices.

You'll find the campground at the entrance to the controversial ancient forest of Clayoquot Arm. The campsites string along a sandy beach. There are no trees, so you'll be exposed to sun and wind. And you're sure to have neighbors. Some people seem to live here all summer. If you have a canoe, you might enjoy paddling the Kennedy River, or up the arm.

After enduring all the tortuous turns and mind-gnawing clearcuts on the highway to Tofino, six miles more on a logging road to a free campground shouldn't seem difficult.

If you're heading west

Drive through Port Alberni. After you pass the marina, on the western edge of town, set your tripometer to 0 on the low cement bridge. Continue toward Tofino.

0 km / 0 mi
On the bridge in Port Alberni.

32 km / 20 mi
Pass the west end of Sproat Lake. You'll soon drive the serpentine road through the MacKenzie Range.

79.7 km / 49.5 mi
Pass the turnoff to the Toquart Bay campground.

81.8 km / 50.8 mi
Arrive at a pullout on your right, just after a bridge. You can park there, then walk to the **unofficial tent camping** down on a rocky beach, where a point juts into Kennedy Lake.

83.7 km / 52 mi
Pass a boat launch on the right.

90.6 km / 56.3 mi
Turn right onto West Main FS Road and head north to Clayoquot Arm.
This major logging road, which crosses the highway continuing in both
directions, is after the highway leaves the shores of Kennedy Lake. Turn
right (north) just before a bridge and a blue sign: Tourist Attraction —
A Walk in the Rainforest. Set your tripometer to 0 as you turn in.

If you're heading northeast

Drive 1.6 kms / 1 mile on Hwy 4 from the Tofino - Ucluelet junction to
the Clayoquot Arm turnoff. It's on the left (northwest) side.

For either approach above, now follow the directions below

0 km / 0 mi
Turning onto West Main FS Road.

2.3 km / 1.4 mi
Bear right at a one-way sign.

6 km / 3.7 mi
Stay right at the junction.

8.9 km / 5.5 mi
Stay straight (right) at the junction. Grice Bay Road goes left.

11.9 km / 7.4 mi
Cross a big bridge over the Kennedy River. Don't take Lost Lake Road.
Immediately turn right, onto Clayoquot Arm Road.

12.4 km / 7.7 mi
Arrive at Clayoquot Arm Beach Provincial Forest Recreation Site.
There's a parking lot on the left, with garbage cans. A nature trail
departs from the right side of the road.

12.9 km / 8 mi
Arrive at the campground, on the end of the cove, just before the long
bridge over Clayoquot Arm.

~

HWY 19: PARKSVILLE TO SAYWARD JUNCTION

COMOX LAKE OVERNIGHT PULLOUTS
Overnight / Weekend (if you're local) / Easy
Room for 20+ vehicles, no tables or designated campsites

This large pullout is on the north shore of the eastern end of Comox Lake — not on the south shore, as the FS map shows. There's now a municipal, pay campground over there. Here you'll find several large, dirt parking-areas along the water, separated by islands of trees. There's no grass and little shade. On hot, summer days it's very dusty. Usually crowded, too. The water's warm enough for swimming, and you do get a view of Comox glacier, but it's still an unappealing spot: exposed, worn out, trashed, and way too busy.

Drive Hwy 19 (either northwest or southeast) to Courtenay

Comox Lake is southwest of Courtenay. From the newer, fast food/gas station/car dealer zone, head to the older, downtown shopping area. If you're entering town from the north, the highway descends a hill as it enters Courtenay. Stay straight. You'll pass Lewis Park on your right and come to a green bridge over the river. Set your tripometer to 0.

0 km / 0 mi
On the green bridge over the river in Courtenay. Drive through the downtown shopping-area. After crossing Cliffe Avenue, stay on Fifth Ave. (Fifth becomes Willemar somewhere after crossing the railroad tracks at 1.0 km.)

1.8 km / 1.1 mi
At Lake Trail Junior High School, go right onto Lake Trail Road. Stay straight on this main road, ignoring all cross streets.

6.5 km / 4 mi
At the 4-way intersection, turn left.

7.9 km / 4.9 mi
Stay straight on the paved road at this intersection.

10.3 km / 6.4 mi
Curve right on the wider, gravel road, then immediately turn left into a big dirt lot beside the lake.

Where the road curved right just before the main turn-in to Comox Lake free-camping, tough-enough vehicles can go left onto a narrow dirt road to perhaps find some peace. Drive around the left side of this cove to park on the shoreline.

Campbell Lake, Vancouver Island

CAMPBELL LAKE
Destination / Easy

Take your pick of 8 campgrounds stretched along the northern shore of this lake, and a few others nearby. Though nearly all were full by 5 p.m. on the long weekend in July, we still found a great site. The water is invitingly clear, and it's cool in summer, not cold. So you don't need a boat or fishing gear to have fun. Just dive in.

Approaching from Campbell River

0 km / 0 mi
At the junction of Hwys 19 & 28, on the western edge of Campbell River. There's a green highway sign: Strathcona Park 49, Gold River 89, Tahsis 153. Turn west on Hwy 28, heading toward Elk Falls and Gold River.

1.6 km / 1.0 mi
After crossing the river, enter Elk Falls Provincial Park.

4.4 km / 2.7 mi
Look for a green highway sign: Elk Falls Park - Loveland Bay (straight) / Strathcona - Gold R - Tahsis (left). To go to the Campbell Lake campgrounds, turn off the main highway, and toward Loveland Bay Provincial Park. Set your tripometer to 0.

If you want a long, driving adventure to two inlets on the Pacific Coast, read the brief description following these Campbell Lake campgrounds.

0 km / 0 mi
At the junction, turning off Hwy 28, going toward Loveland Bay Provincial Park.

0.5 km / 0.3 mi
Cross above the Campbell River, at the John Hart Dam, then curve left around John Hart Lake. Follow the paved road until the next junction.

2.0 km / 1.2 mi
Go left onto gravel at the brown sign: Loveland Bay Provincial Park 10.5 km.

3.0 km / 1.8 mi
Go left at the fork signed: Snowden Forest, Campbell Lake. Continue on a well-graded gravel road.

9.8 km / 6.1 mi
Stay right on the main road. For the Big Bay site down the left road, you really should have a truck or 4WD. It's a steep, washboarded hill.

12.7 km / 7.9 mi
Pass Loveland Bay Provincial Park.

13.1 km / 8.1 mi
The road makes a sharp left on Sayward FS Road. There's a sign: Snowden Demonstration Forest. We can't help but laugh at these

displays. We'd like to see more Demonstration *Ancient* Forests. Those wouldn't need signs. The living giants themselves would stop us all in our tracks.

15.6 km / 9.7 mi
A right turn off the main road goes to **GOSLING LAKE RECREATION SITE #3**, and four campsites. Shoot for one of the sites on huge Campbell Lake, before you go to Gosling.

15.9 km / 9.9 mi
At the turnoff to an **unnamed campground** on the left. There are five sites along this bouldery beach, plus a rough boat launch.

18.4 km / 11.4 mi
Arrive at Gosling Bay. You'll see a stop sign on your left for vehicles coming out. Drive in .5 km / .3 mile.

GOSLING BAY RECREATION SITE #2 (no sign)
4 campsites, 3 with tables, garbage cans, rough boat launch

It's a nice spot with a beautiful rocky beach. You'll enjoy grand views across the widest part of the lake.

19.3 km / 12 mi
Pass another rough road going down to the lake. In this 15-to-23 km / 9-to-14-mile stretch, there are other similar roads leading to **overnight pullouts** beside the lake, but you'll need a high-clearance vehicle.

22.2 km / 13.8 mi
Arrive at the turn-in to another campground. You'll see the back of a stop sign.

CAMPBELL LAKE RECREATION SITE #6
10 great lakefront campsites, 8 tables, garbage cans, shade

You can see all the way to the Coast Mountains on the mainland. Here the beach consists of round rocks.

23 km / 14.3 mi
Arrive at the turnoff to Dogwood Bay. Fork left. You'll see the back of a stop sign.

DOGWOOD BAY RECREATION SITE #7
4 campsites, 3 tables, garbage cans, boat launch, gravel beach, shade

The individual sites are grouped closely together off a circular pullout, making this campground less appealing.

24 km / 14.9 mi
The turnoff to Loon Bay is again marked by the back of a stop sign. At low water, you'll have a sandy beach to play on here.

LOON BAY RECREATION SITE #9
6 campsites, 5 with tables, garbage cans, shade

27 km / 16.8 mi
Arrive at Orchard Meadow.

ORCHARD MEADOW RECREATION SITE #10
6 campsites, garbage cans, boat launch

Two of the sites are more secluded. After you get down to the lake and take a track right, you'll be on a narrow arm. Here you'll find a more intimate site, rather than an expansive, open one.

28.3 km / 17.5 mi
Stay straight (right) at the junction.

30.3 km / 18.8 mi
Arrive at Gray Lake. Turn left and drive in .3 km. Try other campgrounds first. The sites at this one are cramped.

GRAY LAKE RECREATION SITE #11
5 campsites, boat launch

33.6 km / 20.9 mi
Go straight at the junction, onto a wide main road, staying on the east side of Brewster Lake. Apple Point campground is beside the road.

APPLE POINT RECREATION SITE #13
6 tables, garbage cans, boat launch

Follow the main road heading north, to a campground on Mohun Lake and eventually to Hwy 19. Or return on the same road back to Campbell River.

39.4 km / 24.5 mi
See the white back of a stop sign on your left, marking the entrance to **Mohun Lake Recreation Site #15** with 2 campsites.

41 km / 25.5 mi
Pass the turnoff to Morton Lake Provincial Park.

51 km / 31.5 mi
The FS road joins Hwy 19 at the Mac Blo Menzies Bay Division.

If you're heading northwest from **Campbell River to Mohun Lake**, from the junction of Hwys 19 & 28, drive 14.8 km / 9.2 miles to the Morton Lake turnoff.

If you're heading southeast from the **Sayward junction to Mohun Lake**, drive 59.5 km / 37 miles to the Morton Lake turnoff.

For either approach above, at the Mac Blo Menzies Bay Division, turn sharp right along the fence. Follow signs to Morton Lake. Continue beyond that turnoff and turn right at 11.6 km / 7.2 miles.

Remote inlets on the Pacific Coast near Nootka Island

These areas are too far and the access too rough for the purposes of this book. But if you want a long, driving adventure, continue on Hwy 28, past the Loveland Bay and Campbell Lake turnoff. Just after crossing the Gold River at the community of Gold River, turn northwest onto a logging road. At the junction, in a few kilometers, stay left on the main road. If you continue to Tlupana Inlet, there's **Cougar Creek Recreation Site #31** (18 campsites, boat launch, float). On Tahsis Inlet there's **Leiner River Recreation Site #30** (room for about 8 vehicles, in trees next to the river).

If you hang a right at the junction a few kilometers outside Gold River, and cross the river, you can head north to **Muchulat Lake Recreation Site #29.** After the first junction, bear left at two more junctions.

~

Rock Bay on Johnstone Strait, near Little Bear Bay

McCREIGHT LAKE & JOHNSTONE STRAIT
Destination / Easy

This is exciting country north of Campbell River. It's more mountainous than the area just south, and it looks wilder, even though the forest is second growth. Many campgrounds up here feel secluded. McCreight is a great lake for canoeing. Drive past McCreight to idyllic Little Bear campground on Johnstone Strait. Solitude is unlikely here during summer.

If you're heading northwest

From the junction of Hwys 19 & 28, on the north end of Campbell River, drive 41 km / 25.5 miles northwest on Hwy 19. The turnoff you're looking for is 3.4 km / 2.1 miles beyond the Pye Lake West FS Road (if you notice it).

Look carefully for Rock Bay Road, on the right. There's a white sign on the back of a stop sign. The turn is 200 meters before the highway crosses Amor De Cosmos Creek.

If you're heading southeast

From the Sayward junction, drive 24 km / 15 miles southeast on Hwy 19. The turn is 200 meters after the highway crosses Amor De Cosmos Creek.

For either approach above, now follow the directions below

0 km / 0 mi
At the turn north onto gravel Rock Bay Road. It's badly potholed all the way to Johnstone Strait, so watch out.

3.0 km / 1.8 mi
Park in the layby on the left. The sign was missing but might have been replaced. Path and boardwalk quickly lead to Spruce Beach.

SITKA SPRUCE BEACH WALK-IN RECREATION SITE #27

This is a spectacular campsite at the south end of McCreight Lake. Behind the beach is a lovely hemlock-and-cedar forest. You get views of the surrounding mountains and way down the lake.

3.3 km / 2.0 mi
The back of a red stop sign is visible from the road. Turn left for Aldergrove campground, which has a path to a sandy beach.

ALDERGROVE RECREATION SITE #26
A couple campsites in trees, no immediate lakeview,

4.0 km / 2.4 mi
Arrive at the signed turn-in to McCreight Lake campground. The side road cuts back left. The site isn't located as far up the lake as the FS map indicates. Just past the entrance to the campground, there's a rough boat launch that you'll need a truck to use.

McCREIGHT LAKE RECREATION SITE #25
3 well-spaced campsites, 2 with tables, garbage cans

These sites are in lush forest, just above the rocky lakeshore. They're so far apart, you feel you're camping alone. Scramble down to the clear water for a refreshing swim.

7.8 km / 4.8 mi
Go straight (right), following the sign for Rock Bay. Pass a private road on the left.

9.0 km / 5.6 mi
Continue straight on the main road, northeast to Johnstone Strait. The road right goes to **Pye Lake Recreation Site #24.** A brown FS sign marking this turn is visible when heading west. The Pye Lake Road, with lots of big rocks scattered about, is too rough for cars. You can also reach Pye Lake by turning off Hwy 19, 3.4 km / 2.1 miles east of the Rock Bay Road.

11.3 km / 7.0 mi
Stay straight here and also at 13.0 km / 8.1 miles, where a fierce road goes up left.

14.1 km / 8.7 mi
Stay on the main road. Pass a brown FS post marking a rough road going right to **Stella Beach Recreation Site #20.** You need a truck or 4WD to get there. It has eight campsites and a sandy beach.

16.7 km / 10.4 mi
Go left at the junction and descend toward Little Bear Hatchery. (To visit the private, pay campground and small marina, take Rock Bay Road right. When you arrive at a fork in 1.5 km / 0.9 mile, go left.)

17.5 km / 10.9 mi
Having turned left (toward the hatchery) at the junction above, you quickly reach Johnstone Strait where a river flows into it. The free campground is to the right.

LITTLE BEAR RECREATION SITE #21
6 tables, lots of grass below, boat launch

On the rocky ocean edge, the Little Bear campground overlooks Johnstone Strait. If you're a salmon fisherperson, or just want wild scenery, this place will thrill you. But you can expect company. Midweek in July, eight rigs were jammed in here. The best site is straight ahead, on the end, clasped in trees and set off from the others.

~

HWY 19: SAYWARD JUNCTION TO PORT MCNEILL

ELK CREEK RECREATION SITE #28
Overnight / Easy
5 whole tables, one destroyed
(tells you about the mentality of some of the clientele)

This campground is depressing — not because it's near the highway, or in deep trees without views, but because it was totally trashed when we visited. The creek was only a dribble and didn't help muffle the highway noise. You'll probably only want to use it as a place to sleep. Pond-sized potholes on the short access-road might deter you from driving in during or after heavy rain.

If you're heading northwest from the Sayward junction

0 km / 0 mi
At the Sayward junction, where you'll see billboards advertising camping and whale watching tours at Robson Bight.

0.5 km / 0.3 mi
Turn left (south) directly across from a white sign: Aircraft Patrolled. There should be a brown signpost on the left (south) side of the highway. This is also 200 meters before the highway bridge over Lower Elk Creek. Drive 0.3 km / 0.2 mile in.

If you're heading northeast from Woss

The turnoff is 66.7 km / 41.4 miles northeast of the Woss turnoff. When you're getting close, watch for when the highway crosses a bridge over Lower Elk Creek. Drive only 200 meters beyond this bridge, then turn right (south). If you miss the turn, it's only 0.5 km / 0.3 mile back from the Sayward junction. Drive 0.3 km / 0.2 mile in to the campground.

~

KLAKLAKAMA LAKES

If you're heading west

From the Sayward junction, drive 55.7 km / 34.6 miles. Signs warn of the turn for Schoen Lake Provincial Park. This road accesses Schoen's west side and is where you'll turn for Klaklakama Lakes.

If you're heading southeast

From the Port McNeill turnoff, drive 75.7 km / 47.0 miles, or from the Woss turnoff, drive 11.0 km / 6.8 miles, to the Schoen Lake Provincial Park turnoff. Turn south onto the road for Schoen Lake, which also leads to the road to Klaklakama Lakes.

For either approach above, now follow the directions below

0 km / 0 mi
At the turn south off Hwy 19. There might not be a sign by the highway, but there are signs 250 meters in.

250 meters
Go right at the wide Y-junction, where there might be signs for Klaklakama Lakes and Vernon Lake. A sign points left to Schoen Lake. After going right, immediately cross a bridge and curve right.

1.0 km / 0.6 mi
Stay left on the main road at this fork.

2.6 km / 1.6 mi
Come to more signs. Go left first to try for a campsite on Lower Klaklakama Lake.

3.7 km / 2.3 mi
Turn right and arrive at the first campground.

LOWER KLAKLAKAMA LAKE RECREATION SITE #29
Overnight / Easy
5 tables somewhat separated, 2 campsites on the lake, garbage cans

There's a rocky beach and good swimming, but the scruffy, second-growth forest offers little shade. The lake is nice, but the hills were recently clearcut and are no fun to stare at.

From the 2.6 km / 1.6 mile junction, go right to Upper Klaklakama Lake.

7 km / 4.3 mi
Arrive at the upper campground, which has views of worse clearcuts,

but more private campsites. Only come here if you can't get a spot at the lower campground.

UPPER KLAKLAKAMA LAKE RECREATION SITE #30
Overnight / Moderate
3 campsites on the lake, a jumble of tables, garbage cans

There are some enormous old-growth trees still standing here. They're a reminder that this island was once covered by glorious monarchs. Even if the terrain isn't spectacular, the trees are. Vernon Lake is 16 km farther.

~

WOSS LAKE RECREATION SITE #32
Weekend / Easy
20+ campsites with tables, garbage cans, boat launch

A sheltered cove, a float, and a sandy beach enhance the swimming here. The campsites are close together, at the northern end of the lake. Clearcuts glare at you across the cove.

If you're heading southeast

From the Port McNeill turnoff, drive 64.7 km / 40 miles, or from the Nimpkish turnoff, 30.5 km / 18.9 miles to the signed Woss turnoff.

If you're heading northwest

From the signed turnoff to the west side of Schoen Lake Provincial Park, drive 11.0 km / 6.8 miles and look for the signed Woss turnoff.

For either approach above, now follow the directions below

0 km / 0 mi
Turn off Hwy 19, and in 0.7 km /0.4 mile cross railroad tracks.

1.1 km / 0.7 mi
Recross the railroad tracks and immediately curve right. Go left on S. Railway Avenue. You'll see a sign for the campground. Go over the bridge, then right again. (Just after the bridge, left leads to Vernon Lake, which is 22 km distant by way of the Nimpkish River Valley.)

4.3 km / 2.7 mi
Go left at the fork.

4.6 km / 2.9 mi
Go right at the next fork, where there's a sign for Woss Lake. You've arrived.

BONANZA LAKE SOUTH RECREATION SITE #27
Weekend / Difficult
10 campsites, rough boat launch

This medium-size lake is longer than McCreight, but shorter than Woss or the giant Nimpkish. The large, pleasant campground offers an expansive view up the lake. The spacious beach is a good place to sun when it's not too windy. Don't attempt to get to Bonanza from the north end near Telegraph Cove. That road is quite rough. This road is good, allowing you to reach the lake in 15 minutes.

If you're heading southeast

Drive 43.2 km / 26.8 miles southeast of the turnoff to Port McNeill, or 9.0 km / 5.4 miles southeast of the Nimpkish Lake turnoff. Turn east off Hwy 19, on the south side of the Steele Creek bridge, immediately after the Zeballos / Fair Harbour turn.

If you're heading northwest

From the Woss turnoff, drive 21.5 km / 13.3 miles. Turn east off Hwy 19, on the south side of the bridge over Steele Creek, which is next to the Zeballos turn.

For either approach above, now follow the directions below

0 km / 0 mi
Turn east off Hwy 19, by the pink and red flagging on the trees. Cross the railroad tracks and curve right. Do not drive left over the railroad trestle bridge. Ignore the fork going off right.

1.5 km / 0.9 mi
Bear left. At the next minor forks, stay straight on the main road. The trees here are 25 to 30 years old—mere infants as BC trees go. The lower half of the mountain slopes have been cut and replanted the entire length of the valley.

13.7 km / 8.5 mi
You'll get your first view of Bonanza Lake.

15.2 km / 9.4 mi
Bear left and cross the bridge over Bonanza River.

15.9 km / 9.9 mi
Go left immediately before a Forest Fire Hazard sign, and descend to

the lake. The main road continues north along the east side of the lake toward Telegraph Cove.

16.2 km / 10.0 mi
Arrive at the Bonanza Lake campground.

~

ANUTZ LAKE RECREATION SITE
Overnight / Easy
14 tables around a large field

A pretty lake with views north to the Karmutzen Range. Only a couple sites are on the lakeshore. Anutz is only ten minutes from the highway. The same turn off the highway eventually leads to FS campgrounds near the isolated communities of Zeballos and Fair Harbour, on inlets of the Pacific Ocean.

If you're heading northwest

The turnoff is 21.7 km / 13.5 miles northwest of Woss. It's signed for Zeballos and is just north of the bridge over Steele Creek.

If you're heading southeast

At 8.8 km / 5.5 miles southeast of the Nimpkish Lake turnoff, turn right (west) off Hwy 19. This is the Zeballos turn.

For either approach above, now follow the directions below

0 km / 0 mi
This dirt road begins by paralleling the highway.

1.3 km / 0.8 mi
Stay left on the main road. Stay straight at the next two minor forks. At 2.0 km / 1.2 miles, cross a high bridge over the Nimpkish River.

2.4 km / 1.5 mi
Stay straight. Then at **2.8 km / 1.7 miles**, go right for Anutz Lake.

3.1 km / 1.9 mi
Fork right toward Anutz. Left leads 10 km to a FS campground at Atluck Lake. Left is also the way to Zeballos and Fair Harbour.

5.8 km / 3.6 mi
Take the right fork toward Anutz.

6.4 km / 4.0 mi
Fork left. At **6.6 km / 4.1 miles**, go right and continue downhill.

6.8 km / 4.2 mi
Arrive at Anutz Lake and campsites around a large field.

From the 3.1 km / 1.9-mile junction above, proceed left if you want to go to Zeballos and Fair Harbour. Well-signed junctions will get you there.

Zeballos is about 38 km / 24 miles farther; Fair Harbour 71 km / 44 miles. **Resolution Park Recreation Site #32** is about 5 km / 3 miles past Zeballos. It has 7 campsites, a cobblestone beach, and boat launch. 4WD might be necessary for the entrance. **Fair Harbour Recreation Site #33**, with 25 campsites and a boat launch, is one hour beyond Zeballos.

~

NIMPKISH LAKE - KINMAN CAMP
Destination / Easy
24 tables, 6 walk-in tent sites, garbage cans, firewood

NIMPKISH LAKESIDE RECREATION SITE #35
Destination / Easy
20 tables, garbage cans

Nimpkish is a breathtaking lake, long and wide, beneath sweeping mountainsides. Two great campgrounds, a short way off the highway, are ideal for a good night's sleep or a multi-day retreat. The strong, dependable winds make this a fine boardsailing lake. You can just sit on the beach and lose yourself in the grand scenery.

From the Kinman Camp (reached by taking the first right), you have to walk about one kilometer down a slope, on a wide gravel path, to the lake and stone beach. There was only one RV camped here on a long weekend in summer. This campground is provincial-park quality. It was well-thought out and is nicely maintained. The campsites are comfortably spaced, set in tall trees. There's practically a garbage can for every site, which we hope will prevent the area from being trashed, like so many others have been.

The other campground, which is a bit farther, has 16 sites strung along the lakeshore. The sites are not as private as those at Kinman and you'll get blasted by the strong winds, but you'll also have terrific views. If the lakeshore campground is full or too busy for you, there should always be space at Kinman.

Nimpkish Lake, Vancouver Island

If you're heading northwest

The turnoff is 30.5 km / 18.9 miles northwest of Woss, and 8.8 km / 5.5 miles beyond the turn to Zeballos and Fair Harbour.

If you're heading southeast

From the turnoff to Port McNeill, drive 34.2 km / 21.2 miles to the signed Nimpkish Lake turn.

For either approach above, now follow the directions below

0 km / 0 mi
Turn west off Hwy 19, toward Nimpkish Lake (not visible here). There's a gas station beside the highway.

100 meters
Turn right (across from the old gas station) for the Kinman Campground. Immediately cross the railroad tracks and descend the hillside.

1.3 km / 0.8 mi
Arrive at Kinman Campground. A sign/map indicates all the sites. You'll be camping in forest, well above the lake.

If you want a campsite on the lakeshore, continue past the right turn at 100 meters.

0.3 km / 0.2 mi from the highway
At this T-intersection, go left. Signs point left to Sailors and Nimpkish Lake Camp Site.

0.8 km / 0.5 mi
Go right at the sign: LAKE. Then immediately stay left at another fork.

1.0 km / 0.6 mi
Ignore a left fork. Stay straight, proceeding downhill.

1.5 km / 0.9 mi
Arrive at a lakeside campground. Sites are grassy and have open views over the lake. Trees on the hillside back the sites.

~

NEAR PORT HARDY

GEORGIE LAKE RECREATION SITE #3
Overnight / Difficult
4 tables, garbage cans, boat launch

We don't recommend this campground, or this area, to anybody. The topography is uninteresting, and you have to travel through a devastating clearcut—an example of the mindless destruction that is eating away at B.C. Use this campground only if you're heading to Cape Scott and you just need a place to sleep. There's a rim of trees around the lake, and no clearcuts in view from the site.

It takes about twenty minutes to drive to Georgie Lake from the Port Hardy ferry terminal. But, if you're heading to Cape Scott, you're better off investing your time driving farther west to the **Nahwitti Lake Recreation Site #1**, which is beside the road to Cape Scott.

0 km / 0 mi
Across from the cavorting bears on the Welcome to Port Hardy sign. (This is also the turnoff to the Prince Rupert ferry.)

1.3 km / 0.8 mi
Pass the turnoff to Coal Harbour.

2.1 km / 1.3 mi
Turn left (west) toward Cape Scott.

4.7 km / 2.9 mi
The road becomes gravel.

9.2 km / 5.7 mi
Come to a junction and sign: FS Road - Georgie L 5.8 km. Go slow.
There's a small, narrow bridge ahead.

14.8 km / 9.2 mi
Go right at the signed fork and soon arrive at Georgie Lake.

~

MARBLE RIVER RECREATION SITE #23
Destination / Easy
30 campsites, garbage cans, firewood

On a playful, spirited river, this wonderful spot is as well maintained as
a provincial park. Fifteen minutes on paved road takes you all the way
to the campground. Seven campsites with tables back onto the Marble
River. Others are well away from the campground road, with privacy
created by trees and bushes. You can at least hear the river from most
campsites, even if yours isn't overlooking it. A pretty forest provides
shade. Large, grassy areas at many campsites are great for pitching your
tent on, or curling your toes in. Alice Lake is quite close, too. This is as
nice as any free campground in B.C. Expect lots of mosquitoes in summer.

If you're heading northwest from Port McNeill

From the turnoff to Port McNeill, drive 20 km / 12.5 miles to the
Port Alice turnoff on the left, which has a big map and sign.

If you're heading southeast from Port Hardy

From the Welcome to Port Hardy sign with the cavorting bears on it
(also the turnoff to the Prince Rupert ferry) drive 16.4 km / 10.2
miles to the turnoff on the right (south) side of the highway.

For either approach above, now follow the directions below

0 km / 0 mi
Turning south off Hwy 19 onto the paved Port Alice Road. Stay left,
on the main road.

10.6 km / 6.6 mi
Stay straight and pass a dirt logging road crossing the highway.
From that junction, the left route goes to Alice Lake Recreation Site
#22, described after the Marble River campground. The right route
goes to Rupert Inlet campgrounds, described after Alice Lake.

14.6 km / 9.1 mi
Drive over the Marble River bridge. You'll see picnic tables for day

use on the right, in grass beside the bridge. Immediately after the bridge, turn right and follow the dirt road past the big Western Forest Products sign.

15.3 km / 9.5 mi
At the fork, you can go right 100 meters down to campsites in stunning forest and beside the river; or go left to another part of the campground that offers grassy campsites.

~

ALICE LAKE RECREATION SITES #22 & 21
Weekend / Moderate
No tables, room for a dozen vehicles

This spot has an open, rough, wild feeling—totally unlike the intimate, manicured atmosphere of Marble River. This is an open strip-camp on a lakeshore, where RVs line up close together on the stone beach. There are piles of drift-logs blown ashore. The strong winds that often whip across this lovely lake keep the bugs down. The claustrophobic access road makes you feel like you're dropping through Alice in Wonderland's rabbit hole. Light branches over the last stretch might hit the top of a camper or motorhome.

Follow the directions above for the Marble River Recreation Site. Turn left (south) at the 10.6-km / 6.6-mile junction.

0 km / 0 mi
Turning left from the paved Port Alice road, onto Alice Lake Main.

1.2 km / 0.7 mi
Stay right at the fork.

8.2 km / 5.1 mi
Stay right. In 100 meters, go right again onto a narrower road. The trees get closer, reaching over the road.

11.9 km / 7.4 mi
Arrive at Alice Lake.

13.1 km / 8.1 mi
Arrive at Alice Lake campground.

~

RUPERT INLET CAMPGROUND
Weekend / Easy
A few tables, grassy areas, room for 8 vehicles

These campsites on the north shore at the eastern end of this ocean inlet are a good base for fishing. But there's really no other reason to visit, except to see what's here. The scenery isn't spectacular, just vast. The grass and tall trees make this campground feel like a cozy haven from the wind and rain that often buffet northern Vancouver Island. Beyond the large grassy area with one table near the entrance, follow a track left to the ocean and high hedges encircling the campground and another grassy area.

Follow the directions above for the Marble River and Alice Lake Recreation Sites. Turn right (north) at the 10.6-km / 6.6-mile junction.

0 km / 0 mi
Turning right from the paved highway onto Alice Lake Main.

4.4 km / 2.7 mi
Stay straight, ignoring forks.

5.4 km / 3.3 mi
Come to a junction. Stay straight for the campground on the north shore. If you turn back sharply left, you'll arrive in 1.0 km / 0.6 mile at **Rupert Arm Recreation Site #10**. It's a wonderful site on the south side of the inlet that's for day-use only. Local groups, like the Girl Guides, are sometimes allowed to camp. There's a huge grassy play area, two covered eating areas, and firewood.

6.4 km / 4.0 mi
Cross a bridge. Immediately after, stay straight, passing a fork on your right.

7.3 km / 4.5 mi
Turn left between bushes to **Rupert Inlet Campground**.

7.6 km / 4.7 mi
Look for a short spur road left, to a small point where it's possible to camp alone.

7.7 km / 4.8 mi
Arrive at an **unofficial campsite** on the left. This is just a long, dirt pullout, with a boat launch and room for three vehicles beside the water. There are no shade trees, but cloud cover is likely.

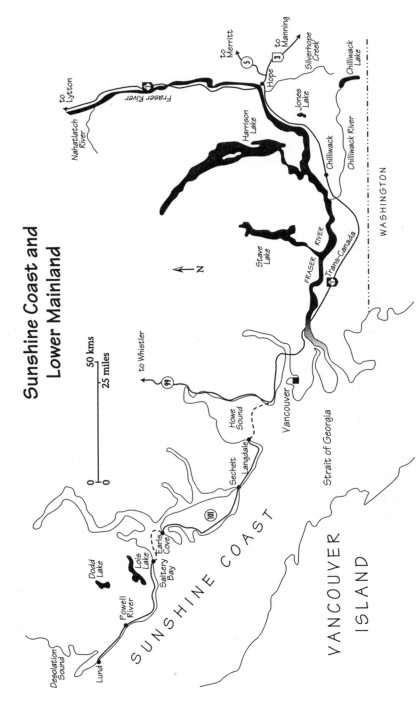

Sunshine Coast and Lower Mainland

N

50 kms
25 miles

to Whistler

to Lytton

Nahatlatch River

Fraser River

to Merritt

5

to Manning

3

Hope

Silverhope Creek

Chilliwack Lake

Jones Lake

Chilliwack

Chilliwack River

Harrison Lake

Stave Lake

FRASER RIVER

Trans-Canada

WASHINGTON

Howe Sound

Vancouver

Strait of Georgia

Sechelt

Langdale

99

100

Earls Cove

Saltery Bay

Lois Lake

Dodd Lake

Powell River

Desolation Sound

Lund

SUNSHINE COAST

VANCOUVER ISLAND

Sunshine Coast and Lower Mainland

SUNSHINE COAST

The Sunshine Coast has high, rugged mountains and luxuriant forests, ocean inlets and long, mysterious lakes. It will stir your soul. From Vancouver, you'll feel you've come a long way from civilization, even though it's only a two-hour drive and an hour-and-a-half ferry ride. Many backroads campgrounds are within a half-hour of Powell River.

On this final northern stretch of Hwy 101, there's one free campground accessible by low-clearance vehicles, between Langdale and Earls Cove. You'll find several others farther along, between Saltery Bay and Lund.

Klein Lake, Sunshine Coast, near Skookumchuck Narrows

LANGDALE TO EARLS COVE

Don't miss walking to these two sites on the ocean.

Smugglers Cove Marine Park
Head northwest from the Langdale ferry to Sechelt, where the road to Sechelt Inlet joins Hwy 101. Continue on Hwy 101 for 19.8 kms / 12.3 miles and turn left onto Brooks Road, just beyond the community of Halfmoon Bay. There's a 1.3-km trail (about 15 minutes walking) to tent sites in the woods. Other trails lead to different parts of the cove.

Skookumchuck Narrows

One kilometer southeast of the Earls Cove ferry terminal, turn off Hwy 101, heading northeast toward Egmont. Set your tripometer to 0. Drive 5.5 km / 3.4 miles to a signed trailhead pulloff on your right. It's before the road heads downhill to the community of Egmont. It's a 4-km walk to the impressive tidal bore of the narrows. This constantly energized water is a good place to see lots of seastars. You can car-camp at Klein Lake. That turnoff is on the south side of the road, 1.7 km / 1.1 miles from Hwy 101.

If you're heading northwest from Langdale

Drive 83.0 km / 51.5 miles northwest, to a junction 1.0 km / 0.6 mile before the Earls Cove ferry terminal. Turn right (east) toward Egmont.

If you're heading southeast from the ferry at Earls Cove

Drive 1.0 km / 0.6 mile south to the Egmont junction.

For either approach above, now follow the directions below

0 km / 0 mi
Turning off Hwy 101, heading toward Egmont.

1.7 km / 1.1 mi
Turn right on the dirt road signed NORTH LAKE FOREST SERVICE ROAD.

3.0 km / 1.9 mi
After passing cottages and nearing the end of North Lake, stay right to Klein Lake.

4.9 km / 3.0 mi
Reach a sign indicating you've arrived at Klein Lake FS Recreation Site. Go right or left to campsites. The road circles the lake.

~

SALTERY BAY TO LUND

The feeling at these long lakes is wild and lonely. The atmosphere is relaxing, yet revitalizing. It's an ideal place to sit and ponder almost anything, or nothing at all. These lakes form the Powell Forest Canoe Route (PFCR) — a good alternative to the busy Bowron Lakes circuit farther north in B.C. A short, rigorous hike up nearby Tin Hat Mountain will give you an impressive view of Georgia Strait and the surrounding lakes and mountains. See Nanton Lake (page 72) for directions.

Lois Lake tent site, Sunshine Coast

LOIS LAKE RECREATION SITE #5
Destination / Easy
8 tables, 5 campsites in the open, 3 walk-in tent sites in trees

If you're heading northwest

11.5 km / 7.1 miles after getting off the ferry at Saltery Bay, turn right off Hwy 101, just before the steel bridge over Lois River.

If you're heading southeast from Powell River

It's 14.5 km / 9.0 miles on Hwy 101, from the town's eastern edge to the FS dirt road into Lois, Khartoum and Nanton Lakes. Turn left (inland) just after the Lois River bridge.

For either approach above, now follow the directions below

0 km / 0 mi
Turning north off the highway, onto a road with these signs: PUBLIC ACCESS TO BR 41 AT ALL TIMES–MACMILLAN BLOEDEL, POWELL FOREST CANOE ROUTE (PFCR), STILLWATER MAIN. This is a wide, maintained, gravel road.

1.1 km / 0.7 mi
Go right at the junction. See signs: PFCR, LOIS MAIN. The left road goes to Khartoum Lake, described below.

4.7 km / 2.9 mi
Go left at the signed junction, and begin descending to Lois Lake.

5.6 km / 3.5 mi
Reach a sign: LOIS LAKE, BCFS RECREATION SITE. Curve right.

5.8 km / 3.6 mi
Arrive at the campground on Lois Lake.

KHARTOUM, NANTON, & DODD LAKES

0 km / 0 mi
Turn north off Hwy 101, at the same place described above for Lois Lake.

1.1 km / 0.7 mi
Go left at the junction. You'll see a sign for the canoe circuit: PFCR.

1.7 km / 1.1 mi
Stay right here. Then go straight at **3.9 km / 2.4 miles**, where a minor road forks off.

5.2 km / 3.2 miles.
Go straight again, on Stillwater Main.

6.7 km / 4.1 mi
There's a nice overnight pullout on the right beside Lois Lake, and another one at 8.5 km / 5.3 miles.

12.3 km / 7.6 mi
Arrive at a signed fork. Left goes to Nanton Lake, right to Khartoum Lake. Set your tripometer to 0. Separate distances are listed below for each lake.

KHARTOUM LAKE RECREATION SITE #4
Destination / Difficult
6 tables, garbage cans, boat launch

Set in a dramatic, steep-sided bowl, Khartoum is a lake we'll always remember. It looks like one you'd have to fly into. (Be careful on the road, or you just might.) There are several campgrounds in the open on the lake's edge, and others in beautiful trees. One is next to a loud creek and, if you use your imagination, a rock-throwing practice gallery. Drive or walk about 2.3 km / 1.4 miles beyond the campground turn-in to get an incredible view overlooking Khartoum Lake from high on the mountainside.

0 km / 0 mi
At the 12.3-km / 7.6-mile, signed fork described above.

7.4 km / 4.6 mi
Pass through Camp B Fish Farm on Lois Lake.

Rock-throwing practice gallery provided at Khartoum Lake, Sunshine Coast

10.0 km / 6.2 mi
The road is now narrow, steep and rocky, but still okay for 2WD.

15.1 km / 9.4 mi
The turn-in to Khartoum Lake is on your right. It's difficult to see because it drops steeply. At the rough entry-road, look for a yellow sign up on a tree, and another sign facing down the road for people coming out: No public traffic Mon-Fri, 5 am-8 pm. Radio controlled!

If you don't see the turn-in here, go 0.6 km / 0.4 mile farther. We missed it the first time, so our calculations might be a little off. If you find you're driving where the road is perched on a cliff without a buffer of trees to your right, and you're getting clear views of the lake way below, then you've passed the turn-in and need to go back.

~

NANTON LAKE RECREATION SITE #8
Weekend / Moderate
13 tables, 15 campsites (a couple on the lake, most in trees)

When it's clear, you'll get views of mountains across the lake. It's about a half-hour drive to Nanton Lake from the highway.

0 km / 0 mi
At the signed fork described above, at 12.3 km / 7.6 miles, on the northwest side of Lois Lake. When heading in from Hwy 101, go left to Nanton Lake. If you're coming from Khartoum Lake, turn right.

0.8 km / 0.5 mi
Stay right on Goat Lake Main.

5.3 km / 3.3 mi
Tin Hat Mountain is visible ahead.

6.6 km / 4.1 mi
For Nanton, go right at the junction, onto the wider road. The left fork goes uphill to Spring Lake and Tin Hat Mtn. To get there, continue to small Spring Lake, on the right. Park 450 meters beyond it. Walk the old logging road that cuts off right. After about two hours, look for a faint trail on the left, heading up the modest, rocky summit in front of you.

7.8 km / 4.8 mi
Arrive at the turnoff for Nanton Lake campground. It's 200 meters down to the site. Continue north if you want to check out Dodd Lake.

12.9 km / 8.0 mi
Arrive at the entrance to Dodd Lake, at the KM 16 sign.

DODD LAKE RECREATION SITE #12
Weekend / Moderate
12 campsites, garbage cans, firewood

It's a pretty lake graced by beautiful mountains, but campsites are in the open, beside the main FS road.

~

THE NORTH END OF HWY 101

DINNER ROCK RECREATION AREA #29
Destination / Easy
12 tables, garbage cans, firewood, rough boat ramp, picnic spots

This campground on the Strait of Georgia, just south of Lund, is well manicured and offers several campsites directly above the ocean. To launch a boat, you have to carry it over rocks for 20 meters.

The turnoff is 15.8 kms / 9.8 miles north of the Petro Canada station on the northern edge of Powell River, or 1.3 kms / .8 mile south of the junction of Hwy 101 and the turnoff to Okeover Inlet. From Hwy 101, drive 1.6 kms / 1 mile on a rough, steeply descending dirt road to the campground. It's closed from October 15 to April 15, to prevent further erosion of this already badly eroded approach road.

~

OKEOVER PROVINCIAL PARK CAMPGROUND
Destination (only if you're boating to Desolation Sound Marine Park) / Easy
5 tables, water pump, firewood (no fires allowed at the sites in trees)

This isn't a great place to stay for more than a night. It's really just a big pullout, with a view over the thrilling expanse of Okeover Inlet — thrilling because you're so far north, not because the scenery is startling. The campsites are crammed together, so there's no privacy. Yet it's usually full in summer.

Just south of Lund, turn east at the junction of Hwy 101 and the road to Okeover Inlet. You'll arrive at the site in 4.2 kms / 2.6 miles from the junction. It's a total of 5 kms / 3 miles from Lund. Read the sign at the junction: One of the last remaining unpolluted mariculture areas on the North American Coast. Help us save this inlet.

~

INLAND LAKE RECREATION SITE
Weekend / Easy
16 tables, 5 cabins (2 at the parking lot) for disabled
people, garbage cans, firewood

This is a very special FS campground, with a 13 km wheelchair-accessible trail around the 5.5 km long lake. It's made from crushed limestone and never exceeds a 4% grade. How wonderful! The lake and trail make this a spot anyone will enjoy, but especially the disabled. There are rest areas along the way and three rustic log-cabins for the disabled to camp in overnight. There are wheelchair-accessible outhouses, fishing wharfs for people to roll their wheelchair onto, and a caretaker at the main campground who'll gladly help anyone who needs it. The rest of you will have to walk one minute from the parking lot to many of the campsites. The road to this campground is better signed than any on the Sunshine Coast, probably because there's a FS office in Powell River.

From Powell River

0 km / 0 mi
In Powell River, at Ash Avenue and Poplar Street, there's a green sign for Cranberry Lake. Look for it where Cranberry Street leaves Hwy 101

(before the bridge over the Powell Lake outlet). Drive through residential streets and pass a sandpit on the left. There are many ways to get through Powell River. You can approach from Cassiar Manson Avenue, if you're coming from the south. Whichever, just head toward Cranberry Lake.

3.7 km / 2.3 mi
Turn at the blue and white sign: 7.6 km Inland Lake Camping. From the east side of Cranberry Lake, head east on Haslam Street.

4.3 km / 2.7 mi
Go left at the clearly marked turn. Sign: Haywire Bay Regional Park 7 km. Stay straight (right) on Inland Lake Road.

11.3 km / 7 mi
Turn left at the junction and drive a short way down the hill.

~

LOWER MAINLAND

SALSBURY & STAVE LAKES
Weekend / Difficult

We don't recommend these campgrounds. You might enjoy driving the paved road through the beautiful farm valley west of Harrison Lake. It's broad and green, with hillsides nearby and looming peaks beyond. But turn around when the dirt begins. It's not worth continuing unless you have a tough vehicle and tough kidneys. Certainly don't come here if you're a tourist. Massive clearcuts are your reward for enduring the long approach and descent to Stave Lake. We'd much prefer to visit one of the big, easily accessible lakes in southern B.C., or the nearby Chehalis River campgrounds. (See the descriptions after this section.) Quite a few gun lovers come out to target practice in this area. We don't like camping, or even driving, where bullets are whizzing around. If you just want to see more of your province, here are the directions.

On Hwy 7, go 1.6 kms / 1 mile west of the tiny town of Dewdney, or 3.2 kms / 2 miles east of Hatzic. Turn right (north) on Sylvester Road. There's no sign for the provincial park at Davis Lake, which is north on this road. That's odd, because provincial parks are always signed. Set your tripometer to 0 at the turn.

0 km / 0 mi
From the gas station on the corner of Sylvester Road and Hwy 7, head north.

3.7 km / 2.3 mi
Bear right at the junction. Sign: Cascade Falls Regional Park 1 km.

11.7 km / 7.3 mi
Continue straight at the junction.

15.4 km / 9.6 mi
Pavement ends. Lost Creek FS Road (gravel) begins.

16.1 km / 10 mi
Bear left at the junction. Lost - Murdo FS Road is on the right.

16.4 km / 10.2 mi
Pass a sign high on a tree to your right: Entering Davis Lake PP.

20.3 km / 12.6 mi
Cross a wooden bridge over an impressive gorge.

22.7 km / 14.1 mi
You'll get a view of Stave Lake, far below in the distance.

23.2 km / 14.4 mi
Continue past the wood sign at the middle of a fork. Go left where a FS signpost on Lost Cr FS Road points to Salsbury Lake.

23.8 km / 14.8 mi
Cross Lost Creek on a wooden bridge. Be careful to avoid the big hole on the left side of this bridge. It could sink a little car. The road starts ascending after the bridge.

24.6 km / 15.3 mi
Pass a gravel pit used for target practice — what a mess! Shortly after, continue straight, passing a road on your left.

26 km / 16.1 mi
Arrive at another junction with a FS signpost: Salsbury. Go right to Salsbury Lake. Lost - Cypress Point FS Road goes left to **Cypress Point Recreation Site #3** on Stave Lake. Don't try it in a motorhome. At Stave Lake, in addition to a small, open area for vehicles, there's a forested area for tenting. A short, steep trail leads to the lake. This access is not a good place to launch even a cartop boat.

26.8 km / 16.6 mi
Go left at the junction, onto Lost Cr FS Road. The mountain ahead suffered a buzz cut.

27.4 km / 17 mi
Arrive at a sign that identifies the disappointing pullout as **Salsbury Lake Recreation Site #2**. It's big enough for a few cars, but only comfortable for one family. There's one table and no view, except of a clearcut and scrawny trees beside the road. There's a 50-meter trail

(portage for small boats) down to the lake. The lake itself is impressive and affords views of nice mountains.

~

CHEHALIS LAKE

Chehalis Lake is in a valley west of Harrison Lake. If you're driving anything less than a truck or 4WD vehicle, go slow and easy. Though the road is wide and the grade is gentle, it's rough. We drove part way and decided it wasn't worthwhile. Lots of stones and sharp rocks jump around, in addition to the usual potholes and washboards. It's an active logging road, closed weekdays 6 a.m. to 6 p.m. Here's how to get started, for those who can tolerate a body-throttling drive and mind-numbing clearcuts.

0 km / 0 mi
In Harrison Mills, turning off Hwy 7, onto Morris Valley Road. Pass the Sasquatch Inn and go left at the four-way stop sign. This road leaves near the Canfor office.

.5 km / .3 mi
Turn left onto Chehalis FS Road. This is directly across from Chehalis Road, which enters a Native reserve.

Chehalis South Recreation Site #6 is on the far south end of the lake and is usually quieter than the next two. When you come to a bridge at 14.5 kms / 9 miles, go up a big hill, then take a fork to the right. After another bridge, go uphill again, then take a left. There's a brown sign marking the site, at about 21 kms / 13 miles.

Skwellepil Creek Recreation Site #7 (about 13 campsites) is two-thirds of the way up the west side of Chehalis Lake. We're told there's often a rowdy crowd here. There's more chance for peace in the over-flow parking up top on the back loop, away from the lake.

Chehalis Lake North Recreation Site #8 is a campground in trees, with a boat launch. To get there, continue driving along the west side of the lake to the far north end.

~

House Hold

If you own a house, it can hold you to it. Maintenance and improvements sap your time and energy. No wonder people try to justify it all by staying home and enjoying the place. If you own a house, but still yearn for adventure, be strong. Break the hold. Go camping. Each time you return, you'll appreciate your house more for what it really is: shelter from the elements.

HARRISON LAKE & CHEHALIS RIVER

This is a beautiful area to explore, even if you don't continue very far up Harrison Lake. The drive along Hwy 7 overlooks the lush, pastoral Fraser Valley and gives views across to the monstrous Cheam and Border Peaks. Weaver Creek and the spawning channel near the southwestern end of the lake are excellent places to see salmon in the first weeks of October. The campgrounds along the Chehalis River are the nicest and most easily accessible ones in the area. Some of the best camping on Harrison Lake is about 30 kms / 18 miles up the rough east-side road, beyond the limits we've set for this book.

If you're heading east on Hwy 7 from Vancouver

Drive Peter Lougheed Hwy 7 to Harrison Mills and a junction. Turn left onto Morris Valley Road. Set your tripometer to 0.

If you're heading east or west on Trans-Canada Hwy 1

Between Chilliwack and Hope, take Exit 135: Bridal Falls, Agassiz, Harrison Hotsprings.

0 km / 0 mi
From Hwy 1, you'll be turning onto Hwy 9. Head north and cross the Fraser River. In about 6 km / 3.7 miles, go left at the junction of Hwys 7 West and 7 East. Follow signs in Agassiz, heading west on Hwy 7, to Harrison Mills.

20.0 km / 12.4 mi
Come to a huge metal bridge over the Harrison River. It's a good place to watch salmon during the October run. Pass a sign: Pioneer - Chehalis.

21.0 km / 13.0 mi
In Harrison Mills, go right onto Morris Valley Road. Set your tripometer to 0 at the turn.

For all approaches above, now follow the directions below

0 km / 0 mi
At the turn from Hwy 7 onto Morris Valley Road. You'll see the following destinations signed: Hemlock Valley Recreation Area, Chehalis River Hatchery 6 km, Weaver Creek Spawning Channel 12 km. In 0.5 km / 0.3 mile, go straight at the junction, on pavement, toward Hemlock Valley and Harrison Lake. The immediate left is the rough road mentioned above that goes to Chehalis Lake.

5.8 km / 3.6 mi
Turn right at the brown signpost. It's next to the stop sign facing drivers exiting. Drive in 0.3 km / 0.2 mile. Arrive at the first and largest Chehalis River campground.

CHEHALIS RIVER RECREATION SITE #17
Weekend / Easy
About 40 campsites, no tables, on a loop, garbage cans

Campsites are well-spaced in forest, beside the river. The river is shallow and wide here, so it's a good place to frolic and enjoy the sandy beach.

6.0 km / 3.7 mi
Turn left (northwest) before the steel bridge, to the second **Chehalis River campground**. This spot isn't as nice. There are five more campsites without tables.

6.1 km / 3.8 mi
Cross a bridge. Just after it, turn left for the worst **Chehalis River campground**. In case the others are full, you'll find five campsites here. They're close together, without tables

Continuing to the west side of Harrison Lake

6.8 km / 4.2 mi
At the junction, stay straight on Morris Valley Road.

7.9 km / 4.9 mi
Go straight at the junction, toward Weaver Creek Spawning Channel. Left goes to Hemlock Ski Area. Set your tripometer to 0.

0 km / 0 mi
At the junction, where roads lead to Weaver Creek and Hemlock.

3 km / 1.9 mi
The road turns to dirt.

3.5 km / 2.2 mi
Cross a bridge and arrive at the spawning channel. If the salmon are running, stop just before the bridge and check out the action in Weaver Creek. The road begins ascending.

5.1 km / 3.2 mi
Continue straight on Harrison West FS Road. The left fork (marked by a brown post) is a rough, steep road heading about 3 kms to **Weaver Lake Recreation Site #20**. Most 2WD vehicles can make it, if the driver's persistent.

5.3 km / 3.3 mi
Arrive at Wolf Lake.

WOLF LAKE RECREATION SITE #19
Overnight / Easy
1 table with a view of the lake, 2 tables beside the road

This campground isn't worth more than a quick overnighter. The small lake, surrounded by thick forest, could be fun for beginning canoeists.

5.5 km / 3.4 mi
Arrive at the turn-in to Grace Lake, by a sign on the right. Big potholes at the entrance. Drive in 150 meters, then take the right fork. Continue another 300 meters. Take care and watch for big depressions.

GRACE LAKE RECREATION SITE #18
Overnight / Easy
3 campsites, 2 with tables, at a pretty lake well off the road

The steep forested sides of Grace Lake give it an intimate feeling of privacy. It's much better than Wolf Lake and should be quiet. You can't really see the lake from the campsites, which are just above it.

Continuing on Harrison West FS Road

7.1 km / 4.4 mi
You'll see a Km 2 sign. These markers are based on an old system, so only use them as landmarks to compare where you are with our descriptions.

9 km / 5.6 mi
After ascending and crossing a peninsula, you come to a viewpoint over Harrison Lake. The road levels now as it heads north and is fairly good: wide, graded, washboarded in spots.

11.7 km / 7.2 mi
Pass a signpost for Francis Lake FS Road veering sharply up to your left. It's a 4WD road to the FS campground up there.

17.5 km / 10.8 mi
Cross a creek.

20.8 km / 12.9 mi
Pass Harrison West - Simms Cr FS Road on your left.

8.5 km / 13.9 mi
Cross a bridge and stay straight at the junction with Harrison West - Walian Cr FS Road.

24.5 km / 15.2 mi
There's a sign on the right, near the Km 20 mark. At this junction, stay right. Stay left at the next small fork with a bad road on the right. Arrive at Wood Lake.

WOOD LAKE RECREATION SITE #12
Overnight / Difficult (because it's a long, tiresome drive)
3 campsites, 2 tables

A view of the distant, glacier-clad Pemberton Mountains is insufficient reward for this drive. It's only worth coming here if you're exploring farther north. If you go another 150 meters on the main road, you'll come to a stop sign marking the turn-in for more campsites.

If you don't mind more bucking around, you can continue north to Twenty Mile Creek and a medium-size campground on the bay.

East side of Harrison Lake

The drive along the southeastern end of the lake is beautiful. Unlike the west side, the road hugs the water's edge for a while. You can see a massive glacier at the north end of the lake. Pay to stay at Sasquatch Provincial Park, if you want to camp on this side. The free FS campgrounds are a long way up the lake, on a rough logging road.

Take Exit 135 off the Trans-Canada Hwy, 36 kms / 58 miles southwest of Hope. The highway sign states: Bridal Falls - Agassiz - Harrison Hotsprings. Set your tripometer to 0 as you exit.

0 km / 0 mi
At Exit 135, off Hwy 1, heading northwest on Hwy 9.

5.5 km / 3.4 mi
Go left at the junction of Hwy 7 West and 7 East. Follow signs in Agassiz, heading west on Hwys 7 and 9. Follow the sign to Sasquatch Provincial Park.

9.3 km / 5.8 mi
Go right at the junction. Follow Hwy 9 North to Harrison Hot Springs.

16 km / 9.9 mi
Arrive at the town of Harrison Hot Springs. Go right at the T-intersection near the lake's end, heading to the east side of Harrison Lake and Sasquatch Provincial Park. Set your tripometer to 0 here.

Now follow the directions below

0 km / 0 mi
At the intersection in Harrison Hot Springs. The roller-coaster road is paved until Sasquatch.

6.3 km / 3.9 mi
Go right at the junction, following the sign to Sasquatch Provincial Park and Hicks Lake. The left road goes to the day-use area. You'll also be following signs for the Forestry Tour Route.

7.4 km / 4.6 mi
Go left at the junction, onto gravel Harrison East FS Road. It's wide, but gets pretty jolty. It's about an hour's drive north from here to **tent camping at Cogburn Beach.** The campground is in ancient forest beside the lake. Some people camp down on the beach when the water's low. It's a five- or ten-minute walk down from parking on the road. There's a small mill and booming-ground in the bay, but it shouldn't be a bother to campers.

~

CHILLIWACK RIVER & CHILLIWACK LAKE

The Chilliwack River and Lake are beautiful places to spend a weekend or more. There are recreation opportunities galore. The hiking, kayaking, boating, fall salmon-fishing, and lounging possibilities are excellent. The town of Chilliwack is 105 kms / 65 miles east of downtown Vancouver.

From Hwy 1 take Exit 119 A: Sardis - Cultus Lake. Set your tripometer to 0. Turn right (south) and pass the fast-food shops and gas stations of Chilliwack. Stay on Vedder Road. Drive 5.5 kms / 3.4 miles to a three-way junction at the metal bridge over the Chilliwack River. Turn left just before the bridge. Head toward Chilliwack Lake. A sign indicates: Chilliwack Lake Provincial Park 42 kms. Set your tripometer to 0 at the turn.

Thurston Meadows campground on the Chilliwack River

0 km / 0 mi
After turning left at the Chilliwack River bridge, starting to drive on the north side of the river.

9.7 km / 6 mi
Slesse Park Road forks off to your left, just before another bridge over the Chilliwack River. Continue straight on the main paved road. There are a number of easy-to-access campgrounds between here and Chilliwack Lake.

If you take the Slesse Park Road to campgrounds on the north side of the river, you'll have to negotiate a rough surface, steep turns, and bad potholes. The north-side road gets really sloppy after rain and takes patience if you're not driving a truck or high-clearance 4WD. You can reach these campgrounds easier and quicker from the eastern end, by continuing on the main highway, then turning in a short way at Foley Creek FS Road. You'll find directions for the north-side campgrounds after our descriptions of the other Chilliwack River and Lake campgrounds.

10 km / 6.2 mi
Come to an **overnight pullout**, in trees on the river.

10.5 km / 6.5 mi
Continue east on the highway for campgrounds farther along the Chilliwack River, or turn right for the campground at Tamihi Creek. Drive in .4 km / .2 mile on the signed Chilliwack - Liumchen Creek FS Road. You'll cross the Tamihi Creek bridge. Don't go left up the Chilliwack - Tamihi Cr FS Road.

TAMIHI CREEK RECREATION SITE #46
Weekend / Easy
30+ campsites, 20 with tables, garbage cans, day-use area with tables

This large campground is provincial-park quality. All the sites are in a healthy deciduous forest, and many are beside the lovely creek. It's a prime salmon-fishing spot in October.

14 km / 8.7 mi
Look for a dirt road on your left, plunging down to the river. A brown post on the right side of the dirt access road marks Allison Pool.

ALLISON POOL RECREATION SITE #45
Weekend / Easy
4 well-spaced campsites with tables, garbage cans, large parking area

15.8 km / 9.8 mi
Look for a large **overnight pullout** on the left, with paths through the bush to the river. It's handy as an overflow area in the busy salmon-fishing season, but otherwise it's not a desirable campsite.

17.4 km / 10.8 mi
Arrive at the turnoff for Thurston Meadow campground.

THURSTON MEADOW RECREATION SITE #44
Weekend / Easy
A couple tables in trees on the river's edge, about 8 campsites, garbage cans

We luxuriated in the sun one beautiful April day at this riverside, meadow spot. We enjoyed views of surrounding mountains and estimated how long it'd take for the sun to melt the snow, so we could hike into the alpine. The campsites are near the highway, but if you camp on the bank above the boisterous riffles, much of the highway noise is muffled. The sites are scattered along the river and around the meadow. Some are in the open, others wedged in trees. There are huge potholes at the road entrance, so drive in carefully.

23.2 km / 14.4 mi
Arrive at the turn-in to Pierce Creek campground. Drive in .3 km / .2 mile on a potholed road between fences.

PIERCE CREEK TRAIL & RECREATION SITE #43
Overnight / Easy
2 tables, garbage cans, a yuk spot

This campground is hard to find if you're following the FS map, because it's marked wrong: away from the creek and not at the trailhead. Actually, the small, grassy, trailhead parking lot with tables next to trees *is* the campground. There are no views, but it's probably quiet at night.

27.4 km / 17 mi
Arrive at the turn-in for Camp Foley. When heading east, it's just 150 meters on your left, after the Chilliwack River bridge with white, wooden sides, and immediately before the Foley Creek FS Road. When you turn in, double back toward the river.

CAMP FOLEY RECREATION SITE #39
Overnight / Easy
3 campsites, no tables, garbage cans

This one's right beside the road, so it's not a desirable campground. But it's convenient, so you're sure to have company here. It's a big pullout with lush trees on two sides, next to the river.

27.4 km / 17 mi
Immediately after Camp Foley, the Foley Creek FS Road joins the highway. It's marked by a large brown sign. Turn left to campgrounds on the north side of the Chilliwack River. Set your tripometer to 0 at the turn.

To continue straight on the main road toward Chilliwack Lake, skip to the directions below this North Side section.

North side of Chilliwack River

0 km / 0 mi
Turning onto Foley Creek FS Road. A sign warns not to exceed 50 km/h. Even in a truck, it's ridiculous and unsafe to drive that fast.

2.1 km / 1.3 mi
Go over a wooden bridge and turn left, passing Foley Cr FS Road on your right. There's a FS campground up that road, but you need a high-clearance 4WD vehicle.

4 km / 2.5 mi
Go left at the junction with Chipmunk Creek FS Road.

4.5 km / 2.8 mi
Arrive at provincial-park-quality Chipmunk campground on your left, beside the Chilliwack River.

CHIPMUNK PENINSULA RECREATION SITE #40
Weekend / Easy (Difficult via Sleese entrance)
13 campsites, most with tables, garbage cans

The campsites are within earshot of the revitalizing sound of rapids, and are well-spaced among old-growth evergreens.

6.8 km / 4.2 mi
Pass Mt. Thurston FS Road.

7.3 km / 4.5 mi
Arrive at Rapids campground.

RAPIDS RECREATION SITE #41
Weekend / Easy (Difficult via Sleese entrance)
3 campsites, 1 table

Roaring rapids will entertain you at this intimate campground. There's a big, sloping rock where you can stretch out and catch some rays. It's too dangerous here for swimming or wading.

8.1 km / 5 mi
Arrive at Eagles Roost campground, with deep pools and roaring white water.

EAGLES ROOST RECREATION SITE #42
Weekend / Easy (Difficult via Slesse entrance)
1 table, room for two vehicles

Continuing toward Chilliwack Lake, past the junction with Foley Creek FS Road

28.8 km / 17.9 mi
The main road becomes gravel and dirt, or mud when it's raining.

30.1 km / 19 mi
Arrive at Riverside campground. About 100 meters farther, on the right, there's a second entrance and parking, where Chilliwack South FS Road heads off.

RIVERSIDE RECREATION SITE #37
Weekend / Easy
Walk-in tent sites 10 meters from the parking area, garbage cans, 8 fire rings

Boulders at each end of the campground block vehicles from interrupting tenters' peace. The sites are well-spaced in deep woods. No sun penetrates here. Though the campground is beside the road, the river muffles most noise.

38.8 km / 24.1 mi
Pass Paulsen Road on your right.

39.8 km / 24.7 mi
Turn left off the highway, to Post Creek campground. Go right at the brown post, which is spray-painted: Post. Drive in .6 km / .4 mile.

POST CREEK RECREATION SITE #36
Weekend / Moderate
12+ campsites, several on the creek, 8 tables, garbage cans

This site is worn out from heavy use and inconsiderate people who've trashed it. It's located at the trailhead to Lindeman and Greendrop Lakes, which is a good early season hike. Most of the campsites are reached via this entrance. At the second entrance (described below), there are two campsites with tables on the creek. Those aren't so good, because people park here and are continually driving in and out.

40.4 km / 25.1 mi
Arrive at the second entrance to Post Creek campgrounds, on the northeast. You'll see a stop sign for drivers exiting. Go 150 meters in, to the Flora Lake trailhead parking on the right. In 300 meters, you'll see campsites and a sign: Lindeman Lake 1.2 km.

41 km / 25.4 mi
Pass the Chilliwack Lake Provincial Park entrance on your right. Arrive at the beginning of the lake. The lakeside road is in pretty good condition, not too rocky and generally flat. Even if you're not staying, drive this fun road and enjoy the great views. After a few curves at the beginning of the lake, the road is directly above the lakeshore.

42.2 km / 26.2 mi
Stop for the view straight south over Chilliwack Lake and the mountains beyond.

42.7 km / 26.5 mi
Here's the best view of Chilliwack Lake, with MacDonald Peak across the way.

48.3 km / 30 mi
Pass a beach and boat launch.

48.6 km / 30.2 mi
Arrive at Paleface campground. For two more campsites, go 150 meters farther and turn right, just before the wooden bridge.

PALEFACE RECREATION SITE #35
Destination / Moderate
1 table and spots for 5 vehicles, garbage cans

This small site, close to the lakeshore, has all the features of a destination campground: a frolicking creek, tall trees, a sandy beach, and a beautiful lake.

~

North side of Chilliwack River via Slesse Park Road

The campgrounds listed below are described in the section above.

0 km / 0 mi
Turning onto Sleese Park Road, just before the Chilliwack River bridge.

2.1 km / 1.3 mi
The road becomes gravel and starts ascending. It gets fairly steep and has broad switchbacks. Pass a sign: Chilliwack Army FS Road.

4.3 km / 2.7 mi
The road levels.

8.2 km / 5.1 mi
Go right at the junction. Chilliwack Bench FS Road goes straight.

9.2 km / 5.7 mi
Come to an **overnight pullout** up on a bench with a mountain view. It's only worth using if the official campgrounds are full.

12.7 km / 7.9 mi
Watch for big potholes across the entire road.

16.1 km / 10 mi
Come to an **overnight pullout** on the north side, before the rockslide area. There's a grassy spot for a tent. 150 meters farther, there's a fabulous **overnight pullout** on a small road that goes back a ways beside the river. It even has a mountain view.

16.4 km / 10.2 mi
Arrive at **Eagles Roost Recreation Site #42**.

17.2 km / 10.7 mi
Arrive at **Rapids Recreation Site #41**.

17.7 km / 11 mi
See a sign for Chilliwack - Mt. Thurston FS Road. Continue on the main logging road.

19.2 km / 11.9 mi
Stop to look down at an arrestingly blue pool below the cliff. It's an excellent spot for watching salmon in October. We saw 50 go by in less than a minute.

20 km / 12.4 mi
Arrive at **Chipmunk Peninsula Recreation Site #40**.

20.4 km / 12.7 mi
Go straight (right) at the junction with Chilliwack - Chipmunk Creek FS Road.

22.4 km / 13.9 mi
Come to the junction with Chilliwack - Foley FS Road. Turn right, toward the highway, and go over a wooden bridge crossing Foley Creek. Straight goes to **Foley Lake Recreation Site #38**, which is only suitable for trucks or 4WD vehicles.

24.5 km / 15.2 mi
Arrive back at the paved highway and a large brown sign: Chilliwack - Foley Creek FS Road.

~

NEAR HOPE

JONES (WAHLEACH) LAKE CAMPGROUND
Weekend / Difficult
13 campsites with tables (2 without), some beside the creek, some overlooking the lake, garbage cans galore

This BC Hydro campground is in the mountains above Trans-Canada Hwy 1. You'll ascend steeply on a very rough road with sharp switchbacks. It's not for big motorhomes. You'll be okay in a low-clearance car if you go slow. Incredible peaks rise above the south end of the lake, but there aren't great views from the campground. The lake itself is fairly large, surrounded by trees. Beautiful fall colors compensate for the low water-levels that time of year.

From Trans-Canada Hwy 1, take Exit 153: Laidlaw / Jones Lake. The exit is 18.7 kms / 11.6 miles northeast of Harrison Hotsprings Exit 135, or 17.3 kms / 10.7 miles west of Hope. Set your tripometer to 0.

For either approach above, now follow the directions below

0 km / 0 mi
Upon exiting the highway, turn onto Laidlaw Road.

.8 km / .5 mi
Cross Jones Creek and immediately veer right. BC Hydro has a blue sign: Jones Lake Recreation Area 9 km - Wahleach Lake. The road gets rough and begins ascending steeply.

3.7 km / 2.3 mi
Stay right on Jones FS Road, at the fork with Lorenzetta FS Road, which veers off left.

4 km / 2.5 mi
The road levels. Your patience is rewarded. The grade relaxes the rest of the way.

8.5 km / 5.3 mi
Go left on Jones Lake FS Road, at the signed junction.

9.7 km / 6 mi
Go straight (right) at the junction, continuing on Jones Lake Road.

10 km / 6.2 mi
Go right and arrive at Jones Lake.

10.5 km / 6.5 mi
You'll find a picnic area and three more campsites with tables.

~

EATON CREEK RECREATION SITE #32
Weekend / Easy
3 tables, 2 enclosed by woods, trail to Eaton Lake

Adventure awaits you in this wonderful, deep, mountain valley. It's worth visiting just for the drive. Silverhope Creek is lively and healthy. Fall colors are exuberant. The road ends at Ross Lake, where you can hike from Hozomeen into the North Cascades.

Eaton Creek is a superb campground, on a bench above the road, where you can contemplate the creek valley and a mountain. There's a very short, rough entrance, but cars can make it in dry weather.

An excellent overnight pullout off the Silverhope Creek Road

From Trans-Canada Hwy 1, take Exit 168: Flood - Hope Rd, Silver Hope Creek. The exit is 32.7 kms / 20.3 miles northeast of Harrison Hotsprings Exit 135, or 3.2 kms / 2 miles west of Hope. Exiting from the west, drive .5 km / .3 mile from the highway. Then set your tripometer to 0.

For either approach above, now follow the directions below

0 km / 0 mi
At the beginning of the Flood Hope Road.

.3 km / .2 mi
Turn south onto the Silver Skagit Road. You'll see a sign: Silver Lake, 38 miles to Hozomeen campground.

2.6 km / 1.6 mi
The road is gravel now.

6.6 km / 4.1 mi
Go left at the signed junction, toward Ross Lake and the Skagit Valley. Right leads to Silver Lake in 1 km.

8.4 km / 5.2 mi
You'll see an **overnight pullout** on your right. It's beside the road under a tree, on the grassy, north end of Silver Lake.

11 km / 6.9 mi
There's an **overnight pullout** to the right, across from a gravel pit. The campsite is 150 meters in from the road, on a large, gravel (almost sandy) bank, on a quiet stretch of the creek. There's room for two vehicles well apart, with a looming mountain-wall to gaze at.

14.8 km / 9.2 mi
You'll see an **overnight pullout** for one vehicle. It's beside the creek, by the fire ring just off the road.

17.2 km / 10.7 mi
Arrive at the official Eaton Creek campground.

~

NAHATLATCH RIVER
Destination / Easy
A wide choice of campgrounds in a beautiful river valley

These campgrounds, near the upper Fraser River, between Hope to the south and Lytton to the north, could also be placed in the Hwy 99 section of this book. Since the fastest way to get here from Vancouver is via Trans-Canada Hwy 1 (which you're also likely to be traveling on if you're coming from the east), we've listed them here, with other areas off Hwy 1 in southwestern B.C.

The Nahatlatch is a fast, glorious, whitewater river, in a sunny valley. Kayakers and rafters love it. Anybody will enjoy camping here. There's a string of campgrounds along the wide, clear water, and along a chain of lakes farther west. It's worth coming out from the city just to sit at one of these spots and relax, fish, or watch rapids from the shore. The river current is way too fast to dip in, but just watching it charge past seems to have a cooling effect.

If you want a bird's eye view of the Fraser River Canyon and snowy peaks above, drive up the Nahatlatch Lookout logging road. This road takes off from the lower, main FS road, near the Apocynum campground.

off from the lower, main FS road, near the Apocynum campground. The soft, silty dirt probably makes the road impassable for 2WD in rain. Otherwise, it's smooth and easy enough for low-clearance cars most of the approximately 16 kms / 10 miles. After 8 kms / 5 miles, the rougher, steeper ascent will strain smaller motors. Near the Km 10 sign, at about 1200 meters elevation, we reached the snowline in early May. From mid-June, you can venture on a hike along the ridge, traveling northwest from the lookout.

Exercise equipment supplied by the Forest Service, Nahatlatch River

Your Keys to the Kingdom

When we were ready to leave Rupert Inlet, on Vancouver Island, it was Craig's turn to drive. I handed him the car keys and said, "Here's your keys to the kingdom." We had a good laugh, thinking of how true it is. Turn the ignition, and away you go: the world is yours.

If you're heading north

From the southeast side of the Fraser River bridge in Hope, drive about 65 kms / 40 miles north. Turn off Hwy 1 at Boston Bar and go through town to cross the Fraser River bridge.

If you're heading south

Take Hwy 1 south of Lytton to Boston Bar and go through town to cross the Fraser River bridge.

For either approach above, now follow the directions below

0 km / 0 mi
In the middle of the Fraser River bridge. When you reach the west side, cross the railroad tracks and head north through North Bend on the paved West Side Road.

7.7 km / 4.8 mi
The paved road becomes well-graded dirt.

10.7 km / 6.6 mi
Bear left at the fork to go above a field. This might be a temporary detour, which soon rejoins the main road.

13.7 km / 8.5 mi
Bear right at the fork.

15.4 km / 9.5 mi
Come to a narrow, wood bridge over the Nahatlatch River. Be sure to stop and peer down at the water roaring through the chasm.

16.7 km / 10.4 mi
After passing the road going down to REO's rafting base, stay left at this junction where a road goes right sharply uphill. Continue on the main road to follow the Nahatlatch River upstream and eventually reach the lakes.

16.8 km / 10.4 mi
Stay left for campgrounds. The signed Nahatlatch Lookout Road goes up to the right.

18.4 km / 11.4 mi
Apocynum Recreation Site #30 is on the left. It has three campsites. The dirt road ends at the river's edge in 0.4 km, so approach slowly to avoid driving straight into the churning flow. There's no barrier or warning sign.

19.9 km / 12.3 mi
Just after passing a road on the right, turn left. Fir Flat Recreation Site

#29 is on the riverside. It has two tables in trees, providing welcome shade in this dry valley.

20.8 km / 12.9 mi
There's an overnight pullout on the left, at the water's edge.

25.4 km / 15.7 mi
Stay left (west) on the main road where a fork goes right (north) up Log Creek.

25.5 km / 15.8 mi
Arrive at Log Creek Recreation Site #28. It has two tables.

25.9 km / 16.1 mi
At the junction, stay straight on the north side of the river. Don't go left, which leads to a bridge over the Nahatlatch.

26.4 km / 16.4 mi
Arrive at Francis Lake Recreation Site #27. It's on a small lake, where the water flows into the river.

28.1 km / 17.4 mi
Arrive at Hannah Lake Recreation Site #26. There's only one table and no privacy from the road.

28.9 km / 17.9 mi
Arrive at Old Hannah Lake Ranger Station Site #25. The cabin here is open to the public, first come, first served. Don't count on it being available. It's usually occupied by squatters, late fall through winter.

31.8 km / 19.7 mi
Arrive at Nahatlatch Lake Recreation Site #24. All three campsites have tables and are on the lake — really a broad river at this point. There's a view up the the lake, toward peaks.

33.2 km / 20.6 mi
Arrive at Salmon Beach Recreation Site #23. It offers plentiful shade, two tables beside the lake, and a view of snowy mountains.

35.9 km / 22.3 mi
Arrive at Squakum Creek Recreation Site #22. Drive .5 km / .3 mile down a rough, rutty road. A Winnebago made it. There are ten shady campsites with fire rings. It's a good spot if you enjoy the stillness of a lake more than the energy of a river. The lake water looks like swill here, but the view is excellent. For a glimpse of truly wild country, drive about a kilometer farther to the road's high point before it descends into the valley.

Roadside view of the upper reaches of the Nahatlatch Valley

~

NEAR LYTTON

STEIN RIVER TRAILHEAD
Weekend, if you're hiking / Moderate
No tables or toilets

Camp here *only* if you're hiking the Stein River Canyon. It's not on the way to anyplace else, and you have to pass through Native land on a small road where traffic is annoying to those living nearby. The hike along the Stein River is spectacular. You walk through a deep canyon, right along the roaring river, which is awesome during the spring runoff. It's worth visiting even if you only walk a few kilometers. Though this is not an official campground, you can sleep at the trailhead parking area, in the pines just above the river. Please respect the Native land.

0 km / 0 mi
Turn off Hwy 1, following the signs for Hwy 12, heading into Lytton. Pass through town and head north.

1.7 km / 1.1 mi
Go over the Thompson River.

2.2 km / 1.4 mi
Pass the Botanie Valley Road on your right. There's a FS campground up there on Botanie Lake. For directions, skip below this Stein section.

2.4 km / 1.5 mi
Go left and descend to the Fraser River.

3.3 km / 2.0 mi
Cross on the free ferry. It runs daily, on demand, 6:30 a.m. to 10:15 p.m., except for half-hour breaks mid-morning and early evening. On the other side, go right and head north on the West Side Road.

3.9 km / 2.4 mi
Ignore a road intersecting from the left.

4.6 km /2.9 mi
Pass Earlscourt Farm on the left.

7.3 km / 4.5 mi
Just after a sharp bend in the road, watch for your turn.

8.1 km / 5.0 mi
Turn left, cutting back on a rutted road that's little more than a track. You'll see a house on your right, across from the turn. This is Native land, so be respectful. Drive 1 km / 0.6 mi to the trailhead, on the south side of the river, where you're not on Native land. If you missed the turn, you'll come to a bridge over the Stein River, 0.6 km / 0.4 mi too far north.

~

BOTANIE VALLEY RECREATION SITE #54
Weekend / Moderate

This is a wonderful area to explore. The slopes of Botanie Mountain are a superb wildflower garden in June. If you're an energetic hiker, walking the old road up the ridge to the lookout will be a rewarding challenge. Just driving part way will give you grand views over the river valleys and the dry interior mountains.

0 km / 0 mi
Turn off Hwy 1, following the signs for Hwy 12, heading into the town of Lytton. Set your tripometer to 0 on the bridge over the Thompson River, just north of town.

0.5 km / 0.3 mi
Turn right on the signposted Botanie Valley Road, which is paved at first. It gradually ascends.

3.5 km / 2.2 mi
Pass a huge escarpment. In another few kilometers you'll pass farms and ranches. Stay on the main road, passing many side roads.

7.3 km / 4.5 mi
Pass Botanie Mountain Lookout Road on your left. If you want to hike to the top, you can drive in about half a kilometer in a low-clearance vehicle. Then you'd have to hoof it. Of course, there are great views up there, but you have to ascend about 1400 meters (4600 feet).

10 km / 6.2 mi
Pass a rougher side road on the right. After this you'll cross several creeks, including Botanie Creek.

17.4 km / 10.8 mi
Arrive at Botanie Lake. A few kilometers farther, come to the small, partially forested FS campground. To tackle the rough road beyond the lake you'll want a truck or 4WD.

33.5 km / 20.8 mi
Turn left at this junction. Follow the Izman Creek Road.

42.6 km / 26.4 mi
Arrive back at Hwy 12, about 19 km / 12 miles north of the Thompson River bridge at Lytton.

Getting Organized

When you're camping out of a car, categorize your stuff. Have several daypacks or small duffel bags for holding specific items. Refer to them as if they were rooms in your home. Which, in a sense, they are — temporarily. For example, if one of us asks, "Where's a knife?" the other can say, "Look in the kitchen." "The map?" "In the library." "My bandana?" "In your room." By the way, when you're traveling, the world is your living room.

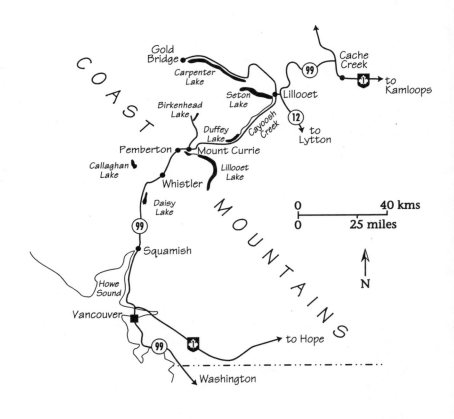

Highway 99: Vancouver
to Whistler to Lillooet

Highway 99: Vancouver to Whistler to Lillooet

SQUAMISH TO WHISTLER

The campgrounds in this area are great bases for exploring the rugged mountains and roaring rivers of the Coast Range. It helps to have these campgrounds so close to the highly developed recreation center of Whistler, so you can escape the bustle and expense.

CAL-CHEAK CONFLUENCE RECREATION SITES #3
Destination / Easy

Camping here can be soothing. The campgrounds are in a lush, glorious forest, beside a roaring river.

If you're heading north from Vancouver

From the turnoff to Horseshoe Bay, continue 86 km / 53 miles north on Hwy 99 to Brandywine Falls Provincial Park. You'll pass Daisy Lake on your right at about 79 km / 49 miles. Then be looking for the park. Set your tripometer to 0 at the entrance to Brandywine Falls Provincial Park.

0 km / 0 mi
Pass the turnoff on the right to Brandywine Falls Provincial Park.

4.1 km / 2.5 mi
For the Cal-Cheak River campgrounds, turn right here, just after crossing the bridge over Callaghan Creek. Set your tripometer to 0.

If you're heading south from Whistler

From the turnoff to Whistler Village (at Village Gate Blvd.), drive Hwy 99 south 5.5 km (3.4 miles) to the Cal-Cheak turnoff on your left.

For either approach above, now follow the directions below

0 km / 0 mi
Turn off the highway onto a wide, well graded, gravel road. You'll see a big sign: Cal-Cheak Recreation Site.

.16 km / .1 mi
Arrive at the first campground, on your right.

BCFS CALLAGHAN CREEK CAMP
5 tables, A-frame cooking shelter, flat spots for tents

Pretty campsites encircle a cleared cul de sac. Please preserve the patches of grass by not pitching your tent on them.

.5 km / .3 mi
Come to a signed junction. Head right on the main road to the south campground. Turn left and drive .3 km / .2 mile for the north one.

CAL CHEAK CONFLUENCE NORTH SITE
9 tables on the river

.8 km / .5 mi
Turn in on the right. Arrive at another campground, a giant stump tells you the ancient forest was logged. The sign was missing the C's in Cal Cheak:

AL HEAK VEHICLE CAMPING
8 tables in a forest, near the river

Drive 100 meters farther and you'll arrive at the turnoff to another campground, just right of a power line structure.

Settled in at Callaghan Creek, Coast Range

CAL CHEAK JCT RECREATION SITE
4 tables, plenty of flat space for tents

This spot is the most attractive. This south campground is also the trailhead for a four km one-way hike to Brandywine Falls. Start by crossing the suspension bridge over Callaghan Creek.

You can only drive to the first campsite. You have to walk a short way from the parking lot to reach the others, but that makes camping here special. There's enough space for about three vehicles in the outer parking area.

~

ALEXANDER FALLS & CALLAGHAN LAKE

The road in gives you good views of mountains few people see as they rush past on the main highway. When you descend on your return to Hwy 99, you get a terrific look at the Black Tusk across the valley to the east. Callaghan Lake is stunning, ringed by rugged peaks, a glacier, and a waterfall. Bring your canoe, or go ambling along the lakeshore.

If you're heading north from Vancouver

From the turnoff to Horseshoe Bay, continue on Hwy 99 north 86 km / 53 miles to Brandywine Falls Provincial Park. You'll pass Daisy Lake on your right at about 79 km / 49 miles. Then be looking for the park. Set your tripometer to 0 at the entrance to Brandywine Falls Provincial Park.

0 km / 0 mi
Pass the turnoff to Brandywine Falls Provincial Park.

4.1 km / 2.5 mi
Cross the bridge over Callaghan Creek and pass the entrance to the Cal-Cheak campgrounds on your right. Just after the four-lane section of highway ends at the north end, look for a dirt road on the left.

4.4 km / 2.7 mi
Look for a sign on the right: Km 45. You'll see another sign on the left: Callaghan Lake FS Rd. The sign Mad River Nordic Centre will probably still be there too. Set your tripometer to 0.

If you're heading south from Whistler

From the turnoff to Whistler Village (at Village Gate Blvd.), drive Hwy 99 south 5 km / 3 miles to the Callaghan Lake turnoff on your right.

For either approach above, now follow the directions below

0 km / 0 mi
Turn off Hwy 99 onto Callaghan Lake FS Road.

.4 km / .3 mi
See a sign on the right: Callaghan L, Mad L, Alexander Falls. The road is stony and rough. Drive through a recovery area and see a clearcut hillside to the west.

9 km / 5.5 mi
Come to a dark green sign at a junction. Drive less than 200 meters to the left for Alexander Falls campground. Continue on the main road to reach Callaghan Lake.

ALEXANDER FALLS RECREATION SITE #4
Overnight / Difficult
2 tables, level spot for a tent

You can drift off to sleep here while listening to the crashing falls in the gorge below.

9.2 km / 5.7 mi
You'll cross a creek, then pass a huge pullout with views over the forest. The road climbs, but isn't terribly steep. Expect bad washboards for several kilometers. The potholes are shallow and not continuous.

9.5 km / 5.9 mi
Pass a rough road on the right, just as the main road starts uphill. There's a small campground up there at Madely Lake. You'd need a truck or 4WD to get there.

16 km / 10 mi
The road deteriorates, but is okay for 2WD. A Mazda sports car flew past us.

17.7 km / 11 mi
Arrive at Callaghan Lake.

CALLAGHAN LAKE RECREATION SITE #5
Weekend / Difficult
3 campsites, 2 with tables

The campground itself isn't very nice. It's just a huge dirt parking lot. But you probably won't complain when you see the lake and mountains. There are about three spots where you can pitch a tent facing the lake.

~

NORTHWEST OF PEMBERTON

MEAGER CREEK HOT SPRINGS RECREATION SITE #16
Weekend / Moderate

This is an extremely popular campground because of the wonderful hot springs. It's possible to have as many as 600 people here at once, so don't come expecting quiet. In 1996 the springs were officially closed because the Ministry of Health determined that the contaminated water was unsafe for bathing. Don't drive up here without first checking with the Squamish FS office (898-2100) for current information. There are usually swarms of horseflies in summer, so camping can be unpleasant, unless you're enclosed in screen or immersed in water.

It's worth the trip just to see the pastoral Pemberton and Lillooet river valleys cradled by high mountains. Hikers should explore the Stoltmann Wilderness Hiking Route, which you can access 6.5 km / 4.0 miles beyond the hot springs parking lot. Contact the Western Canada Wilderness Committee at (604) 683-8220 for a trail description and directions to the trailhead.

Logging trucks are hauling on the road, so you can only drive on weekends, or before 6 a.m. or after 6 p.m. weekdays.

0 km / 0 mi
At the edge of Pemberton, at the 3-way intersection on Hwy 99, by the Petro Canada gas station. Go north into town. Cross the railroad tracks. At the T-junction in 1 km / 0.6 mile, turn right, heading toward Hurley River FS Rd.

2.8 km / 1.7 mi
Turn left to head northwest on Pemberton Valley Road. In 20 km / 12 miles, watch for signs directing you to Meager Hot Springs and Gold Bridge via the Hurley River FS Rd.

25.0 km / 15.5 mi
At the sign for Meager Creek, Gold Bridge, and Lillooet, go right to the Hurley River / Upper Lillooet River FS Road.

26.5 km / 16.4 mi
Cross the small bridge over the Lillooet River. The road is dirt after the bridge. This is Mile 0 on the FS road. Set your tripometer to 0.

0 km / 0 mi
Starting the Lillooet River FS Road.

7.6 km / 4.7 mi
For Meager Creek and the Stoltmann Wilderness, stay left at the junction. The Hurley River Road goes right and jitters 60 km / 37 miles over washboards and potholes to Gold Bridge. At a slow speed, 2WD vehicles can do it. From there you could visit Carpenter Lake and its many campgrounds (see page 116), or drive through 168 km / 105 miles to Lillooet.

40.2 km / 25.0 mi
Turn left at the signed junction, crossing the Lillooet River for the last leg to Meager Creek. Continue about fifteen minutes more, bearing left at all forks. The road climbs above the creek valley.

47.2 km / 29.3 mi
Stay left past an old building and some machinery. Cross the bridge over Meager Creek. Continue uphill for about 1 km / 0.6 mile to the parking area and campsites in Douglas firs. It's a five-minute walk down staircases to the hot springs.

~

NORTH OF PEMBERTON, THE BIRKENHEAD ROAD

You can explore this spectacular mountain-and-river country from these campgrounds near the Cayoosh Range. In the Pemberton Valley to the northwest, the stirring Coast Mountains are the backdrop for calming fields. To the northeast, steep mountains cradle gorgeous turquoise Birkenhead Lake.

If you're heading northeast to Lillooet

From the edge of Pemberton, at the 3-way intersection by the Petro Canada gas station, continue on Hwy 99 east 7.1 km / 4.4 miles to Mount Currie.

If you're heading southwest from Lillooet

From the Joffre Lakes Recreation Area pullout, continue 23.5 km / 14.6 miles to the 3-way junction in Mount Currie.

For either approach above, follow the directions below

0 km / 0 mi
In Mount Currie at the 3-way intersection, follow the road north to D'Arcy and Birkenhead.

4.6 km / 2.8 mi
Just after crossing Owl Creek, there's a sign parallel to the highway

for the Owl Creek campgrounds. Turn right, under a power line at a small station. Drive in 0.3 km / 0.2 mile and cross the railroad tracks. Come to another FS sign. You can go left or right to various campsites.

OWL CREEK RECREATION SITE #7
Destination / Easy
13 tables, lots of shade

This is a wonderful campground on the frolicking Birkenhead River, in a mixed forest, next to high mountains. Campsites are well separated from each other. Look around to choose your special spot.

6.6 km / 4.1 mi
Take the first right for this **overnight pullout**, after you cross the Birkenhead River. Use it only if Owl Creek campground is full. There is room for 2 vehicles and flat space for tents.

12.2 km / 7.6 mi
Look for a FS sign parallel to the highway: Recreation Site. Turn here and drive in 0.3 km / 0.2 mile to Spetch Creek campground. The area is not as open or spacious as Owl.

SPETCH CREEK RECREATION SITE #8
Overnight / Easy
6 secluded campsites with tables, near the creek

34.6 km / 21.5 mi
Turn left at the sign for Birkenhead Provincial Park. On the right in 1.5 km / 0.9 mi, you'll see the FS sign: Blackwater Rd.

35.9 km / 22.3 mi
Be cautious here. The pavement ends right away and you'll cross a rough wooden bridge.

43.0 km / 26.7 mi
Arrive at the Blackwater Lake campground.

BLACKWATER LAKE RECREATION SITE #9
Weekend / Easy
3 tables, 6 campsites

Though this campground isn't appealing, it'll probably be quiet. The campsites are private, huddled in a horseshoe of brush and trees. You could spend the night here and enjoy the day at Birkenhead Lake Provincial Park. Tiny Blackwater Lake doesn't compare to the grandeur of Birkenhead.

50.2 km / 31.1 mi
Arrive at Birkenhead Lake. There's a pay campground here, a day-use area near the water, a sandy beach, a grassy lawn and a lakeshore hiking trail.

~

LILLOOET LAKE

This long, beautiful lake offers a spectacular campground and a couple other fairly nice ones. A few of the campsites are especially good for setting up a tent on the beach, away from the road.

If you're heading northeast to Lillooet

Drive 7.1 km / 4.4 miles east of the 3-way intersection at the edge of Pemberton, by the Petro Canada gas station, to Mount Currie.

0 km / 0 mi
At the 3-way junction in Mount Currie, turn east toward Lillooet.

10.2 km / 6.3 mi
Turn right onto a dirt road as the highway begins ascending a hill. It's marked with a sign: In-SHUCK-ch FS Rd. You'll see it just before a large green highway sign pointing to Lillooet, and before the winter closure gate. Set your tripometer to 0.

If you're heading southwest to Pemberton

Look for the Joffre Lakes Recreation Area pullout, and continue driving 13.2 km / 8.2 miles to the In-SHUCK-ch FS Road, which will veer off on your left. It's directly after the winter closure gate, at the bottom of the steep hill.

For either approach above, now follow the directions below

0 km / 0 mi
At the start of the In-SHUCK-ch road. Continue southeast along the lake.

6.8 km / 4.2 mi
A FS sign on the right announces your arrival at the first campground.

STRAWBERRY POINT RECREATION SITE #10
Destination / Moderate
Beach tent-camping only, 2 tables, several sites

It's only a five-minute walk down to the lake and this special camp-ground. You don't see any clearcuts or power lines from here. You get good views across the lake, including a glimpse of a glacier. It's a peaceful place to enjoy a weekend away, without having to backpack to a lonely spot. You'll find lots of driftwood to make fun creations. Please use the existing fire rings; don't mar the beach by starting more.

9.2 km / 5.7 mi
Continue straight on the main road. Twin One Creek Haul Road goes up to the left.

9.8 km / 6.1 mi
Arrive at the second campground.

TWIN ONE CREEK RECREATION SITE #11
Overnight / Moderate
2 tables in the open beside the lake, 3 tables in trees

This is an okay campground, but not great. The campsites are close together. It was full on the first weekend in October. There's one **overnight pullout** just before this side road goes back onto the main FS road. You can hear the creek there, and you're away from other campers, which could be helpful if they're staying up late jabbering.

11.3 km / 7 mi
Pass Lillooet Lake Lodge and the pay campground.

15.3 km / 9.5 mi
Look for a yellow Km 16 sign, to your right, on a tree. There's one **campsite** here in trees at the end of Lizzie Bay, with a table, beach and boat launch.

15.5 km / 9.6 mi
Arrive at the turn-in to Lizzie Bay. Drive .3 km / .2 mile down.

LIZZIE BAY RECREATION SITE #12
Destination / Moderate
9 tables, flat space for tents

This is the best campground along Lillooet Lake. The campsites are well spaced, surrounded by trees, on the waterfront, looking north up the lake. Only one campsite has a sandy beach on this rocky shore.

16.1 km / 10 mi
Continue straight on the main road, passing Lizzie Cr Branch FS Rd on your left. That's where you turn if you're here to hike in the Stein.

17.2 km / 10.7
Arrive at the turn-in to the last campground. It's only 200 meters down.

DRIFTWOOD BAY RECREATION SITE #13
Weekend / Moderate
3 tables

Though it's beside the lake, this campground is not attractive. Power lines and the road are directly on your left and there's a clearcut across the lake. It's also more open than the Lizzie Bay campground. Nonetheless, if the other campgrounds are full, this could be enjoyable for a weekend of fishing and boating. The trees over the entrance road are too low for motorhomes.

~

Duffey Lake, along Hwy 99

HWY 99 NORTH: THE DUFFEY LAKE ROAD

Often people buzz through this valley just to get from Pemberton to Lillooet, or vice versa. But they should spend more time here. This is a very scenic area. On the western end, there are impressive glaciers and mountain vistas. After passing Duffey Lake, the road meanders along delightful Cayoosh Creek. There are at least half a dozen one-lane wooden bridges — still standing from the days when travel was slower and more intimate. Southwest of Lillooet, the road works through a deep, rugged canyon, hugging the cliffsides, then careening down to Lillooet Valley.

This is a special place for free-camping because the campgrounds are all easily reached off a paved highway. In addition to the abundant FS campgrounds along Cayoosh Creek, there are overnight pullouts galore where you can find your own spot on the water's edge. This is a beautiful area all year, and particularly pretty in October. It can be chilly in early October, even on a clear, sunny day.

If you're heading northeast to Lillooet

The Heading Southwest directions follow this section.

From the 3-way intersection at the edge of Pemberton, follow Hwy 99 for 17.3 km / 10.7 miles. You'll pass through Mount Currie and arrive at the north end of Lillooet Lake. Soon after you cross a small arm of the lake, be looking for the junction described below. Set your tripometer to 0 there.

0 km / 0 mi
On the Duffey Lake Road, where the In-SHUCK-ch FS Road turns off, at the north end of Lillooet Lake. This is where the highway begins rising up a hill, just before a large green sign pointing to Lillooet and before the winter closure gate.

13.2 km / 8.2 mi
You'll see the **Joffre Lakes Recreation Area** parking lot on your right. Don't miss hiking here. In 2 hours, you can reach Upper Joffre Lake beneath Matier Glacier and Joffre Peak.

32.2 km / 20 mi
Look for a blue boat-launch sign on the right, and shortly you'll come to the launch and a BC Parks sign at the northeast end of Duffey Lake.

32.8 km / 20.4 mi
Arrive at Duffey Lake campground.

DUFFEY LAKE EAST RECREATION SITE #1
Overnight (longer if you can stand the noise) / Easy
5 tables

Stupendous views of the peaks at the other end of the lake make this an extremely picturesque campground. It's set in trees, but unfortunately it's right beside the road. Expect to hear traffic all day and scattered through the night. Leaping frogs provide entertainment on this marshy lake end.

35.1 km / 21.8 mi
Come to an **overnight pullout** on the left, just above Cayoosh Creek. It's between Kane Creek to the northeast, and Blowdown Creek to the southwest.

Campsite view of Cayoosh Creek, along Hwy 99 – the Duffey Lake Road

41.4 km / 25.7 mi
Another **overnight pullout** for one vehicle, right beside the creek and the highway.

43.6 km / 27.1 mi
This **overnight pullout** allows you to get a little farther off the highway than others do. It's on a large gravel bar on the creek.

45.2 km / 28.1 mi
Arrive at the official Cayoosh Creek campground.

CAYOOSH CREEK RECREATION SITE #3
Weekend / Easy
6 tables, very pretty campsites, all in trees and on the creek

Turn left before you cross the one-lane bridge. If you're heading southwest, turn right after the bridge.

45.9 km / 28.5 mi
Come to an **overnight pullout** on the creek, on your right.

49.4 km / 30.7 mi
Arrive at the first turn-in to the official campground at Roger Creek.

ROGER CREEK RECREATION SITE #4
Weekend / Easy
4 tables at the first area; 5 campsites and 4 tables at the second area

The campsites at the first area feel private. They face dense forest and the creekbed. The second site is .5 km / .3 mile farther on the road. It's more open, so it's especially good for big rigs. In early October, no sun reaches the sites until 11:30 a.m.

51.5 km / 32 mi
Arrive at Gott Creek campground, at the confluence of Cayoosh and Gott Creeks. The campsites are worn-out looking, similar to those at Roger.

GOTT CREEK RECREATION SITE #5
Overnight / Easy
2 tables on the creek

58.9 km / 36.6 mi
Where there's a sign on the right, turn off left for the Cottonwood campground.

COTTONWOOD RECREATION SITE #6
Weekend / Easy
7 tables, all campsites well spaced near the creek, but not on it

There's plenty of room for big rigs here, amid thin pines and tall cottonwoods. Downton Creek Road is just north of the campground.

60.0 km / 37.3 mi
Come to an **overnight pullout** on the creek.

62.5 km / 38.8 mi
Arrive at Cinnamon campground, 19.6 km / 12.2 miles southwest of Lillooet. It's a pretty spot with views across a dry, rugged mountainside.

CINNAMON RECREATION SITE #7
Weekend / Easy
7 tables, a couple on the creek and a few just off it.

77.8 km / 48.3 mi
Arrive at the signed entrance: BC HYDRO SETON DAM CAMPGROUND. It's at the valley bottom, before reaching Lillooet. The nearby highway sign states: Pemberton 100 km, Whistler 134 km, Vancouver 255 km.

SETON LAKE RECREATION AREA
Weekend / Easy
29 campsites with tables, garbage cans, firewood,
separate tent-camping area

A sign in the campground labels it CAYOOSH CREEK. Mountain goats roam on towering cliffs across the valley. Most sites are not beside the creek, but only a minute's walk away. There's a beach and picnic area across the highway, at Seton Lake. This is one campground that provides free firewood, or you might look at it as free toys for imaginative campers.

There's more to do with firewood than just burn it.
Seton Dam campground near Lillooet

82.1 km / 51.0 mi
The junction of Hwys 99 and 12 in Lillooet, on the west side of the Fraser River.

If you're heading southwest on Hwy 99 from Lillooet

For descriptions of these campgrounds, see the Heading Northeast section above.

0 km / 0 mi
At the junction of Hwys 99 and 12 in Lillooet, on the west side of the Fraser River.

4.3 km / 2.7 mi
Arrive at the signed entrance: **BC Hydro Seton Dam Campground**. It's in the valley bottom, just before the highway begins climbing through the canyon toward Duffey Lake.

19.6 km / 12.2 mi
Arrive at **Cinnamon Recreation Site.**

23.2 km / 14.4 mi
Arrive at **Cottonwood Recreation Site.**

30.6 km / 19.0 mi
Arrive at **Gott Creek Recreation Site.**

32.7 km / 20.3 mi
Arrive at **Roger Creek Recreation Site.**

36.9 km / 22.9 mi
Arrive at **Cayoosh Recreation Site.**

49.3 km / 30.6 mi
Arrive at **Duffey Lake Recreation Site.**

68.9 km / 42.7 mi
Arrive at **Joffre Lakes Recreation Area.**

82.1 km / 51.0 mi
Turn left for **Lillooet Lake Recreation Sites** and see page 106.

EAST OF LILLOOET

KWOTLENEMO (FOUNTAIN) LAKE RECREATION SITES #47 - 50
Weekend / Easy
Campsites in a grassy open area, and in cottonwoods

Fountain Valley and Lake are located over the mountains, just east of Lillooet. The area gets less rain than farther west in the Coast Mountains, so it's a good place to come in spring for an early taste of summer. Or, if it's hot in the Fraser River Canyon, you'll find it's cooler up at the lake because it's about 500 meters higher. The lake is roughly at the crest of the rise. Dry, rugged mountains surround the valley.

The gravel road is good, with only a few rough spots. Motorhomes should have no trouble. You can get to this lake from the south (16 kms / 9.9 miles) or from the north (10.5 kms / 6.5 miles).

If you're heading north on Hwy 1

Skip below for directions Heading West on Hwy 12 and Heading Northeast from Lillooet.

From Hope, travel 129 kms / 80 miles north to Lytton and the junction of Hwys 1 and 12.

0 km / 0 mi
Turn off Hwy 1, following the signs for Hwy 12, heading into Lytton.

1.2 km / 7.4 mi
Drive through downtown Lytton and head north on Hwy 12.

1.7 km / 1.1 mi
Continue over the Thompson River.

2.2 km / 1.4 mi
Pass Botanie Valley Road on your right.

2.4 km / 1.5 mi
Pass the turn-off to the Fraser River ferry.

39.5 km / 24.5 mi
Turn right onto the Fountain Valley Road. This is the south entrance, 22.4 kms / 13.9 miles south of Lillooet. Set your tripometer to 0 here.

If you drive 28 kms / 17.4 miles through the Fountain Valley, you'll rejoin Hwy 12, at which point you'll be 13.9 kms / 8.6 miles northeast of Lillooet.

0 km / 0 mi
At the start of the Fountain Valley Road.

10 km / 6.2 mi
You'll pass small Native reserves and ranches in the valley.

16 km / 9.9 mi
Arrive at Kwotlenemo Lake South campground, in an open, grassy area.

17.5 km / 10.9 mi
Arrive at Kwotlenemo Lake North campground, set in cottonwoods.

23.4 km / 14.5 mi
You get a view of the Camelsfoot Range.

28 km / 17.4 mi
Rejoin Hwy 12.

If you're heading west on Hwy 12

0 km / 0 mi
At the junction of Hwys 12 and 97.

28.8 km / 17.9 mi
Marble Canyon Provincial Park is on your left, beside the road. The mountains are stunning here. Crown Lake is small, but pretty. Camping is free in the off-season. It's still quite cold here until April. We were surprised to have so many cars driving past late at night in mid-March, so we recommend going to Fountain Valley for quiet.

43.4 km / 26.9 mi
Pass through the community of Pavilion.

61.4 km / 38.1 mi
Arrive at the north entrance to Fountain Valley. (Lillooet is 13.9 kms / 8.6 miles farther southwest on Hwy 12.) Set your tripometer to 0 here. Drive 10.5 kms / 6.5 miles to Kwotlenemo Lake North campground. The south campground is 1.5 kms / .9 mile farther.

If you're heading northeast from Lillooet

0 km / 0 mi
In Lillooet, on the bridge over the Fraser River.

13.9 km / 8.6 mi
Turn right onto the Fountain Valley Road. Set your tripometer to 0.

0 km / 0 mi
At the north end of the Fountain Valley Road.

10.5 km / 6.5 mi
Arrive at **Kwotlenemo Lake North campground**.

12 km / 7.4 mi
Arrive at **Kwotlenemo Lake South campground**.

~

CARPENTER LAKE
Destination / Difficult because it's so far

There are several FS campgrounds and a new BC Hydro camp-ground on the north shore of this long lake. It's about a 45-minute drive from Lillooet to the east end of the lake. Numerous side roads lead to smaller lakes and more free campgrounds.

The terrain is dry. Pines and firs are scattered on the sloping mountainsides. When it's rainy in the Coast Mountains or farther south near Hope, you might find sunshine here.

If you're a hiker, plan a minimum of five days in the area and spend at least three days backpacking from Taylor Basin into the Southern Chilcotin Mountains. From the Tyax junction, follow directions to Tyaughton Lake. This is a sumptuous range of wondrous red-and-mauve soil and meadowed slopes. From the basins you can walk gentle, skyscraping ridges and look south to the rugged Coast Mountains nearby. Get our hiking guidebook, *Don't Waste Your Time in the B.C. Coast Mountains*, for a full trail description.

0 km / 0 mi
In Lilloett, at the junction of Hwys 99 and 12, on the west side of the Fraser River. Head north into downtown Lilloett, following signs to Gold Bridge. Be sure your gas tank is full.

0.8 km / 0.5 mi
After crossing the railroad tracks, turn right onto Main Street. Drive north through town.

2.9 km / 1.8 mi
Immediately turn left, after the green highway sign: Gold Bridge 101 km, Shalath 69 km. This is just before the Old Mill Mall.

9.0 km / 5.6 mi
Cross the narrow, impressive chasm of Bridge River.

9.4 km / 5.8 mi
Continue straight on the main road. It's paved for a while, then well-graded gravel, and later alternates. Pass Slok FS Road on the right.

33.8 km / 21.0 mi
Stay left toward Gold Bridge at the signed junction. Descend to the river. Right is the Yalakom Road.

35.4 km / 22.0 mi
Cross the Yalakom River. You're now in a deep, narrow canyon. The road becomes gravel in 10 km / 6 miles.

50.0 km / 31.0 mi
If you're eager to camp now, rather than continuing to attractive sites beside the lake, you can turn left here, then drive right 0.4 km to desperate-looking **Mission Dam FS Recreation Site #33**. The campsites with tables are on the right next to scrubby trees. You'll probably sleep better above the dam, however, so proceed a bit farther and drive over the dam to nearby campsites.

50.9 km / 31.6 mi
Arrive at Terzaghi Dam junction. Stay right, heading to the better campgrounds on the north side of Carpenter Lake. Or turn left onto Mission Mtn Rd, cross the dam, and go through the tunnel. From the junction, it's 1.6 km / 1.0 mile to tiny **Carpenter Lake Recreation Site #34**, which is across the road from the lake.

69.6 km / 43.2 mi
Turn left and drive down to the **BC Hydro Campground at Bighorn Creek**. It's on the lake, with 10 campsites, a boat launch and day-use area.

72.0 km / 44.6 mi
After crossing the creek, an unsigned but obvious dirt road on the left leads to **Jones Creek Recreation Site #32**. Bushes and trees that close over the narrow road might scratch your vehicle. Don't plan to drive a motorhome down. This is a special campground on Carpenter Lake, because it's so far off the road.

Drive 150 meters down and go left at the FS sign. At 0.5 km, go left on the better road. This is a pretty forest with lots of aspen. After reaching the first 3 sites with tables, you can continue 200 meters to a campsite next to the creek, but without a table, and 3 other sites in trees.

72.2 km / 44.8 mi
Come to a junction. Stay left on the main road for campgrounds farther

west, and for Gold Bridge (33 km farther). If you go right to ascend the Marshall Lake Road, you'll arrive in 3.0 km / 1.9 miles at the turnoff to **Carol Lake FS campground**. Take the side road to the right (east).

If you're out to explore, you can continue on the Marshall Lake Road for approximately 13.5 km / 8.4 miles, where you'll see a turn-in on the left for a small FS campground at **Marshall Creek**. Just over 3 km / 2 miles farther, there's a rough entrance on the left to **Marshall Lake Recreation Site #12**. This campground is larger and more open, but low-clearance cars might have a hard time getting in.

Continuing on the main road along Carpenter Lake

95.7 km / 59.3 mi
On the left, directly below the road, is **Tyax Junction Recreation Site #60**. It has two tables, but is really a campsite for just one party. There's also a rough boat launch.

95.8 km / 59.4 mi
Arrive at the major, signed Tyax Junction. Continue straight (left) on the main road if you're heading to Gold Bridge. Or ascend right for a campground on a small lake (Mowson Pond) or the tiny campsite on beautiful Tyaughton Lake. Set your tripometer to 0.

0 km / 0 mi
Starting up Tyaughton Lake Road. It's dirt and climbs steeply.

2.0 km / 1.2 mi
At the top of the climb, on your left, is **Mowson Pond FS Recreation Site #19** with 5 well-spaced campsites. The trees are scraggly, but you can see the mountains.

3.5 km / 2.2 mi
Continue past the rough Gun Creek Road, on your left. Follow signs for Tyax Lodge.

6.0 km / 3.6 mi
Pass a road going left. Immediately there's a fork. Curve, descending left on the main road, and pass Hornal Road on your right.

8.2 km / 5.1 mi
Look for a sign: **Friburg Recreation Site #20**. Turn right there to the small campground on Tyaughton Lake.

8.6 km / 5.3 mi
Stay straight and 200 meters farther, go up left. Tyax Lodge is down to the right.

For the Taylor Basin trailhead, continue to a steep descent around a ridge at 13.5 km / 8.4 miles. Reach a 3-way junction at 14.2 km / 8.8 miles. Mud Cr-Taylor Cr FS Road continues right (north). The extreme left road might still be marked by a partially hidden sign on its right side: TAYLOR CREEK. You should have a truck, or at least a low-clearance 4WD. This road can get really muddy and there are deep ruts to negotiate. The alternative is to park at the pullout and walk the road 6.5 km / 4 miles to the trailhead.

Continuing on the main road along Carpenter Lake, back at the 95.8-km / 59.4-mile Tyax Junction.

99.5 km / 61.8 mi
Gun Creek Recreation Site #18 is on the left at the creek's mouth. It has 7 tables, but room for 12 parties. The sites are a couple-minute walk from the lake.

107.5 km / 66.7 mi
Reach the west end of Carpenter Lake and a junction. A left here will take you across Bridge River to Gold Bridge and Bralorne. If you want to drive the Hurley FS Road southwest to the Pemberton Valley, go straight toward Gun Lake. 250 meters up that road, turn left at Gwyneth Lake Road following the sign to Pemberton. The Hurley is a rough road, but doable in 2WD if you go slow over the washboard sections.

From this junction, a free campsite on cottage-rimmed Gun Lake is straight. You won't enjoy an away-from-it-all feeling here. It's better to camp on Carpenter Lake, unless you just want to overnight before heading into the Chilcotin Mountains via the Gun Creek trail to Spruce Lake.

0 km / 0 mi
Going up Gun Lake Road. 250 meters up stay straight on pavement.

1.3 km / 0.8 mi
Go left on Gun Lake Road West. At 2.0 km / 1.2 miles, drive beside the ugly bowl of Downton Lake. Compelling Mt. Sloan is southwest.

5.7 km / 3.5 mi
Stay left at this fork, and at **6.8 km / 4.2 miles**, on Gun Lake Road.

10.2 km / 6.3 mi
Finally arrive at **Gun Lake South Recreation Site #17**, comfortable for 5 parties. It's in trees on a bench above the lake.

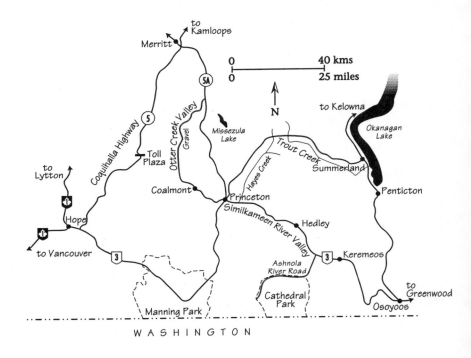

to Kamloops

Merritt

5A

0   40 kms
0   25 miles

Coquihalla Highway

5

Otter Creek Valley

Gravel

Missezula Lake

N

to Kelowna

Okanagan Lake

Trout Creek

Hayes Creek

Summerland

Toll Plaza

to Lytton

Coalmont

Princeton

Similkameen River Valley

Penticton

Hope

Hedley

to Vancouver

3

Ashnola River Road

Keremeos

3

to Greenwood

Cathedral Park

Osoyoos

Manning Park

W A S H I N G T O N

South Thompson Plateau:
Coquihalla Hwy 5,
Manning Park to Merritt,
Princeton to Summerland,
Similkameen River

South Thompson Plateau: Coquihalla Hwy 5, Manning Park to Merritt, Princeton to Summerland, Similkameen River

NEAR MANNING PARK

CASCADE RECREATION AREA
Overnight / Easy
Just a big gravel parking lot

If you need an easy place to park just for an overnight sleep, you might want to look for this spot. It's the trailhead for the Dewdney and Whatcom Trails. Even though it's near the highway, there is a buffer zone of trees and it's probably quieter than the pay campgrounds in Manning Park.

If you're heading east into Manning Park

On the western, narrow section of the park, soon after you pass the turnoff to Sumallo Grove — where Hwy 3 makes an abrupt turn north from its southern course — you'll pass Rhododendron Flats. Be looking for the Cascade turnoff in a short distance on your left (north), just before the highway turns south again.

If you're heading west through Manning Park

The Cascade parking lot is located 31 kms / 19.2 miles from the Manning Info Centre, 21.2 kms / 13.2 miles from Allison Pass in Manning Provincial Park. The turnoff is on your right (north).

~

MANNING UNOFFICIAL FREE CAMPING
Overnight / Easy
About 6 spots well-spaced in the trees

This large overnight pullout beside Hwy 3, on the Similkameen River, is useful if you want a free night and you're exploring Manning Provincial Park, or you're continuing on and just need to sleep. It's actually just as good as the pay campgrounds in the park, which are also right along the highway.

Near the east edge of Manning Park

Just outside the park's east side, look for the private Bonnevier Camping—marked by a big, brown sign. 0.8 km / 0.5 mile northeast of it is the free camping area — an obvious, large, cleared area on the east side of the highway, at the KM 60 sign.

There are two good spots for tents. One is between the gravel roads on the left and right. Walk over the grass to the ledges just above the river. The other spot is off to the left, just below the end of the gravel ridge. A flat, grassy area is somewhat shielded from road noise.

~

COPPER CREEK RECREATION SITE #85
Overnight / Easy
2 tables beside the river, 2 more on a bench above,
12+ campsites across the river

Northeast of Manning Park and south of Princeton, this is an excellent place to know about when traveling. You can hear road noise (especially from trucks rounding the bend) since the campground is close to the highway, but the creek helps muffle it. During hunting season, the noise will be secondary to the marauding men and their 4WD vehicles.

If you're heading south from Princeton

0 km / 0 mi
In Princeton, at the Petro Canada station, by the blue bridge over the Similkameen River.

34.9 km / 21.6 mi
Continue past Sunday Summit (1232 m), which is 6.7 kms / 4.2 miles before the turnoff.

41.6 km / 25.8 mi
Turn left off the highway, just before it crosses Copper Creek and starts ascending out of the hairpin turn. There's a dirt pullout at the turn. On

the left, at the neck of the hairpin, you'll see a stop sign at the dirt road. The access road descends a little to the first campground, just off the highway, to your right.

Drive across the log bridge at the end of this campground and you'll come to a superb **camping area** on the other side of the river. The bridge has deteriorated, but all types of vehicles were crossing it. Just choose your route carefully. There's room for about a dozen vehicles on the left of the road, and some on the right. Both areas are beside the river, with pine trees and a little grass.

If you're heading north to Princeton

Set your tripometer to 0 as you pass the Manning Park Lodge. Drive 24 kms / 15 miles northeast. The small road to this campground is off a tight hairpin turn. Be looking as you head left and down into a sharp turn, immediately after the highway goes over Copper Creek. You'll see a stop sign on the right, at the neck of the hairpin. There's a dirt pullout at the turn. This will help you make a safe turn, since this highway is often busy.

If you pass Sunday Summit, you've missed the campground. Turn around and drive back 6.7 kms / 4.2 miles.

~

NORTH OF PRINCETON

The scenery on the east side of Hwy 5A isn't as pretty as just across on the west. So if you want to try one area, spend your time at The Plateau Lakes first, unless you want to boat on the longest lake in the area — Mizzuela. For just pretty camping and more choices, the west is best. Some people call the plateau area, between the Otter and Allison Creek valleys, *the Gulliford Lakes*, but we call them *the Plateau Lakes*.

The Tulameen River valley, northwest of Princeton, is beautiful meadow country with numerous cattle ranches, cradled by low forested mountains. Unlike the Okanagan, this is a peaceful, undeveloped valley.

MARTINS LAKE RECREATION SITE #75
Overnight / Easy
2 tables

This one's just outside Princeton, on the road to Summerland, in the Okanagan. Though it's handy, most people won't want to spend more than a night here. It's actually a pond, right across from the highway. The forest cover is sparse. There are homes nearby, so there's no sense of wildness. But if we'd known it was here years ago, we would have gladly used it instead of the awkward spots we ended up at.

0 km / 0 mi
In Princeton, at the junction of Hwy 5A and the turnoff to the Old Hedley Road. Get here by turning left (west) off Hwy 3 at the Petro Canada station, just before the blue bridge. Take the first right, onto Tapton Ave. Cross the Tulameen River. In almost 1 km / .6 mile, turn onto the Old Hedley Road. Shortly, go left at signs onto the Princeton - Summerland Road.

1.1 km / .7 mi
You'll see an **overnight pullout** to the right. It could be the local Lovers' Lane. This area in sparse trees overlooks an industrial plant.

3.2 km / 2 mi
Turn left at the white sign on your left: Princeton Sierras Unit Crew. There's also a yellow sign depicting a burning match: Our Forests Are Vital, Please Be Careful. At the first fork, go right and arrive at the Martins Lake campground.

~

GRANITE CREEK RECREATION SITE #74
Weekend / Easy
A few tables, about 2 dozen campsites, several on the river's edge

The Tulameen is a pretty river valley — not stunning, but pleasant. The long-gone mining town of Granite Creek had over 200 buildings and was one of the liveliest gold towns in B.C. during the 1880's. The campground, in Ponderosa pines, has a large meadow and is sometimes used as a base for tree-planting crews. You can walk about a kilometer back to Coalmont, and have a meal at the hotel or a drink in the pub.

0 km / 0 mi
In Princeton, at the Petro Canada station, just south of the blue bridge over the Similkameen River. Follow the sign to Hwy 5A. This will take you left (north) onto Bridge Street. Drive through the historic downtown. Soon cross the Tulameen River and come to a T-intersection. Just after, there's a sign pointing left: Coalmont 18 km, Tulameen 25 km.

Turn left, heading toward Coalmont, west of Princeton. At first, the small, curvy road parallels the Tulameen River, then ascends through a forested canyon. We noted "dry forest." It certainly is. Two weeks later this area was in flames. As you're nearing Coalmont, look for a large meadow across the river on your left. You'll soon be crossing a bridge to get there.

20 km / 12.4 mi
Reach Coalmont and the historic hotel established in 1912. On the left corner of Parrish Avenue, you'll see a sign: Rice Road 2 km, Granite Creek 2 km, Blakeburn 10 km. Turn toward Granite Creek.

If you want to go up to the Plateau Lakes near here, continue northwest past Coalmont, and read below.

21.6 km / 13.4 mi
Don't take the road to the right. It goes to Lodestone Lake and Blakeburn.

21.7 km / 13.5 mi
Cross another bridge. Take the road to the left for Granite Creek campground.

~

Thalia Lake, north of Princeton, on the Interior Plateau

RICKEY, GOOSE, THALIA, & LODWICK LAKES
Weekend / Moderate from the east, Difficult from the west
Not for motorhomes from either approach

This is a pleasant area of aspen, pine, meadows, and at least ten small lakes, all at about 6,000 feet (1,800 meters) elevation. Your 2WD vehicle will get you to several of the lakes, but not all. You could spend many days exploring this plateau, even if you don't fish. It's a lot of fun just driving the winding, soft, graceful roads, which are also great for mountain bikes. Sometimes the main road is little more than two tire tracks, but it's smooth enough for low-clearance vehicles. Once you're up on the plateau, it's clear what's the main road and what's not.

Wheeling along the narrow, lighthearted roads up here might remind you of driving jalopies on set tracks at amusement parks when you were 8 or 9 years old. You won't enjoy traveling in this area if you're the kind of person who gets tense when things get a little confusing in the back of beyond. Go gently and enjoy.

The side roads to various lakes are just tracks. During or after rainy weather, the depressions fill and you might be unable to reach some lakes. Don't drive anywhere you can't get out if a storm transforms the tracks into creeks and ponds. Decide where to venture *after* you get up on the plateau. That's the fun of it.

Reaching these lakes was one of our best adventures exploring back-roads campgrounds. We entered via the rougher approach from the Otter Creek Valley on the west, which the map shows as barely a road. But with care and patience, we made it. Big RVs or timid drivers definitely should not head up the plateau from the west. We give directions for both approaches.

The easier approach to the Plateau Lakes, from Hwy 5A on the east

Skip ahead to find directions for the western, more difficult approach.

0 km / 0 mi
In Princeton, at the Petro Canada station, just south of the blue bridge over the Similkameen River. Follow the sign to Hwy 5A, turning left (north) onto Bridge Street. Turn right at the first street, marked by a green highway sign: Tulameen - Merritt. Soon cross the Tulameen River and come to a junction.

1 km / .6 mi
Turn north onto Hwy 5A. Head toward Missezula Lake and Merritt. The Old Hedley Road, which has many FS campgrounds on the Similkameen River, is to the right. (See this description farther along.) Osprey Lake, on the Summerland Road, is signed to the right. You'll see highway signs: Merritt 90 km, Kamloops 188 km. You'll also see a green sign: Missezula Lake.

9.3 km / 5.8 mi
Pass Summers Creek Road on the right.

31.7 km / 19.7 mi
Come to the north end of Allison Lake.

35.6 km / 22.1 mi
See a yellow sign on the right, depicting trucks entering the highway. If you're in a truck or 4WD, you can explore the Hornet Lk FS Rd leading

to a campground on Loosemore Lake. The first ascent is rugged. Most of us will continue on the highway.

37.8 km / 23.5 mi
Arrive at **Guilliford Lake Rest Area**. You can park here overnight, if you don't want to drive to a better campground off the highway.

39 km / 24.2 mi
Turn left for the Plateau Lakes. A sign for A & P Guest Ranch, just before a small lake, marks the turn. Continue on Hwy 5A to Missezula Lake. Read the description below for the campground there. Set your tripometer to 0.

0 km / 0 mi
Starting on the dirt road. Just off the highway there's a sign: Pike Mtn FS Rd.

1 km / .6 mi
Stay straight, passing A & P Ranch on the right.

1.9 km / 1.2 mi
Go right at the junction (on the right side of the triangle). Follow the sign to W H Ranch. You'll see Robertson Lake Road signposted on the left.

3.9 km / 2.4 mi
Go left at the second triangle-junction. See more signs to W H Ranch.

4.3 km / 2.7 mi
Go right at the fork.

7.6 km / 4.7 mi
Come to a beautiful **overnight pullout** in aspen and meadows, with views over the plateau.

9.2 km / 5.7 mi
Arrive at another triangle-junction. Continue straight for Thalia Lake. If you want to try Lodwick Lake, look for a road cutting back to your left. The approach could be too muddy for 2WD after rain.

LODWICK LAKE NORTH RECREATION SITE #51
Weekend / Moderate
3 campsites

Just another simple, small, quiet, plateau lake. If you're lucky, you'll hear the loons in a yodeling frenzy. It's hypnotic and summons the wildness in you.

11.8 km / 7.3 mi
Come to a fork and see a yellow arrow on a tree. The right tree has three stripes. The entrance to Thalia Lake is on your right.

THALIA LAKE SOUTH RECREATION SITE #48
Weekend / Moderate
5 tables, room for others to crowd in

Glades with wildflowers brighten this pleasing lakeside campground in aspen and pines. Craig asked some campers what the elevation is, and a guy wearing camouflage standing beside his spread-out camp said, "Oh, you must be a pilot." Craig, hiding his laugh, answered, "No, I just want to know why it's so cold in mid June." The camper said, "I'm pretty sure it's about 2100 meters."

If you want to try **Goose Lake Recreation Site**, which has an eight-unit campground on the south end (reached by a road along its west side) and a two-unit campground on the north end (about .2 km off the main road), explore the small roads (tracks) heading south between Thalia and Rickey Lakes.

12.6 km / 7.8 mi
Arrive at Rickey Lake.

RICKEY LAKE RECREATION SITE #45
Weekend / Moderate
2 campsites beside the road

There are two, big, grassy areas on the lake's end, which is cluttered with cattails and deadfall.

22.4 km / 13.9 mi
Exit the plateau area on the west side, in the Otter Creek Valley, after negotiating the small, rough, adventurous road.

The difficult approach to the Plateau Lakes, from Otter Creek Valley on the west

Read the campground descriptions above, in the *easier approach*. The dirt access road to these lakes is much longer from the west than depicted on the FS map.

0 km / 0 mi
In Princeton, at the Petro Canada station, just south of the blue bridge over the Similkameen River. Follow the sign to Hwy 5A. This will take you left (north) onto Bridge Street. Drive through the historic downtown. Soon cross the Tulameen River and come to a T-intersection. Go left where the highway sign marks the turn: Coalmont 18 km, Tulameen 25 km.

20.1 km / 12.4 mi
Arrive in Coalmont. Then continue to Tulameen. Stay on the main road.

29 km / 18 mi
Arrive in the town of Tulameen. Tulameen reminded us of isolated Lake City, Colorado, nestled in the Rocky Mountains. Not far outside Tulameen, peaceful Otter Lake Provincial Park boasts horseshoe-pits for campers.

40.1 km / 24.9 mi
The pavement turns to a good gravel road. It would make a great road-cycling trip from Princeton up to here. It's pretty country, and there's little traffic.

58.6 km / 36.4 mi
Turn right onto narrow Youngsberg Road, near a small wooden bridge. This is before the Km 22 mark. Set your tripometer to 0.

59.2 km / 36.8 mi
You'll see the old Kettle Valley Railway, crossing the road overhead on a trestle, near where the old Thalia station was. You've gone too far. Turn back.

If you want to travel through to Hwy 5, and come out south of Aspen Grove, continue following the road through a tight, twisting canyon. In 9.7 kms / 6 miles, it travels through open woods and meadows, and arrives at the highway in about that much again.

0 km / 0 mi
Entering the Youngsberg Road, heading up to the Plateau Lakes. The road is rough, steep and rutted, as it begins ascending through an old clearcut. Stay on the main dirt road when a steep one goes off left. You'll be fine in a low-clearance car, as long as you enjoy this kind of adventure and you go slow.

4 km / 2.5 mi
Jostle through a rough, rutty section.

7 km / 4.3 mi
Come to a quiet **overnight pullout** in an open area, almost at the top of the plateau.

9.2 km / 5.7 mi
Go left at the fork.

9.8 km / 6.1 mi
Arrive at **Rickey Lake Recreation Site #45**.

10.6 km / 6.6 mi
Arrive at **Thalia Lake South Recreation Site #48**.

12.6 km / 7.8 mi
Go right to **Lodwick Lake North Recreation Site #51**.

15.5 km / 9.6 mi
Arrive at an **overnight pullout** next to a meadowy hill.

23.2 km / 14.4 mi
Arrive at Hwy 5A, on the east side of the plateau.

~

MISSEZULA LAKE RECREATION SITE #62
Weekend / Moderate
8 tables, boat launch, all campsites jammed together,
motorhome accessible

This lake is just east of Hwy 5A, between Merritt and Princeton. If you can decipher the confusing maze of logging roads, it's possible to spend a week fishing and exploring the many smaller lakes in this area. We had three maps and they all disagreed, so we had to put the pieces together at each junction we approached. There were two other parties doing the same thing. You'll be especially happy at this lake if you get one of the three lakefront properties.

If you're heading south from Merritt

From the Merritt Interchange, at the junction of Hwys 5 and 5A South, head toward Princeton on 5A South (which is twinned at this point with Connector Hwy 97C). At 23 km / 14.3 miles, you'll reach Aspen Grove. From there, drive about 11.0 km / 6.8 miles farther south on 5A to the turnoff for Missezula Lake. It's signed on the left: Dillard Cr FS Rd, and is easy to spot in the open grassland.

If you're heading north from Princeton

0 km / 0 mi
In Princeton, at the Petro Canada station, just south of the blue bridge over the Similkameen River. Follow the sign to Hwy 5A, turning left (north) onto Bridge Street. Turn right at the first street, marked by a green highway sign: Tulameen - Merritt. You'll cross the Tulameen River and in about a kilometer come to a junction. Pass the Old Hedley Road going right. Just beyond it, turn north onto Hwy 5A, heading toward Missezula Lake and Merritt.

9.3 km / 5.8 mi
Pass Summers Creek Road, continuing north on Hwy 5A. Summers Creek Road goes all the way to Missezula, but we don't recommend it. You'd need a 4WD for the road around the east side of the lake before you could reach the free campground on the north end.

39 km / 24.2 mi
Continue north, past the turn for the Plateau Lakes.

48.8 km / 30.3 mi
Pass a yellow sign: Trucks entering highway.

49.1 km / 30.5 mi
Turn right (east) off the highway, for Missezula Lake. Set your tripometer to 0.

For either approach above, now follow the directions below

0 km / 0 mi
At the turn. No sign indicates where the road goes. After driving over a cattle guard, see a sign: Dillard Cr FS Rd.

1.6 km / 1 mi
Stay straight at the fork. The road is wide and well-graded, just a bit rocky and bumpy. Pass through unimpressive forest.

4.2 km / 2.6 mi
Go left at the fork, staying on Dillard Road. Right goes to Ketchan Lake. We drove 7.3 kms / 4.5 miles to the right, through ugly country, to miserable, shallow, swampy Ketchan "Lake." It's not worth anybody's time.

6.7 km / 4.3 mi
Go right at the fork. Left heads sharply to Bluey Lake. We started up that road, but it got pretty sketchy and the scenery was dismal. Bluey Lake road could be impassable when wet. You should have 4WD if you want to explore in that direction.

7.6 km / 4.7 mi
Go right at the fork, for Missezula. If you're in a low-clearance vehicle, be on the lookout for lone rocks tumbled in the road. The left fork goes north on a rough road to Loon Lake, and eventually to Hwy 97C.

9.7 km / 5.8 mi
Take the road on the right, going down to the end of the lake and the unsigned campground.

Most people will return the same way to Hwy 5A. But if your vehicle has good clearance and you're in the mood, upon leaving the Missezula campground go right.

12.1 km / 7.5 mi
At this junction, a left on the Dillard-Galena Crk FS Road will take you back to the Loon Lake Exit and Hwy 97C Connector. But it's a long way on rough dirt.

~

Gifts on the Wind

Out of the city you'll have a new nose. Be aware of all the stimulating smells wafting your way. Urgent blossoms, wet moss, golden grass, moist dirt, a freed cloudburst, warm rocks, a fishy stream, crunchy leaves, pine bark, cool shade on a hot day, a sun-baked picnic table. Notice all these and how the senses meld to create sumptuous sensations.

PRINCETON TO SUMMERLAND, HAYES & TROUT CREEKS

This valley is quite settled. There's a crowd of private homes on all the lakes, so it's harder to find solitude here compared to other areas. The terrain of low, forested hillsides isn't anything special. We wouldn't go out of our way to get here. But it's a nice alternative if you're traveling between the Okanagan and the Coast. It's a good gravel road, so it probably isn't a much longer drive than if you go south on Hwy 3A. It's always nice to camp beside a lake, and there are plenty of campgrounds along the way to do just that.

If you're heading east to the Okanagan

Directions for heading west from Summerland are below this section.

In Princeton, follow the signs to Hwy 5A. Turn west onto Bridge Street, which is just south of the Petro Canada station and the blue bridge over the Similkameen River. Then turn right immediately at the green sign, toward Tulameen and Merritt. Soon cross the Tulameen River. You'll have driven .8 km / .6 mile to a junction of roads: left for Tulameen and Coalmont, right for the Old Hedley and Summerland Roads. Set your tripometer to 0.

0 km / 0 mi
Go right onto the Old Hedley Road. In .3 km take the signed road to Osprey Lake, on the Princeton - Summerland Road.

36.6 km / 22.6 mi
Arrive at Chain Lake campground, right beside the road.

CHAIN LAKE RECREATION SITE #65
Weekend / Easy
20 tables, most campsites on the lake, boat launch

41.6 km / 25.7 mi

Turn right on Agur Road, for the Link Lake campground. Set your tripometer to 0.

Or continue on the highway for Osprey and Thirsk Lakes

LINK LAKE RECREATION SITE #66
Overnight / Easy
2 tables, 3 more campsites without tables, boat launch

The campground at this small lake isn't as nice as the others along this corridor. It looks as if it were just tossed in there as an afterthought. Private cabins and homes are nearby.

From the turn-in, drive .8 km / .5 mile, past the private homes and three campsites scattered in trees, before you get to the official campground. To drive the loop around the lake, go left at the next fork, soon pass the boat launch, and you'll arrive back at the highway in 3.1 kms / 1.9 miles.

You can also get to Link Lake by entering on Link Lake Road, .8 km / .5 mile past Agur Road, at 42.2 kms / 26.2 miles.

Set your tripometer to 0 upon turning onto Link Lake Road. Immediately go left, then right at the junction where a green sign points to Link Lake. At the fork with Osprey on your left, go right onto the main road. Pass the boat launch. In 1.8 kms / 1.1 miles, go right at the T-intersection. Just beyond is an **overnight pullout**, useful if you can't find space at the campground. Drive .5 km / .3 mile farther to arrive at Link Lake campground. You'll pass more campsites along the road leading out to the highway.

Continuing past Link Lake, at the 41.6 km / 25.7 mile turnoff above, to Osprey and Thirsk Lakes

43.8 km / 27.2 mi
Arrive at Osprey Lake.

OSPREY LAKE RECREATION SITE #67
Overnight / Easy
4 tables, rough boat launch

This one is far enough below the road so noise won't be too bothersome. The more densely forested hillside across the lake is prettier than the scenery at Link Lake.

45 km / 27.8 mi
The gravel road is wide and well graded.

46.6 km / 28.8 mi
At the junction, continue straight toward Summerland. Trout Cr FS Road will take you to Peachland and Headwater Lakes farther north. But why go? They're ugly.

52 km / 32.3 mi
Come to an unmarked junction. Go right to continue on the main road, toward the Okanagan. Immediately past the intersection, a small road through lodgepole pine leads to **unofficial campsites** on the stumpy, swampy western end of Thirsk Lake, before you're actually at the water. Stay on the main road, however, for the official Thirsk Lake campground.

52.8 km / 32.8 mi
Arrive at signed Thirsk Lake campground, beside the road.

THIRSK LAKE RECREATION SITE #110
Weekend / Easy
Table on the beach, room for 1 or 2 others farther east, garbage can

53.1 km / 33 mi
Come to more official **campsites**. There are two tables, one on a point which you can't drive to, and places for two or three vehicles overlooking the lake.

54.1 km / 33.6 mi
See an **overnight pullout** for one vehicle, on your right, beside Trout Creek.

55.4 km / 34.4 mi
Cross Trout Creek.

67.5 km / 41.9 mi
Come to another **overnight pullout** on the right, in trees, beside the creek.

68.3 km / 42.4 mi
See another **overnight pullout** on the right. Also Munro FS Road.

68.6 km / 42.6 mi
Feint fork to the right. Stay straight on the main road. Just beyond, on the left, a narrow track goes down to the creek and an **overnight pullout** for one party.

70.5 km / 43.8 mi
Arrive at the official Trout Creek campground, just before a bridge.

TROUT CREEK CROSSING RECREATION SITE #111
Weekend / Easy
4 tables, but only 3 campsites

Set in pines and cottonwoods, this campground is the nicest one along this road. The creek is loud, which enhances the atmosphere. Nobody was here Thanksgiving weekend, while there were crowds at the lakeside campgrounds. People must like lakes better.

82.1 km / 51 mi
An **overnight pullout** drops below the road and widens out. You get a panoramic view looking east toward the Okanagan Valley.

83 km / 51.5 mi
Pavement resumes.

84.4 km / 52.4 mi
Continue straight on Bald Range Road, to Summerland. Darke Lake and Meadow Valley are to the left, off Fish Lake Road.

90.2 km / 56 mi
Turn left at the junction, to Summerland. The road curves downhill.

94.1 km / 58.4 mi
Arrive at the junction of Prairie Valley and Victoria Roads, at Giant's Head in Summerland. Continue east on Prairie Valley, toward Okanagan Lake.

95.3 km / 59.2 mi
Arrive at Hwy 97, at the IGA Shopping Centre.

If you're heading west from Hwy 97 in Summerland

This route starts in a beautiful valley above Okanagan Lake. Come just for the drive to Km 11, even if you don't plan to camp farther west. The campgrounds and lakes are described in the section above.

0 km / 0 mi
From Hwy 97, at the IGA Shopping Centre, head west on Prairie Valley Road through the center of town.

1.3 km / .8 mi
Arrive at a junction with Victoria Road. Continue straight on Prairie Valley Road, toward Rutherford Farms. The road begins climbing in about 2.4 kms / 1.5 miles.

5 km / 3 mi
Go left on Bathfield Road. Basically, follow the yellow line on the main road going up. At the white signs with a red outline, curve right for Meadow Valley and Princeton.

11 km / 6.8 mi
Continue straight on Bald Range Road. Fish Lake Road curves away to the right.

12.4 km / 7.7 mi
Pavement ends.

24.8 km / 15.4 mi
Arrive at **Trout Creek Crossing Recreation Site**.

42.5 km / 26.4 mi
Arrive at **Thirsk Lake Recreation Site**.

51.5 km / 32 mi
Arrive at **Osprey Lake Recreation Site**.

54 km / 33.5 mi
Arrive at the turn-in for **Link Lake Recreation Site**.

58.9 km / 36.6 mi
Arrive at **Chain Lake Recreation Site**.

95.3 km / 59.2 mi
Arrive in Princeton, at the junction with the Old Hedley Road.

~

"Be Free," the sign says. We got a boost when we spotted it near Hedley, in the Similkameen River Valley.

OLD HEDLEY ROAD, SIMILKAMEEN RIVER
Weekend if you're rafting or fishing, otherwise Overnight / Easy

The Similkameen is a beautiful river. Even if you're not staying overnight at one of the campgrounds here, drive this old road instead of Hwy 3, so you can go slowly, enjoy the scenery, and get out to admire the river. It's ideal for rafting, canoeing or fishing. The campgrounds aren't special. You don't get any privacy from other campers, or from the Hedley Road, and you can hear cars across the river — unless you're camped right by a loud rapid.

If you're heading northwest from Keremeos

From the community of Hedley, be looking in 6.5 kms / 4 miles for a turnoff on your right. It's immediately before the highway bridge over the Similkameen River. Turn right, onto the Old Hedley Road. You'll easily spot the campgrounds along the river.

If you're heading east from Princeton

0 km / 0 mi
In Princeton, turn west (left if you're coming from the south) off Hwy 3, at the Petro Canada station, just south of the blue bridge over the Similkameen River. At the first street, turn right where a green highway sign points the way to Tulameen and Merritt. Soon cross the Tulameen River.

1 km / .6 mi
Turn right at the junction, onto the Old Hedley Road. You'll be traveling on the north side of the Similkameen River, past homes, then campgrounds. Hwy 3 is on the other side of the river.

8 km / 5 mi
Arrive at the first campground on the Old Hedley Road.

DEWDNEY RECREATION SITE #76
Overnight / Easy
1 table, room for 2 vehicles

This signed campground is too close to both roads to be peaceful. There's not even any vegetation shielding it from the Old Hedley Road. But that probably won't bother you for a night's sleep. There's also an **overnight pullout** past a group of trees.

18.2 km / 11.3 mi
You'll see an **overnight pullout** on the river. There's room for two vehicles comfortably apart. The highway is not visible.

25.8 km / 16 mi
The river narrows here.

31 km / 19 mi
Now you're past all the houses. Arrive at another official campground.

OLD HEDLEY RD WEST RECREATION SITE #77
Weekend / Easy
5 tables, pit toilet across the road

31.9 km / 19.8 mi
Arrive at an **unnamed campground** with eight tables, one across the road. River rapids muffle the noise of cars across the way.

34.3 km / 21.3 mi
Arrive at the next official campground.

OLD HEDLEY RD EAST RECREATION SITE #78
1 table, 2 pit toilets across the road

~

The Ashnola River, an example of why B.C. stands for Boating Country

ASHNOLA RIVER, NEAR CATHEDRAL LAKES PARK

This area between Princeton and Penticton gets a lot of sunny weather, except for the mountain plateau at the top of Cathedral Lakes Provincial Park, which averages about 7,000 feet elevation. It can snow up there in summer. The Ashnola River Valley has a great camping climate from April until November. Even if you're not going up to the Lakes to hike, you'll enjoy this scenic drive through a deep mountain valley along a roaring river. There are many free FS campgrounds along the way, so you can probably find a site even on busy weekends.

We highly recommend hiking from the Quiniscoe Lake basecamp up to the lakes on the plateau. You can pay for a jeep ride up, or start hiking from the Lakeview Creek Trailhead at 23.8 kms / 14.8 miles. It's a 14.5 km / 9 mile ascent. There's a sign at the trailhead: Gain on Lakeview trail: 1357 m; Quiniscoe to Ladyslipper Lake 150 m, 5 km.

The access road is signed, 66 kms / 40.5 miles southeast of Princeton, on Hwy 3, at the western edge of Keremeos. A white BC Parks sign announces: 24 km - Cathedral Lakes Provincial Park. After that, only two of the FS campgrounds are signed.

0 km / 0 mi
On the Red Bridge over the Ashnola River, just after turning off Hwy 3 toward Cathedral Lakes Provincial Park.

10 km / 6.2 mi
Pavement turns to gravel. There's a **campsite** on the right, beside the raging Ashnola River. It's comfortable for two vehicles if you're both quiet, or for one big group.

12.2 km / 7.6 mi
A road on the left side leads to a **campground**. There are nine attractive campsites in the trees beside the river. A couple have tables. There's a beautiful river pool. Enter carefully if you're going swimming. The riversong is just enough to drown out other campers' noises.

13.4 km / 8.3 mi
There are three **campsites** without tables on the left side. It's easy to miss, because the road drops steeply here. You might want to walk down first if you're driving a motorhome.

13.7 km / 8.5 mi
The road on the left leads to two comfortably-spaced **campsites**. This isn't as nice as other spots. There's little shade.

15.3 km / 9.5 mi
Turn left to **Horseshoe Canyon Recreation Site**. It has one table, but room for two vehicles.

15.6 km / 9.7 mi
More **campsites** here, close to the road.

One of many riverside campsites along the Ashnola River, near Keremeos

15.9 km / 9.9 mi
Come to a junction with Ewart Creek. Go right, to the resort and trailhead camping.

18.2 km / 11.3 mi
Arrive at a **meadow campsite** with a bit of shade. Or you can go down on the river to a larger campsite with a table and lots of shade. There's also one in the trees to the left that's a little more difficult to get into.

18.8 km / 11.7 mi
Turn left to another **campground** with no name or table. A park info sign is across the road. There are two spacious sites on terraces above the river.

22.2 km / 13.8 mi
Pass Cathedral Lakes Resort Base Parking, unless you're using their services. You can take a jeep from here. Jeep pick-up times: 10 am, 2 pm, 4 pm. Call (604) 499-5848. It's about $50 roundtrip per person. Otherwise, continue a bit more to the trailhead.

23.8 km / 14.8 mi
Arrive at the turn-in to **Lakeview trailhead and campground**, with walk-in tent sites beside the river.

~

HWY 5: COQUIHALLA COUNTRY

This area looks like a continuation of the Interior Plateau's featureless, rounded, forested mountains, rather than part of the rugged Cascade Mountains as maps label it. Driving south to Hope, only the last twenty minutes of scenery are spectacular. All along the route, however, the vastness is impressive, even if the mountains themselves are not.

These campgrounds are all reached from the major, easy-to-see interchanges on Coquihalla Hwy 5. Once you exit the interchanges, check the *heading south* section below for further directions.

GILLIS LAKE RECREATION SITE #30
Weekend / Moderate
6 tables, rough boat launch, crude dock, plenty of flat ground for tents

Gillis is an okay campground, but not great. Don't spend your time here if you live far away. It might be pleasant for a weekend, if you're from Merritt or the Lower Mainland. Your activities will have to center around the lake. There's really no place to walk or explore. The whole lake is in a tight bowl, with forested sides rising abruptly. Some people will feel cozy, nestled in such a small pocket; others will feel too closed in.

If you're heading north from Hope

From the junction of Hwys 3 & 5, east of Hope, drive approximately 80 kms / 50 miles north on the Coquihalla Hwy to the Coldwater Exit (also known as Kingsvale Interchange).

If you're heading south from Merritt

From the junction of Hwys 5 and 5A in Merritt, head south on the Coquihalla Hwy for 30 kms / 18.7 miles. Take the Coldwater Exit (also known as Kingsvale Interchange).

For either approach above, now follow the directions below

After exiting the highway, go north on the paved road paralleling west of Hwy 5. You'll soon come to a sign listing destinations south: Brookmere 10 km, Thynne Mtn 8 km, Merritt 30 km. Set your tripometer to 0.

0 km / 0 mi
Starting north, after exiting the highway.

2.6 km / 1.6 mi
In Kingsvale, go left before the railroad overpass. See the sign, up on the left: Murray Lake Rd. Cross the bridge, then go left. Take the Maka - Murray FS Road.

6.5 km / 4 mi
The road starts ascending.

7.1 km / 4.4 mi
Stay high and straight (left) at the fork.

7.9 km / 4.9 mi
Gillis Lake is now visible below. You've arrived at the first entrance. Head left, steeply down the road, off the main logging road. This first entrance skirts the lake to arrive in 1 km at the campground in trees. It's on a bench, well below the road.

8.9 km / 5.6 mi
This second entrance is very short — a little bumpy, but okay for 2WD. There's a rough spot just after entering.

Playful campers encourage their straggling buddies, Gillis Lake, Coquihalla

~

MURRAY LAKE RECREATION SITES #41 & 42
Weekend / Difficult
13 tables, flat grassy areas for tents, boat launch

Murray is a narrow, unremarkable lake in the woods. The access road is horrible, but passable with 2WD. Be brave and patient. It's definitely not for motorhomes. At the top, along the lake, there are inflatable-pool-size potholes. It's certainly not a place we expected to see such huge, opulent cabins. Though it's a hard drive getting here (only twenty minutes from the highway, but seems longer) the nice campground compensates for it. Stay off this road in rain. The section at the top could turn into very sucky mud.

If you don't want to charge up this steep, rough road, and you just want a place to park and sleep for the night, there's a decent **overnight pullout** off the Juliet Exit, heading south. We'll first explain how to reach that, then give directions for the Murray Lakes.

If you're heading north from Hope

From the junction of Hwys 3 & 5, east of Hope, drive approximately 63 kms / 39 miles north on the Coquihalla Hwy. Get off at the Juliet Interchange. Set your tripometer to 0.

If you're heading south from Merritt

From the junction of Hwys 5 and 5A in Merritt, head south on the Coquihalla Hwy. You'll pass the Coldwater Interchange in 30 kms / 18.7 miles. In a total of 47.3 kms / 29.4 miles, get off at the Juliet Interchange. Set your tripometer to 0.

For either approach above, now follow the directions below to the overnight pullout

0 km / 0 mi
Off the Juliet Exit, at the beginning of the Maka - Murray FS Road. Head south on the frontage road, which is on the west side of the highway.

2.3 km / 1.4 mi
Continue under the highway, then head north on the frontage road, which is on the east side now. Just before the highway entrance, turn right (east).The one-vehicle **overnight pullout is** in trees, to the right, next to a drainage.

For either approach above, now follow the directions
below to the Murray Lakes

0 km / 0 mi
Just off Hwy 5, at the Juliet exit. Head straight toward the hill, then go right after a big cattle guard. Turn onto the signed Maka - Murray Lake Road. It's narrower here than at the north end near Gillis Lake. Stay left, above the canyon on your right.

.9 km / .5 mi
Make a hairpin turn where the road is close to the other side of the canyon. You'll climb steeply here for a bit.

5 km / 3 mi
Arrive at **Murray Lake South campground**. This one is really a pond with three tables. In fall, this end can be bathed in late-afternoon sun.

6.9 km / 4.3 mi
Arrive at **Murray Lake North campground**, with views down the forest-enclosed lake. There are ten tables, and a broad, grassy clearing. The very small beach is mucky. There's a smooth area to launch boats.

~

ZUM PEAK RECREATION SITE #68
Overnight / Difficult
No tables, no appeal, just a pit toilet

Warning: Don't come here unless you intend to hike and just want to sleep here the night before. It's a very unpleasant pullout, cramped next to a hillside and across from a clearcut. You won't want to bring your new vehicle on this rough road. Or your old one — it might fall apart.

0 km / 0 mi
Just north of the toll booth, take Exit 228 for Upper Coldwater - Coquihalla Lakes U-Turn Route and Rest Area. Set your tripometer to 0. Head south. Turn right. Cross a metal bridge over the Coldwater River. Follow a paved road bending west. Pass some highway maintenance buildings.

1.6 km / 1 mi
Start on the Upper Coldwater FS Road.

2.1 km / 1.3 mi
Stay straight at a seeming fork. Zum Peak looks like a boring forest-covered peak.

4 km / 2.5 mi
Stay straight at the fork. The road improves now that it's out of the river bottom.

6.5 km / 4 mi
Drive through logging destruction and over very rough rocks.

8.4 km / 5.2 mi
Arrive at the campsite, on your left, just before another bridge.

~

OVERNIGHT PULLOUTS NEAR THE COQUIHALLA TOLL BOOTH
Overnight / Easy

Get off just north of the toll booth at Exit 228, for Upper Coldwater - Coquihalla Lakes U–Turn Route / Rest Area. Follow the road over the highway, as if going to Coquihalla Lakes.

0 km / 0 mi
Set your tripometer to 0 after exiting.

1.1 km / .7 mi
Angle off to the left. You'll see a big flat area on your left, just off the Coquihalla Lakes Road, before the Tulameen FS Road. The **overnight pullout** is just past a grated cattleguard, before the pavement ends.

Continue .5 km / .3 mile south on the Tulameen River FS Road, and take the smaller right fork. For another nice **overnight pullout**, go down .6 km / .4 mile to a small, narrow lake. The drawback is that you can hear cars on the highway from here.

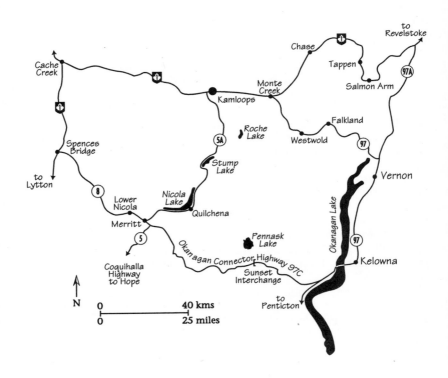

North Thompson Plateau:
Kamloops to Merritt on Hwy 5A,
Connector Hwy 97C,
Kamloops to Okanagan Lake

North Thompson Plateau: Kamloops to Merritt on Hwy 5A, Connector Hwy 97C, Kamloops to Okanagan Lake

CACHE CREEK TO MERRITT

WILLARD & BARNES LAKE RECREATION SITES #3 & 4
Weekend / Easy

These campgrounds near Ashcroft, south of Cache Creek, are good to know about because they're close to Hwy 1. It's about a 15-minute drive from Ashcroft to the lakes. Willard Lake has two campsites and a cartop boat launch. Barnes has a boat launch and room for about 20 campers. Both campgrounds get heavy use. This grasslands country has a scattering of pines. The vast openness is grand, cleansing for the soul.

From Cache Creek, at the junction of Highways 1 and 97, drive south 4.2 kms / 2.6 mi on Hwy 1. Turn left (southeast) at the northern junction leading into Ashcroft and drive 6.2 kms / 3.8 miles. **Or from Spences Bridge**, drive north about 39 kms / 24 miles on Hwy 1. Then turn right (east) at the southern junction leading into Ashcroft and drive 5.0 kms / 3.1 miles. Set your tripometer to 0 in Ashcroft, at the northwest side of the Thompson River bridge.

For either approach above, now follow the directions below

0 km / 0 mi
In Ashcroft, cross the bridge and go south on Hwy 97C.

7.8 km / 4.8 mi
After generally going south, the highway loops north.

9.2 km / 5.7 mi
Where the highway turns abruptly south, look for a sign marking Barnes Lake Road. Turn left (north) on the paved road. In .4 km / .25 mile, a sign marks 4400 Road.

10.0 km / 6.2 mi
Arrive at the south end of Willard Lake. Look for a couple overnight pullouts on the shore.

11.1 km / 6.9 mi
Arrive at the south end of Barnes Lake. You'll find pullouts along the lake.

12.8 km / 7.9 mi
Official campsites, a couple tables, and a pit toilet are at the northwest end of Barnes.

If you're interested in seeing how industrial muscle mangles the earth, continue southeast on Hwy 97C toward Logan Lake. You'll pass the Highland Valley area and what some say is the second largest open-pit copper mine in the world. It's not our idea of a noteworthy site, but some people might think so.

~

N'KWALA RECREATION SITE #17
Weekend / Easy
7 tables, lots of spaces, shade, a sandbar to pitch your tent on
near the river, good wading in shallow water

In this warm, dry valley, the Nicola River and shade trees are welcoming. You drive through the pretty Nicola River Valley on Hwy 8, which connects Hwy 1 at Spences Bridge with Hwy 5 in Merritt.

If you're heading southeast from Spences Bridge

Drive 42.8 kms / 26.5 miles to the N'Kwala turn-in, by a cement road-guard at an abrupt curve.

If you're heading northwest to Spences Bridge

0 km / 0 mi
On the Merritt Interchange, near the Tourist Information Centre, at the junction of Hwys 5 and 97C . Head northwest for a bit on Hwy 97C.

4 km / 2.5 mi
Follow the signs to Logan Lake and Spences Bridge. You'll see a sign: Spences Bridge 63 km, Cache Creek 111 km.

8.9 km / 5.5 mi
Stay straight, heading west on Hwy 8 toward Spences Bridge. Pass the turn to Logan Lake, which is north on Hwy 97C.

12.6 km / 7.8 mi
Continue on the highway through Lower Nicola, to reach N'Kwala campground.

If you want to drive up on the plateau, to good fishing-lakes a long way off the highway, turn on Aberdeen Road. You'll see a sign: Chataway Lake Resort 27 kms. The road is paved for about 6 kms / 3.7 miles, then becomes good gravel, then the inevitable rougher gravel. The road junctions are well signed. At the 14 km / 9 mile junction, go left to Chataway. Be looking for the **Tyner Lake Recreation Site #7**, near the No. 4 Rd marker, after a total of about 20 kms / 12 miles. Chataway Lake is farther north. At the 22.5 km / 14 mile junction, turn right onto Skuhun Creek Road. You'll arrive at Chataway Lake lodge in a total of 33 kms / 20.5 miles.

26.1 km / 16.2 mi
Arrive at the turn-in to N'Kwala. Go left just before a cement road-guard and an abrupt curve north. Two big, dark boulders mark the entrance. A short, rough road takes you down to the riverside campground.

N'Kwala campground, Nicola River, west of Merritt

~

HWY 5A: SOUTHEAST OF MERRITT

0 km / 0 mi
Set your tripometer to 0 at the Merritt Interchange, at the junction of Hwys 5 and 5A South. Follow signs to Connector Hwy 97C and Hwy 5A. Turn onto Hwy 5A going toward Princeton and Kelowna.

9.4 km / 5.8 mi
Look carefully by a cattleguard for a turn left (east) if you're going to Marquart and Lundbom Lakes. Set your tripometer to 0.

Continue on Hwy 5A for the more pleasant Kane Valley campgrounds.

0 km / 0 mi
Turning off Hwy 5A. Shortly, you'll come to a junction. Go left. Pass through rolling, bare grassland. It's a rocky, rough road, with many small potholes.

2.7 km / 1.7 mi
Arrive at Marquart Lake.

MARQUART LAKE RECREATION SITE #24
Overnight / Easy
4 tables, boat dock

This campground without shade or shelter is beside a very shallow, unappealing lake. We don't understand why so many people camp here when the larger Lundbom Lake or the more pleasant Kane Valley campgrounds are so close.

Drive approximately two kilometers farther to Lundbom Lake.

LUNDBOM LAKE RECREATION SITES #25 & 26
Weekend / Easy
Over 34 campsites

One site at this grasslands lake is on the southwest end, and another is on the northeast.

Continuing on Hwy 5A, past the turnoff to Marquart Lake

14.3 km / 8.9 mi
A sign warns of the Kane Valley turn.

14.5 km / 9.0 mi
Turn right (west) at the top of the rise, at a white sign. A highway sign on the left gives the distances: Merritt 18, Princeton 72, Kelowna 112. Set your tripometer to 0.

KANE VALLEY RECREATION SITES
Weekend / Easy

Even if you don't camp here, but you want to get a better feel for the country, drive in for a picnic, or cross-country skiing in winter. You'll find a chain of small lakes and meadows set in ponderosa pines and aspen. It's a good dirt road for cruising on your mountain bike. Cattle will keep you company while you're fishing or sunbathing.

The prevalance of cows will be a constant reminder this isn't wilderness. But as long as people continue to eat beef, it's nice these cows are allowed to wander this pretty country rather than being stuffed into factory farms.

This area is much easier to get to and prettier than the Elkhart - Hatheume area, which is farther east off Connector Hwy 97C.

0 km / 0 mi
Turning off Hwy 5A. The road is well graded and fairly flat.

3.7 km / 2.3 mi
Stay straight (right) on the main road. Pass several lakes.

9 km / 5.6 mi
Arrive at the south end of Lower Kane Lake.

KANE LAKE RECREATION SITE #27
5 tables and room for more, open grassy area, close to the pretty lake

9.2 km / 5.7 mi
Arrive at the next campground, unsigned.

HARMON LAKE WEST RECREATION SITE #29
Fairly open campsites with fewer trees

9.8 km / 6.1 mi
Turn off the road just before the cattleguard. Drive about 200 meters in to the campground.

HARMON LAKE EAST RECREATION SITE #28
4 tables, the most spread-out campsites we've seen

10.3 km / 6.4 mi
Come to a nice **overnight pullout** in trees above the lake.

11.9 km / 7.4 mi
Arrive at an **overnight pullout** at Englishman Lake.

~

GRASSLAND COUNTRY —
HWY 5A BETWEEN KAMLOOPS & MERRITT

The grassland country along Hwy 5A between Merritt and Kamloops has sweeping valleys, high hillsides, and long, beautiful lakes. The country feels open and lonely — far different from the busy routes along Hwy 1 or the Coquihalla. Consider taking Hwy 5A, instead of the Coquihalla Hwy 5, south or north to the Trans-Canada. Though 5A is a little slower, it's much more scenic. The road is good and not too curvy.

These campgrounds are great for a weekend retreat, or useful simply as an overnight stop if you're traveling between Vancouver and Shuswap Lake. They're 24 kms / 15 miles south of Kamloops. The access roads are smooth, wide and flat.

Roche Lake, Interior Plateau, south of Kamloops

ROCHE LAKE RECREATION SITES #16-19
Destination for fisherpeople, Weekend for others / Easy
27 tables, boat launch

These campgrounds are nicely organized with well-spaced sites, like a provincial park. You'll find they're worth the drive, even for just an overnight stop. Although the area is heavily used, enough sites are provided that you should always find room to camp. This large, backcountry, grassland lake gives you an expansive feeling. Some campsites are in the pine trees, where you can hide from the sun or other campers.

If you're heading north from Merritt

Once you get to the Quilchena Store on Nicola Lake, set your tripometer to 0. Look for the turnoff to Roche Lake, on your right in 47.7 km / 29.6 miles. It's just north of Trapp Lake.

If you're heading south from Kamloops

0 km / 0 mi
Just west of Kamloops, turn south onto Hwy 5A, from the junction with Trans-Canada Hwy 1.

17.7 km / 11 mi
After passing Shumway Lake, be looking for the turnoff.

23.2 km / 14.4 mi
A sign announces Roche Lake Road is up ahead.

23.7 km / 14.7 mi
Turn left (east) at the white sign: Roche Lake Rd. There's also a big white sign: Roche Lake Resort 11 km. Drive through pretty, rolling grassland. Set your tripometer to 0.

Continue south on Hwy 5A for the turnoff to Peter Hope Lake, described below, after the Roche Lake directions.

0 km / 0 mi
Turning onto Roche Lake Road.

7.1 km / 4.4 mi
Stay on the main road.

8 km / 5 mi
Go right at the junction. See a FS sign on your right: Roche Lk West. Drive through a tall forest.

8.2 km / 5.1 mi
Stay straight at the next junction and negotiate some potholes. The right fork leads in 1 km to a **small campground** where all four campsites with tables overlook the lake.

9.8 km / 6.1 mi
Go left and continue uphill.

10.5 km / 6.5 mi
The boat launch is to your right. The campsites are in trees, away from the lake.

From the 8 km / 5 mi junction above, set your tripometer to 0 again. The left way goes to Roche Lake Resort and more FS camping. You'll pass ponds, a marsh, and thick cattails.

1 km / .6 mi
Come to an **overnight pullout** at a marshy lake.

2.6 km / 1.6 mi
Arrive at Roche Lake campground.

ROCHE LAKE RECREATION SITE
5 tables, 8 campsites, lakeview

Here's a wonderful site — alone, open, grassy, close to the lake. The area has a grass lakefront with a sprinkling of trees. The lake is surrounded by forest and has a picturesque rock island. Especially beautiful in fall.

2.8 km / 1.7 mi
Arrive at a boat launch and a pullout along the lakeside.

3 km / 1.8 mi
Arrive at more **official campsites**. You'll find two tables and room for five well-spaced vehicles, in trees beside the lake.

~

PETER HOPE RECREATION AREA
Weekend / Easy
4 tables at the first area, 12 tables and a boat launch at the second

Another pretty and relaxing, though unremarkable lake. There's very little shade to give relief from the summer heat, but there is a sprinkling of trees. We saw fish jumping. The second campground has lots of open, lumpy grass for kids to play on. Across the dirt road from this campground, there's a nice meadowy forest where kids can safely roam.

If you're heading north from Merritt

Once you get to the Quilchena Store on Nicola Lake, set your tripometer to 0. Look for the turnoff to Peter Hope Lake, on your right in 21.7 kms / 13.5 miles. It's just before you reach Stump Lake.

If you're heading south from Kamloops

0 km / 0 mi
Just west of Kamloops, turn south onto Hwy 5A, from the junction with Trans-Canada Hwy 1.

23.7 km / 14.7 mi
Pass the turnoff to Roche Lake, described above.

37.4 km / 23.2 mi
You'll see Stump Lake.

42 km / 26 mi
Arrive at **Stump Lake Rest Area**. This is a huge lake held by gentle, grassy hillsides. Parking is down on the left, a bit below the highway, so headlights won't hit you directly if you're parked overnight. There are many tables lined up beside the lake. We didn't see any *No Camping* signs. Check if any new signs have been erected.

If you want a quiet, pretty campground off the highway, look in 6.5 kms / 4 miles for a turnoff to the easily accessible Peter Hope Lake.

49.1 km / 30.5 mi
Pass the brown sign: Peter Hope Lake Resort 8 km.

49.6 km / 30.8 mi
Turn left (east) by a huge professional wooden sign on the left. Set your tripometer to 0. The road is washboarded at first, as it gradually climbs. But it's wide and not nearly as bad as the FS map indicates.

For either approach above, now follow the directions below

0 km / 0 mi
Turning off Hwy 5A, onto the Peter Hope Road.

6.5 km / 4.0 mi
Come to a junction on your left. Follow the signed route to Government Camping.

7.6 km / 4.7 mi
Arrive at the first **campground**. It's a grassy flat area, with four tables in the open, on the water's edge.

7.8 km / 4.8 mi
Arrive at the second **campground**, on the reedy side of the lake.

You can drive beyond Peter Hope's eastern edge, about 11 kms / 6.7 miles to **FS campgrounds** on the northern and southern shores of **Glimpse Lake**. Turn right at the junction, 8.4 kms / 5.2 miles south of Peter Hope Lake.

The following distances continue back on Hwy 5A, from the Peter Hope turnoff at 49.6 kms / 30.8 miles.

60.4 km / 37.5 mi
Come to a **rest area** on impressively long Nicola Lake. We don't think you're supposed to park here for even a short sleep overnight. There are a couple picnic tables and garbage cans. You might be able to overnight at the **pullouts** north or south of the rest area.

66.3 km / 41.2 mi
Pass the Douglas Lake Road, which joins the highway from the left (east). You can drive this smooth, wide, dirt road north to Westwold, on Hwy 97.

71.3 km / 44.3 mi
Arrive at the settlement of **Quilchena**, on Nicola Lake. There's an impressive historic building here, with a dining room and general store.

83.4 km / 51.8 mi
Arrive at the town of Nicola. You might enjoy getting out to stretch and admire several cute houses that exude community pride.

91.8 km / 57 mi
Hwy 5A joins the Coquihalla Hwy 5, just before Merritt.

~

LAKES OFF OKANAGAN CONNECTOR HWY 97C

SUNSET INTERCHANGE

Pinnacle, Hatheume, Brenda and MacDonald Lakes have beautiful campgrounds and are easy to reach from the highway. They're at the top of the plateau, so they're also cooler than Peachland and Headwater Lakes. We had fog and light snow in October at MacDonald. Peachland Lake is in a heavily logged area and is just about the ugliest site in this book. Headwater Lakes are small and don't warrant the long drive through mining and logging debris.

These lakes are all reached from the Sunset Interchange. Once you get off the highway, you have to drive east on the dirt logging road paralleling the highway, before turning north or south to the lakes. The roads are smooth and well-signed to Pinnacle and Hatheume Lakes on the north side of the highway, and to Brenda and MacDonald Lakes on the south side. The roads on the north side are excellent. We averaged 60 to 70 kph / 35 to 40 mph. On the rougher south-side roads, we averaged 40 kph / 25 mph.

If you're heading east from Merritt

Set your tripometer to 0 at the junction of Hwys 5 and 97C, by the Tourist Info Centre. Drive 62.5 kms / 38.8 miles east to the Sunset Interchange.

If you're heading west from the Okanagan

0 km / 0 mi
Set your tripometer to 0 at the junction of Hwy 97 and Connector Hwy 97C, on the west shore of Okanagan Lake, between Peachland and Westbank.

1.6 km / 1 mi
Pass a highway sign: Merritt 108 km.

33.3 km / 20.7 mi
You've reached Pennask Summit and can see Pennask Lake to the north.

42.5 km / 26.4 mi
Get off at Sunset Main Interchange. Set your tripometer to 0.

For either approach above, now follow the directions below

PINNACLE & HATHEUME LAKES

Small Pinnacle Lake has an intimate atmosphere. Hatheume is larger and has an expansive, wild feeling, as though you were farther up in the lonely north. It only takes 20 minutes from the highway to these lakes. Either one is a good base for exploring nearby Pennask Lake, which is accessible only by truck or 4WD.

0 km / 0 mi
Cross south under the Connector Hwy. There's a sign at the T-intersection indicating Hatheume and Headwater Lakes to the left. Sunset is a wide, well-graded road, but still has a few loose, sharp rocks kicking about.

5 km / 3.1 mi
Head left (straight) at the junction, toward Hwy 97C.

6.1 km / 3.8 mi
Curve left.

6.4 km / 4 mi
Bear right. See signs on a tree for Hatheume and Headwater Lakes.

6.8 km / 4.2 mi
Come to an intersection and a sign: Hatheume - left / Headwaters -

right. Cross north (left) under the highway for Hatheume Lake. This Bear FS Road heading north is even better than Sunset.

If you're heading to Brenda and MacDonald Lakes, go right on the same road as for Headwater and Peachland.

9.3 km / 5.8 mi
Go right on Bear Road, near the Km 9 mark.

13.7 km / 8.5 mi
Come to a sign: Pennask FS Rd - Public access farther.

14.2 km / 8.8 mi
Pass another sign: Pennask Park 6 km - recommend use of high clearance vehicles. Just after the sign, stay straight on the main road at the fork.

18.7 km / 11.6 mi
Come to a sign for Hatheume, near the Km 18 mark.

19 km / 11.8 mi
Go left at the junction, where a sign indicates public access to the left and Hatheume Lake Lodge to the right.

21.3 km / 13.2 mi
Go left to the Pinnacle Lake campground. Continue right for Hatheume Lake.

PINNACLE LAKE RECREATION SITE #101
Weekend for locals, Overnight for travelers / Easy
3 tables, garbage cans galore, boat launch

It's a pretty lake, ringed by forest, but you'll probably prefer Hatheume.

22.2 km / 13.8 mi
Go right at the fork, after which the road narrows and deteriorates.

22.9 km / 14.2 mi
When you see the sign on your left, you've arrived at Hatheume Lake.

HATHEUME LAKE RECREATION SITE #102
Weekend / Easy
7 tables within ten feet of the water, garbage cans galore

A healthy forest surrounds the lake. The trout jumping in October were louder and more active than we'd ever heard. You can see the fishing lodge way across the lake.

S.O.S.

Just when you want privacy, it vanishes. Many times after breakfast or dinner, in some quiet spot where we've seen no one, we'll start to brush our teeth. Instantly somebody shows up. It happens to us all the time, even on the loneliest backroads. It's annoying. But we've realized it could come in handy. If we ever need help, we'll whip out a toothbrush, its powers will call, and a savior will appear.

~

BRENDA & MACDONALD LAKES

These restful lakes are south of the Connector Hwy. They have a peaceful feeling, despite the mining and logging that has penetrated nearby.

Get off the Connector Hwy 97C at the Sunset Main Interchange, as described above for Hatheume & Pinnacle Lakes. Or, if you're coming out from those northside lakes, take the Sunset FS Road at the 6.8 km / 4.2 mile intersection described below, where you set your tripometer to 0 again.

0 km / 0 mi
Cross south under the Connector Hwy and go left at the T-intersection, where there's a sign: Hatheume and Headwater Lakes - left. You'll be following the signs toward Headwater. Sunset is a wide, well-graded road.

5 km / 3.1 mi
Head left (straight) at the junction, toward Hwy 97C.

6.1 km / 3.8 mi
Curve left.

6.5 km / 4 mi
Bear right. You'll see signs on a tree for Hatheume and Headwater Lakes.

6.8 km / 4.2 mi
Turn right at the intersection, toward Headwater and Peachland Lakes, if you want to go to Brenda and MacDonald Lakes. Set your tripometer to 0.

0 km / 0 mi
At the signed junction of Sunset Lake FS Rd and Bear FS Rd, head southeast toward Brenda Lake, on Sunset FS Rd.

5 km / 3 mi
Come to a well-marked junction. For Brenda Lake, go left on Brenda FS
Road. Headwater Lakes are to the right.

6.7 km / 4.1 mi
Stay straight on the main road at the junction. An unmarked road goes
left. Just .5 km / .3 mile beyond, you'll see a sign on a tree. Turn left to
arrive at the Brenda Lake campground, in scattered trees beside the lake.

BRENDA RECREATION SITE #104
Weekend / Easy
2 tables, 3 or 4 vehicles could squeeze in, flat areas for tents,
excellent boat launch, garbage cans

If you're heading to MacDonald Lake, continue past the Brenda Lake turn.

8 km / 5 mi
Turn left at the junction. There's a brown signpost on the northeast
corner: MacDonald Lake. Soon bear right at the fork, to arrive at
MacDonald Lake campground.

MACDONALD RECREATION SITE #105
Weekend / Easy
3 tables (2 together), room for 2 more, right beside the lake; 2 tables &
garbage cans in a clearing just above the lake, room for lots more

~

PEACHLAND & HEADWATER LAKES

We don't recommend either place. The whole area is featureless. There
are larger, more scenic lakes not far away. It's better to go to Brenda or
MacDonald. The drive past clearcuts and mine tailings is discouraging
if your intent is to get away from it all. You need a high-clearance vehicle
for the campground at Headwater Lake, so you can get over a rough,
rocky spot uphill beyond the dam. But in case you just want to see all
the lakes in the area, here are directions.

*Continue past Brenda Lake on the route described above, using the same distances
from the 8 km / 5 mile junction, where the left way goes to MacDonald Lake.*

8 km / 5 mi
Go right at the junction, following the sign to Headwater Lakes. The
road steeply descends and gives a view of the Brenda Mine slag heap.
Pass signs indicating unstable ground. Don't go hiking here; apparently
it's easy to fall and die. It's so abused, you won't want to stop anyway.

12.9 km / 8 mi
At the junction, stay on pavement to the right. A gate and mine entrance are to the left. There are signs here pointing up toward MacDonald and Hatheume Lakes.

15.1 km / 9.4 mi
Pass a gravel road to the right (west). A blue sign advertises: Headwaters open all year - cabins, camping, boats, motors, snowmobiling, skiing - 6 miles. This is one of the optional routes to Headwater Lakes.

17.2 km / 10.7 mi
You'll see a brown FS signpost on the left at this junction: Peachland Lake straight, Headwater Lakes right. We first went left to Peachland. Directions for Headwater continue below.

17.7 km / 11 mi
Arrive at Peachland Lake.

PEACHLAND LAKE RECREATION SITE #106
Overnight / Difficult because it's a long, ugly way
2 tables, room for 15 vehicles around a big,
gravel parking lot, garbage cans, boat launch

This unpleasant place should be called Pitland Lake. There are virtually no trees at the campground, and the surrounding clearcuts jolt your senses — at least they should. There's one pullout to the left, at the bottom of a small hill, with some grass. Fire rings are scattered about.

To reach Headwater Lakes, go right at the 17.2 km / 10.7 mile junction described above. The road gets rougher and smaller, but is still okay for 2WD.

20.6 km / 12.8 mi
Turn left at the junction. There's a brown FS signpost indicating directions to Headwater Lakes and Peachland Lakes.

21 km / 13 mi
Come to at an unmarked, poor **campsite**. It's on the right, next to a small lake. Just beyond, ignore the blue sign for Headwaters south. Turn right on the road marked by a FS post indicating Whitehead Lk - right, and another sign announcing Peachland FS Rd.

21.3 km / 13.2 mi
Come to another unmarked, poor **campsite** on the lake, across from cabins.

23 km / 14.3 mi
Turn left at the brown FS post on the right indicating Headwaters Lakes left, Whitehead Lake straight. The side road might be too narrow for motorhomes.

23.8 km / 14.8 mi
Arrive at Headwater Lake, but continue across the berm for ten camp-sites straight ahead in the trees. There's a lot of deadfall in the water. There are no views beyond the surrounding trees.

~

ELKHART INTERCHANGE

These lakes aren't as pretty as those off the Sunset Interchange, but here are the directions.

If you're heading east from Merritt

Set your tripometer to 0 at the junction of Hwys 5 and 97C, near the Tourist Info Centre. Drive 50.7 kms / 31.4 miles east on Hwy 97C, to the Elkhart Interchange.

If you're heading west from the Okanagan

Set your tripometer to 0 at the junction of Hwy 97 and Connector Hwy 97C, at Okanagan Lake. Drive 54.3 kms / 33.7 miles west on Hwy 97C, to the Elkhart Interchange. It's 11.8 kms / 7.3 miles west of the Sunset Interchange.

Once you exit at Elkhart, don't take the first road on the right. Drop down toward the tunnel. Turn right onto Bob's Lake Pit Road, at the green highway sign. It's a wide, level, well-graded road. Set your tripometer to 0 again.

Typical Forest Service road, near Bob's Lake, north of Connector Hwy 97C

0 km / 0 mi
At the highway sign: Elkhart L 2 km, Paradise L 6 km, Island L 7 km.

5 km / 3.3 mi
Pass an unnamed lake on the right.

5.7 km / 3.5 mi
Arrive at the turn-in to Bob's Lake. Or continue on for a better campsite.

BOB'S LAKE RECREATION AREA #37
Overnight / Easy
2 tables

There's not much to say about this insignificant pond in the woods, except that it might be good for sleeping. The loop road to the lake circles back to the FS road, but the second road entrance is rougher than the first.

7.2 km / 4.5 mi
Pass the Paradise Lake turn-in. There are nice cabins to rent if you get tired of camping. The road worsens from here and has big dips.

7.5 km / 4.7 mi
Go left at the four-way junction.

7.7 km / 4.8 mi
Head left on a small road. Arrive at the campground. You can see Island Lake.

ISLAND LAKE RECREATION AREA
Weekend / Easy
5 nicely spaced tables, boat launch

This is a large, pretty lake in full forest. It's way nicer than Bob's, even if you encounter several other vehicles here.

~

HWY 97: FALKLAND AREA

JOYCE & PILLAR LAKES

Drive to Falkland, which is on Hwy 97, between Monte Creek on Hwy 1 and Vernon. A paved road from Falkland leads you to Pillar Lake, then becomes an excellent gravel road, called the Falkland-Chase Road. Some people use it as a cutoff going from Hwy 97 to the Trans-Canada. There's good swimming and fishing at Pillar Lake. You can also ogle the lake's namesake: an 80- or 90-foot pillar you can reach in a ten-minute walk.

0 km / 0 mi
In Falkland, turn north off Hwy 97, at the Chase-Falkland Road. A green highway sign on the south side points to Pillar Lake.

7.2 km / 4.5 mi
Stay straight. You'll see a sign: Chase 43 km.

10.1 km / 6.3 mi
Come to an **overnight pullout** in trees on your left, just after a small bridge at Bolean Creek. There's a suitable spot for a tent. There's another **overnight pullout** in trees, 150 meters farther. Just beyond that, you arrive at the official Joyce Lake campground, on a small lake beside the highway. It's not signed.

JOYCE LAKE RECREATION SITE #65
Overnight / Easy
3 tables, boat launch

12.9 km / 8 mi
See Pillar Lake on your left.

13.5 km / 8.4 mi
Arrive at the campground just below the highway, beside the lake. Walk up to the pillar — an interesting geological formation off the east side of the highway.

PILLAR LAKE RECREATION SITE #64
Overnight / Easy
2 campsites, boat launch, no tables, no garbage cans, no toilets

15.9 km / 9.9 mi
Arrive at Chase Creek. The campground is on the right (east), just before crossing a small bridge.

CHASE CREEK RECREATION SITE #63
Overnight / Easy
3 campsites beside the highway, no tables

This isn't a nice place camp, but if the other sites are full, all you want is an overnight pullout, and you don't mind vehicles buzzing by, it could be alright. It's in a clearing, beside trees and a tiny creek. It might be quieter than Joyce for sleeping, but Joyce will be more appealing during the day.

~

BOLEAN, ARTHUR & SPA LAKES

Bolean Lake, scenery typical of small lakes on the Interior Plateau

Three peaceful lakes, surrounded by forest, each about a mile long, are tucked in the hillside at 5,000 feet elevation. Fisherpeople will enjoy the area, but it doesn't offer others much to do, unless you just want to sit and relax. There's a fishing lodge on Bolean Lake, but no place special to hike or explore. It's good for an overnight stop and a peaceful morning. It's about a half-hour drive in — not far, but steep. Cars can make it, perhaps not motorhomes. Vantage points along the way afford views of the beautiful Salmon River valley.

You reach the lakes from Falkland, which is 43.5 kms / 27 miles northwest of Vernon, or 69 kms / 43 miles southeast of Kamloops, on Hwy 97.

0 km / 0 mi
In Falkland, at the Petro Canada station on Gyp Road. Head east, out of town.

.8 km / .5 mi
Turn north onto Silver Nails Road. East of Falkland, there's a blue highway sign before the turn: Bolean Lake Lodge 10 km.

1.1 km / .7 mi
Turn left on Ord Road. The lakes are on top of the hillside you're looking at. The gravel road switchbacks steeply. It's washboarded, bumpy, and gets quite narrow. Our car needed to be in first gear much of the way, to have enough power to climb. A small motorhome can make it, if the driver's up to it. There are some pullouts for passing.

9.7 km / 6 mi

Come to a junction and sign: Bolean Lake. Stay on the main road, passing a 1984 clearcut on the right. You'll come to another sign, on a tree to your right: Arthur and Spa. Go straight if you're going to Arthur Lake and refer to the directions after Bolean. To go to Bolean, bear left at the next fork, shortly after this one.

10 km / 6.2 mi

Where you come to the lodge and cabins of Bolean Lake, go left on a deeply potholed road to the FS campground.

10.2 km / 6.3 mi

See a sign: Bolean Lake Rec Area.

10.5 km / 6.5 mi

Arrive at the campground.

BOLEAN LAKE RECREATION SITE #68
Weekend / Moderate
4 tables, 2 campsites overlooking the lake,
room for 3 more, rough boat launch

If you're venturing to Arthur and Spa Lakes, go straight at the 9.7 km / 6 mile junction above, set your tripometer to 0, and continue with the directions below.

0 km / 0 mi

At the junction.

2.9 km 1.8 mi

Go right at the junction, onto the higher road. See an orange sign on a tree: Spa. This surface might require 4WD when wet. But it's rough even in dry weather, with many protruding rock slabs. Better tackle it with 4WD, or a snowmobile as signs suggest.

4.2 km / 2.6 mi

Arrive at a sign and turnoff for Arthur Lake, on the right. Drive .7 km / .4 mile in to the campground.

ARTHUR LAKE RECREATION SITE #67
Weekend / Difficult
3 campsites, 1 with a table, eroded boat launch

Don't come here unless Bolean is full. You can't really see the lake from the campsites, which are at the weedy end. The lake itself is very pretty. Continue on the rough road to Spa Lake if you want more punishment, or more privacy.

~

PINAUS LAKE RECREATION SITE #71
Weekend / Difficult
About 25 campsites and a boat launch on a medium-size plateau lake

You'll probably want a high-clearance vehicle for the last section of this road. But we mention Pinaus in case you're already in the area with your truck or 4WD and want to explore more than nearby Bolean and Pillar Lakes.

If you're heading east

Turn onto Ingram Creek Road, which is 2 kms / 1.3 miles east of the Westwold School, on Hwy 97. At the signed turnoff, follow the directions starting at the 13.4 km / 8.3 mile point below.

If you're heading west

0 km / 0 mi
In Falkland, at the junction with the Falkland-Chase Road, continue west on Hwy 97. There's a green highway sign on the south side of the highway: Westwold 18 km, Monte Creek 43 km, Kamloops 69 km. Travel through ranch country, in a broad, picturesque valley.

10 km / 6.2 mi
See a blue sign on the right indicating a left turn to Pineas Lake Resort.

10.3 km / 6.4 mi
Pass the old, gravel road to Pinaus Lake. This one is narrow, curvy and steep. A sign warns: Large RVs and trailer towing vehicles use Ingraham Road 3 km north.

13.4 km / 8.3 mi
Turn left (south) on Ingram Creek FS Road. It's signed for Pineas Lake Resort. This is the easiest way for everybody. At 8 or 9 km and a turn left, the road joins Pineas Lake Road. It's good gravel to the lodge, but the last few kilometers to the FS campground are very rough and not recommended for low-clearance vehicles.

~

SALMON RIVER RECREATION SITE #58
Weekend / Easy
A big, grassy, flat area, ideal for group camping

This is the former site of a Dominion ranger station. If a group hasn't already claimed it, you'll have room to fling a frisbee, or play ball with your kids. Located on the Douglas Lake Road, it's accessible from both Hwys 97 and 5A. The approach described here, driving south from Hwy 97, is on a smooth, wide road. If all you need is an overnight pullout, try parking near the narrow bridge, soon after turning onto Douglas Lake Road.

0 km / 0 mi
Turning south off Hwy 97, onto paved Douglas Lake Road, just west of Westwold. At this intersection, a highway sign announces: Monte Cr Jct 27 km, Kamloops 55 km, Westwold 2 km, Falkland 18 km Vernon 63 km. Another sign states SALMON LK RESORT 35 KM.

8.0 km / 5.0 mi
Pavement ends. Continue on well-graded dirt. Pass homes scattered through the river valley.

14.0 km / 8.7 mi
Look for the turnoff on your left. The campground is between the road and the river.

~

HWY 1: CHASE TO SALMON ARM

HARPER LAKE RECREATION AREA #85
Overnight / Difficult
5 tables crowded on uneven ground in a dirt pullout,
a couple tables at the grassy end

The turnoff for this campground is near Chase, just southwest of Little Shuswap Lake. Harper is a small, pretty lake surrounded by forest, with nice cattails on the north end. Your reward for negotiating the rugged access road is a free place that's quite nice for camping. You could have a quiet break from the highway rush, do a little fishing, maybe have a swim on a hot summer day.

This half-hour driving adventure includes a steep climb, tortuous turns, and dances with potholes. This road won't be a problem for a patient driver or an ambitious backroads fan. Just don't go when it's rainy or threatening to rain, unless you have 4WD. The initial climb up the hillside has a steep dropoff that could be scary at night. We don't recommend tackling it after dark.

Remember these backroads driving suggestions. If you get in a tough spot and can't turn around, stay cool. You'll probably find a doable turn soon, or maybe you can back out. If the road looks like it might get too rough for you or your vehicle while driving in, make a mental note of spots where you could turn around if you have to reverse.

If you're heading northeast from Kamloops

Drive 53 kms / 33 miles northeast of Kamloops. Be looking for the turn 4.0 kms / 2.5 miles before Chase. Turn right (south) onto signed Harper Lake Road. If you reach Shuswap-Chase Cr Rd, you've gone .3 km too far.

If you're heading southwest from Chase

Just out of town, be looking for the green highway sign showing the distance to Kamloops. Set your tripometer to 0 there.

0 km / 0 mi
At the highway sign: Kamloops - 55 km.

1.4 km / .9 mi
Pass another highway sign: Pillar Lake, Falkland 45 km. There's a white sign above a stop sign: Shuswap-Chase Crk Rd. Start slowing down.

1.7 km / 1.1 mi
Turn left (south) at the white sign: Harper Lk Rd. Set your tripometer to 0.

For either approach above, now follow the directions below

0 km / 0 mi
At the turn onto Harper Lake Road.

3.4 km / 2.1 mi
Come to a junction with a sign indicating to go right.

5.8 km / 3.6 mi
Arrive at Harper Lake. Go left to the campground.

~

SKIMIKIN RECREATION SITE #16 or 88
Weekend / Easy from the east, Moderate from the west
About 6 campsites on each of 2 small, pleasant lakes

The setting is not awesomely beautiful, but it's pretty and soothing. Campsites are scattered in meadows, or pine, alder and aspen trees, beside small lakes that are prettier in spring when the water level is high.

You can reach Skimikin Lakes via a paved road from Hwy 1 on the eastern approach. Or, if you're heading northeast from Chase and want a taste of quiet backroads, drive through pleasant Turtle Valley from the west side, then exit at Hwy 1 farther east.

The longer approach, if you're heading east from Chase

0 km / 0 mi
On Hwy 1, at the rest area beside Chase Creek.

9.1 km / 5.6 mi
After passing the BC Parks sign for Roderick Haig-Brown, you'll see a white sign: Squilax-Anglemont Rd. Get into the right turn-lane. At 9.5 kms / 5.9 miles, turn right going uphill. In .5 km / .3 mile turn left onto paved Turtle Valley Road, which becomes dirt in 1 km / .6 mile.

13.2 km / 8.2 mi
See a yellow sign: Welcome to Turtle Valley.

15.5 km / 9.6 mi
At the Y-junction, go left. Chum Lake is on the right.

16.8 km / 10.4 mi
Stay straight here and at another fork in 2 kms. Follow signs for Tappen.

19.4 km / 12.0 mi
Bear left on the main road. In the next 8.2 kms / 5.1 miles, stay straight where roads fork off right.

27.8 km / 17.2 mi
Turn right for the first entrance to Skimikin Lakes. The next access road is .7 km / .4 mile farther, just after you pass the lakes. You can continue east on pavement 10 kms / 6.2 miles to Tappen on Hwy 1.

The easier approach, if you're heading east from Chase

If you don't want to drive the long, dirt access road from the west, continue to the easier approach from the east. Drive 35 km / 21.7 miles from Chase. Then look for the signed Turtle Valley turnoff on your right, across from the lumber mill at Tappen Bay.

The easier approach, if you're heading west from Salmon Arm

From the Salmon River bridge, on the west edge of town, drive 10.5 kms / 6.5 miles north and look for the turnoff on your left, just after the Co-op station, and across from the lumber mill at Tappen Bay. There's a sign on the left: Salmon Arm 14 km, Skimikin Lake 5 km.

For either approach above, now follow the directions below

0 km / 0 mi
At the turn, northwest onto Tappen Valley Road. Drive 4 kms / 2.5 miles, and turn left (west) at the signed junction.

10 km / 6.2 mi
Come to a sign for the larger **campground** on the southernmost lake. The entrance is to the left, just off the pavement, across from houses with addresses 1627 - 1631. The FS map incorrectly shows the pavement ending way before the lakes. Meander through the trees to find your choice spot.

10.6 km / 6.6 mi
If you continue beyond the first entrance, you'll pass the lakes on your left and come to the entrance for another **campground**. If you turn down to the lake, there are two tables on a point in the open. Or you can quickly turn right upon entering and head slightly uphill to campsites in the trees, sheltered from wind, but without tables.

~

OKANAGAN LAKE RECREATION SITE #52
Destination / Easy
17 tables, boat launch

This is the only free campground we've found on the shores of popular Okanagan Lake. And it's farther off the highway than most of the expensive provincial parks. So cherish it. There's great swimming here from several pocket beaches scattered among the campsites. You'll have lots of pines for shade, and water lapping at your feet. Previous users had really trashed this site. Please help keep it clean.

If you're near Vernon

Drive to the junction of Hwys 97 and 97A, north of Vernon, at the north end of Swan Lake.

0 km / 0 mi
At the turn west onto Hwy 97, toward Kamloops.

5.8 km / 3.6 mi
Turn south onto the Westside Road, which is along the west shore of Okanagan Lake.

24 km / 14.9 mi
After reaching the top of a rise and passing through trees high on the roadside, you'll come to an open view of the lake. Take the dirt road on the left, going downhill. It's easily seen from the pavement. Across from it, there's a dirt road that goes to Sugarloaf Mountain and a yellow sign: Caution - Radio controlled logging.

25 km / 15.6 mi
You've arrived at the Okanagan Lake campground. You'll see a sign:

BC Forest Rec Site. To the left of the boat launch is the best campsite, facing the lights of Vernon.

The problem you might have on this popular lake is noisy campmates. The night we stopped, there was an RV with an atrocious generator charging at 9:30 pm, a van with likeable boardsailors blasting a stereo, and two rough families roaring away.

So at 10 p.m. we drove up the Sugarloaf Mountain Road and found a pullout. It's easy enough to do if you're self-contained. If you need this outlet, the best **overnight pullout** on Sugarloaf Road is about 1.6 kms / 1 mile up. Drive past the refuse dump, until you see a crude sign: hiking trail - right. Stay left at that fork. When you come to an island in the road, where a blue arrow on a tree points left, go right to the pullout. Keep all your food inside. We heard a black bear rustling up the hillside.

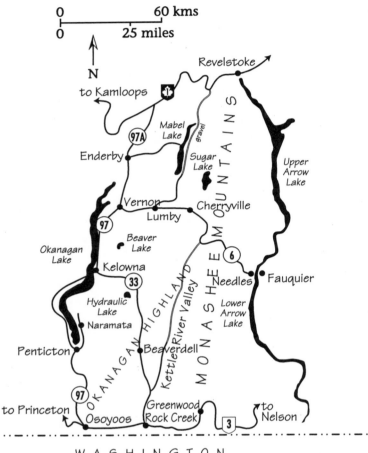

Okanagan Highland
and Monashee Mountains

Okanagan Highland and Monashee Mountains

OKANAGAN HIGHLAND: NEAR KELOWNA

This is not a great area for sightseeing because the topography is fairly dull: just low, forested hills above the lakes. But if you're already nearby, it's a pleasant place to relax and escape the crowds of the Okanagan. If you're on vacation and need a cool break from the Okanagan Valley heat, or if you've had enough lounging in the sand, drive up to the lakes to go fishing or walking in the woods.

CHUTE LAKE RECREATION SITE
Weekend / Moderate

The drive to this forest-rimmed, kilometer-long lake starts in picturesque orchard and vineyard country with views over Okanagan Lake. Chute Lake, at 3,950 feet elevation, is cooler than the Okanagan Valley. It's a good base for exploring the historic Kettle Valley Railway (KVR). It's fascinating to drive on the railbed beyond Chute Lake, to the western approach to scenic Myra Canyon. You can even drive on a towering trestle bridge, over the chasm of Bellevue Creek. At the road's end, you can walk or bicycle along the railbed over twelve trestle bridges.

0 km / 0 mi
Starting in Penticton, at the southern end of Okanagan Lake, where Front Street (at the waterfront) runs into Vancouver Avenue, on the east end of town. Vancouver Avenue soon becomes Naramata Road. Follow it north toward Naramata.

11.8 km / 7.3 mi
Continue straight on the main road for Chute Lake. You can follow Smethurst Road, going uphill on your right, to a trailhead. There, you can walk or cycle the KVR along its switchbacks, gaining 3000 feet and passing through two tunnels.

You'll pass Robinson Avenue and others veering off left down to Naramata's beaches. The main road becomes Chute Lake Road. You'll see a few signs along the way pointing to Chute Lake.

19.6 km / 12.2 mi
At the fork, go right and start climbing. The road gets rougher. The left road goes to a subdivision.

25 km / 15.5 mi
Stay right at a fork. The left way leads to Okanagan Mountain Park trailhead.

29.8 km / 18.5 mi
Chute Lake Road levels out.

30.8 km / 19.1 mi
Stay straight (left) at the junction, just below Chute Lake.

31.2 km / 19.4 mi
Chute Lake Resort is on the west side of the lake. The FS was planning to re-establish the free campground, probably on the north end. It should be ready when you arrive.

The road continuing northeast past Chute Lake is fun to drive because it's obvious you're on the railbed. In the narrow, blasted-out rock chasms, you can imagine the old trains chugging through. You can drive about 24 kms / 15 miles to where Little White Road, coming up from Kelowna, joins the railbed. Park your vehicle to the right, just beyond the junction, and continue on foot or bicycle into Myra Canyon.

The Old Kettle Valley Railway trestle bridge in Myra Canyon,
near the Chute Lake campground, above Kelowna

From East Kelowna you can take McCulloch Road to June Springs Road, which leads to Little White Road and access to the western side of the canyon. Or you can take McCulloch to Myra Road, for access to the eastern side of the canyon.

~

BEAVER (SWALWELL) LAKE RECREATION SITE #41
Weekend / Moderate
11 tables, 2 campsites overlooking the water, boat launch

The lake is broad, set in a shallow, forest-covered valley. Purple lupine was flourishing in the sun at the forest edges in mid-June.

Go to the town of Winfield, which is on Hwy 97, north of Kelowna. Turn east at the Turbo gas station. Look for the sign: Beaver Lake 17 km, Dee Lake 26 km.

If you have a bicycle, when returning to Winfield from Beaver Lake, let your companion drive while you freewheel down these exciting turns. You might want to wait to start until you're on pavement, which is also where you get the best views of the Okanagan Valley below.

0 km / 0 mi
At the turn onto Beaver Lake Road. Go straight over the railroad tracks, staying on Beaver Lake Road. You'll see signs along the paved road: 7 km more to Beaver Lake.

8.5 km / 5.3 mi
Pavement ends, but the gravel road is wide and well-graded, with only a few washboard sections.

15.6 km/ 9.7 mi
Go left at the junction. You'll see a big brown sign: Beaver Lake Resort, right 200 meters. Don't go there. Go left at the yellow sign: Boaters. There are also white signs for the Dee Lake Fishing Lodge and the Government Access Road.

18.4 km / 11.4 mi
Turn in at the brown FS sign on your right: Public Use Area. Arrive at the Beaver Lake campground.

For Island Lake, continue on the main road through a previously logged area that's now growing back.

24.3 km / 15.1 mi
You'll see a sign: Public Use Area. You've arrived at Island Lake.

ISLAND LAKE RECREATION SITE #40
Weekend / Moderate
7 tables, boat launch

Don't drive out of your way to come here, unless you're a fisherperson who likes to explore new lakes.

~

IDEAL LAKE RECREATION SITE #1
Weekend (only if you're a fishing fiend) / Difficult
3 tables, 30 campsites scattered about

We had a miserable time bagging this campground."Ideal?" Hardly. It should be called Devil's Road and Hell Lake. The road doesn't just turn to gravel, it gets mean: hellaciously rocky and washboarded. And while you're being jostled, you're treated to panoramic views of horrible clearcuts. You have to be very persistent or just plain oblivious not to give up and turn around. It takes about 40 minutes to drive the logging road in, but it seems much longer.

The campground is undeveloped and unappealing. You can't see the water from many campsites. So why were so many people camped there? Beats us. Earnest anglers, maybe. Or just woefully short of imagination. Only go if you live in the area. B.C. has better places to explore.

If you're heading northwest on Hwy 33

From Beaverdell, drive 61.8 kms / 38.3 miles. In Three Forks, the community just before the turnoff to Ideal Lake, you'll see a yellow sign warning you of the right turn. Set your tripometer to 0 at the turn.

If you're heading east from Kelowna on Hwy 33

From the junction of Hwys 33 and 97 in Kelowna (near Leckie Road), drive 21 kms / 13 miles to the Ideal Lake turnoff. Just before the community of Three Forks, look for a paved road ascending on your left. Set your tripometer to 0 there.

For either approach above, now follow the directions below

0 km / 0 mi
Turn northeast onto paved Philpot Road. Pass lots of country homes.

2.4 km / 1.5 mi
Stay on the main road. Continue past the Cardine Cr FS Road on your left.

6.6 km / 4.1 mi
You're now on a wide, gravel road.

7.7 km / 4.8 mi
Continue past the Darley Cr FS Road on your left.

16 km / 10 mi
From this junction, stay straight on Philpot Main. Continue past Mugford Road on your left. The road gets rockier, and the surroundings worse: you'll go through a 1987 clearcut.

Turn left at the next junction where there's a FS sign: Ideal Lake. From there it's another slow 3.6 kms / 2.2 miles to the lake. This side road gets narrower. Stay straight (left) at the fork. The forest will be on your left, a clearcut on your right. Potholes aplenty here, but even in rain the road should be passable — the holes are shallow. Go right at the sign: Belgo Dam Rec Site. In .5 km / .3 mile you'll come to a camping area beneath the dam.

~

HYDRAULIC & McCULLOCH RECREATION SITES #51 & 52
Weekend / Easy

Hydraulic Lake is also known as McCulloch Lake. The FS map labels it Hydraulic. Locals call it McCulloch — the name of a Kettle Valley Railway engineer.

The KVR passed by the lake. You can hike, bike, or drive your 4WD vehicle along the railbed to Myra Canyon, where an impressive section of trestle bridges begins.

If you're heading north on Hwy 33

From the Beaverdell Hotel (in Beaverdell, of course), drive 42.3 kms / 26.3 miles to the Hydraulic Lake turnoff. It's just after a blue highway sign, at a large pullout with garbage cans, on your left. Set your tripometer to 0.

If you're heading southeast from Kelowna on Hwy 33

From the junction of Hwys 33 and 97 in Kelowna, drive 40.5 kms / 25 miles to the Hydraulic Lake turnoff. Look for a large pullout with garbage cans, on your right. You'll also see a sign for the lake. Set your tripometer to 0.

0 km / 0 mi
At the turn onto McCulloch Road.

.8 km / .5 mi
Go straight at the junction. You'll see a sign for McCulloch Lake Resort. Drive through a recent clearcut.

If you go left here, onto Okanagan Falls FS Road, you can continue all the way south past Greyback Mountain to **Idleback Lake Recreation Site #8,** *which is about 28 kms / 17 miles from Penticton.*

4.5 km / 2.7 mi
Go left at the brown FS sign: Public Use Area. Cross the KVR railbed. Drive .5 km / .3 mile to the Hydraulic Lake campground.

HYDRAULIC LAKE RECREATION SITE #51
5 tables, 6 or 7 campsites without tables but with fire rings

If you drive through this campground and follow the dirt road out the other side, you'll come to a much nicer site on an isthmus between two lakes. Go slow. This stretch of road has lots of deep potholes.

6 km / 3.7 mi
Arrive at the nicer campground on Hydraulic Lake.

McCULLOCH RECREATION SITE #52
7 campsites with tables, garbage cans, 11 campsites without tables

One three-day weekend there were seven vehicles at the first campground, but none here.

~

ARLINGTON LAKES RECREATION SITE #50
Weekend / Easy
5 tables, 7 campsites

This campground is next to the old Kettle Valley Railway, so you'll love it if you're a history buff or want to mountain bike on the railbed. Along the road in are several overnight pullouts — attractive and quiet, unless it's fall and the chainsaw firewood frenzy is underway. The official campground is on pretty Arlington Lake.

If you're heading north on Hwy 33

From Rock Creek, at the junction of Hwys 3 and 33, drive 46 kms / 28.5 miles to the town of Beaverdell. Set your tripometer to 0.

0 km / 0 mi
Starting at the Beaverdell Hotel — one of the oldest in B.C.

1.4 km / .8 mi
Pass the Beaver Creek Road on your right. It goes to Lassie and Cup Lakes and the east fork of the Kettle River.

8 km / 5.1 mi
Continue through the small settlement of Carmi, soon passing the Carmi Creek FS Road on your left.

17.5 km / 10.9 mi
Continue straight. Pass the Trapping Creek FS Road on your right.

24.3 km / 15.1 mi
Turn left onto a gravel road. You'll see a small brown sign on the left pointing upward: Arlington Lake. The road is rough, but okay for 2WD cars. Set your tripometer to 0.

If you're heading south from Kelowna on Hwy 33

From the junction of Hwys 33 and 97 in Kelowna, drive 58.5 kms / 36.3 miles to the signed Arlington Lake turnoff. Set your tripometer to 0.

For either approach above, now follow the directions below

0 km / 0 mi
At the turn into Arlington Lakes.

2.9 km / 1.8 mi
Pass a marshy pond on your right, under an old cutblock. Continue as the road bends to your left.

3.4 km / 2.1 mi
Come to an **overnight pullout** for one vehicle, overlooking the lake. Just beyond, there's a campsite on your left: one table, overlooking the lake, across from a forested hillside.

3.7 km / 2.3 mi
Fork to the right, hugging the lake road.

3.9 km / 2.4 mi
There's an **overnight pullout** on your left. You'll find room for one vehicle. You're so close to the water here you can sit and admire your reflection.

4 km / 2.5 mi

There's a one-vehicle site with a table, on your left. A sign indicates you've arrived at the official Arlington Lakes campground.

~

The Adventure Begins

Searching for a campground in the Okanagan, our wheels still on the pavement, we asked a man driving a luxury coupe, "Is this the road to Ideal Lake?" He answered, "Sorry, I don't know. I've never heard of it. But the road ends just up ahead." We kept going. We knew the road continued. It just turned to dirt. That's usually where the adventure begins, because that's where most people stop.

KETTLE RIVER VALLEY

This scenic, pastoral valley is located in extreme southern B.C. between the Okanagan and the Monashee Mountains. The flat, winding road is ideal for a day or two of road cycling. There's little traffic and a foot-wide shoulder much of the way. You can get here off Hwy 3, between Osoyoos and Greenwood, or off Hwy 33, south of Kelowna.

If you're heading south from Kelowna

You have two choices: (1) You can stay on pavement, driving south on Hwy 33 to the junction at Westbridge. From there, turn sharply left (north). You'll be on the west side of the east fork of the Kettle River. Then follow the directions under *heading north*, starting at the 13.7 km / 8.5 mile point, going toward Christian Valley. Or (2) you can take the Beaverdell Creek Road east from Beaverdell, and come out at the campgrounds on the north end of the Kettle River. It's an easy gravel road, so you'll make good time. For this approach follow the directions below.

0 km / 0 mi

From the junction of Hwy 33 and the Beaverdell Creek Road, head northeast.

5.7 km / 3.5 mi

Stay straight (right) at a junction with the Wallace Cr FS Road. Don't turn left on Sago Creek Road.

24.3 km / 15.1 mi

Go right. Left is a 4WD road to Maloney Lake.

25.6 km / 15.9 mi
Stay straight (right). Left goes to Cup and Lassie Lakes, which might be doable in 2WD if a big pothole near the turn isn't filled with water.

31.5 km / 19.6 mi
Arrive at the junction with the road along the Kettle River. Just a short way to the left (north) is **State Creek Recreation Site #7** — the worst of the campgrounds along the Kettle. Turn right (south) for better campgrounds, the first one in another 6 kms / 3.7 miles. The descriptions are below this *heading north* section.

If you're heading north from near the U.S. border

0 km / 0 mi
Head north from the intersection of Hwys 3 West and 33 North, at the community of Rock Creek. A highway sign indicates north to Beaverdell and Kelowna.

6.5 km / 4 mi
Pass Kettle River Provincial Park.

13.7 km / 8.5 mi
You're in Westbridge. Go straight at the silver bridge to Christian Valley. Coming from Kelowna, turn sharp left (north).

33.8 km / 21 mi
If you want to stay indoors, Double Camp offers cabins here.

41 km / 25.5 mi
Stay straight on the main road if you're going to the Canyon Flats campground.

The Thone Lake - Lost Horse Creek FS Road heads off right. To go to small **Thone Lake Recreation Site #9**, turn here, cross the bridge over the Kettle River and continue about 7 kms / 4.2 miles. It offers good swimming but gets busy.

44.4 km / 27.6 mi
Turn right, just before the Km 31 sign. Arrive at the Canyon Flats campground. There's no sign on the road, but there might still be a red marker on a tree across from the turn-in.

CANYON FLATS RECREATION SITE #45
Weekend / Easy
7 campsites, 2 with tables

Two campsites are next to the Kettle River. Others are wide, flat, grassy areas surrounded by forest. Very pretty.

45.5 km / 28.2 mi
Canyon Creek campground is just before the Fourth of July Cr FS Road.
The other landmark to look for is a Km 32 sign on the right side of the road.

CANYON CREEK RECREATION SITE #10
Weekend / Easy
2 tables on the river, room for 3 vehicles but best for only 2

This stretch of river is slow and quiet, so you won't be lulled to sleep by
water music. But there's a big swimming hole and a good sandy beach.

45.7 km / 28.4 mi
Pavement turns to gravel.

52 km / 32.3 mi
At a wide intersection stay straight on the main road.

53.3 km / 33.1 mi
Arrive at the road to the Kettle Bench campground. There's no sign.
Turn right, drive a short way down to the river, and you'll see it.

KETTLE BENCH RECREATION SITE #46
Weekend / Easy
2 tables, lots of wide, flat spots

This pleasant campground is on a bench, above the river. The State Creek
FS Road is nearby, opposite a big barn. It goes over the hill to Beaverdell.

Swimming hole at Kettle Canyon, Okanagan Highland

54.7 km / 34 mi
Look on your right for the turn-in to this campground, near the Km 41 sign.

KETTLE CANYON RECREATION SITE #8
Weekend / Easy
3 tables in trees, next to the creek

Enormous swimming holes and a small waterfall await you in a steep-sided canyon. Lots of big, flat rocks for sunning. Gorgeous! You could enjoy several summer days here, splashing in the water and snoozing on the shore.

58.4 km / 36.3 mi
A branch of the State Creek FS Road is on your left. Turn here if you're going up to Cup and Lassie Lakes, or over the hill to Beaverdell. Read the directions below State Creek Recreation Site.

60.7 km / 37.7 mi
Look for a sign indicating State Creek Site #7, on the right side of the road.

STATE CREEK RECREATION SITE #7
Overnight / Moderate
2 tables, 4 campsites

Barely off the road, this site is little more than an overnight pullout. The creek is dinky and overgrown with brush. All the previous camp-grounds along the Kettle River are quieter (at least 150 meters away from the main road) and much more scenic.

Going over the hill to Beaverdell

0 km / 0 mi
At the 58.4 km / 36.3 mile point mentioned above, set your tripometer to 0. This road will join the State Creek FS Road in 2 kms /1.2 miles, on its way to tiny Cup and Lassie Lakes.

6 km / 3.7 mi
If you turn right, you might be able to make it to Cup and Lassie Lakes. We were stopped here by a deep dip filled with water. The camp-grounds at the lakes are in 6.5 kms / 4 miles.

Cup Lake Recreation Site #24 is a small, heavily used campground. **Lassie Lake Recreation Site #19** is a large, forested campground that has a boat launch and is popular on weekends. There's a 1-km hiking trail to a campground at **Joan Lake.**

The main road, to the left, continues to Malone and Beaverdell Creeks. It passes a campground and offers you a smooth gravel surface all the way back to Hwy 33 — about a fifteen-minute drive.

7.2 km / 4.5 mi
Continue on the main road. Turn left at the signed junction, onto the Beaverdell Creek Road. Right is a 4WD road to Malone Lake.

13.7 km / 8.5 mi
Arrive at Sago Creek campground.

SAGO CREEK RECREATION SITE #27
Overnight / Moderate (from Hwy 33)
3 tables, room for 4 vehicles

This campground is right beside the road. It's almost ugly. The trees are scrawny. The land worn out. Creek? Leaky faucet is more like it. A big sign labeled *Campsites and Trails in the Kettle Lakes Area* indicates "You are Here" — at Lassie Lake. Very helpful. One appreciative camper permanently scratched in his comment: "Bullshit." This is also the trailhead for walk-in campsites at Clark and Joan Lakes.

25.9 km / 16.1 mi
Curve left (south) on the main road. The Wallace Cr FS Road is to the right.

30.6 km / 19 mi
Gravel turns to pavement at the north end of Beaverdell.

31.5 km / 19.6 mi
Arrive at Hwy 33.

~

SAUNIER LAKE RECREATION SITE #50
Weekend / Easy
2 tables at a small, intimate campground on a weedy but pretty lake

You'll enjoy the lonesome, soothing atmosphere here, as long as noisy campers don't show up. A couple minutes walk on a trail leading south from the tables is a tiny trickle that's supposed to be a potable spring. But this is cattle country, so we wouldn't drink without first purifying the water.

0 km / 0 mi
Go south on Hwy 33 from the Beaverdell Hotel — one of the oldest in B.C. It's in Beaverdell, of course. There's also a Petro Canada station here.

6.9 km / 4.3 mi
Turn right on Tuzo Creek Road. Follow this narrow but smooth road into a very pretty, narrow valley. In fall you'll see golden cottonwoods, aspen and larch. Watch for scattered rocks on the road that fall from the steep hillside on your right.

13 km / 8.1 mi
Arrive at Saunier Lake. The campground entrance is on your left, just before a small wooden bridge across the outlet stream.

~

HWY 3: OSOYOOS TO GRAND FORKS

JOLLY CREEK RECREATION SITE #17
Weekend / Easy
3 tables, 1 group site

This is a small, little-used gem, set in a lush meadow with a few trees beside the creek. It's in a ravine, in an area of low, gentle mountains. Though the meadow is bumpy, probably from ground squirrels, the campground is fine for tents. Come for wild rose in spring, golden larch on the mountainside in fall.

If you're heading east from Osoyoos

Be looking for the turn 2.7 kms / 1.7 miles northeast of Bridesville.

If you're heading west from Greenwood

Be looking for the turn 12.7 kms / 7.9 miles west of the junction of Highways 33 & 3, at the settlement of Rock Creek.

0 km / 0 mi
At the turn north off Hwy 3, toward Mt. Baldy Ski Area. You'll see a highway sign, just west of Rock Creek Canyon bridge.

2.9 km / 1.8 mi
Turn right on Canyon Road (Baldy goes left). Go down to the bottom of the hill.

4 km / 2.4 mi
Arrive at Jolly Creek campground, across from an historic cabin.

~

GREENWOOD VISITORS CAMP

This community offers a wonderful service to travelers: free overnight camping in a meadow beside a creek, with a shelter and tables. It's on the north end of town. Thanks for your generosity, Greenwood. Campers, please be respectful of the town and its residents. Let's not give them any reason to revoke our camping privileges.

Greenwood is a pleasant and interesting town to walk around. It was a booming mining town in the 1890's. Many of its historic buildings have been renovated. So you might enjoy an overnight stay here on your way between the Okanagan and the Kootenays. Even if you're just passing through, get out to stretch your legs and get a taste of the town.

~

OLD DEWDNEY TRAIL OVERNIGHT PULLOUT
Overnight / Easy
Two separate campsites in trees above the river

This unmarked campsite is hidden from the road, just above Boundary Falls. The waterfall muffles any road noise.

From Midway, drive 7.2 kms / 4.5 miles northeast on Hwy 3. **Or, from Greenwood**, drive southwest 5.4 kms / 3.3 miles (passing Boundary Creek Provincial Park halfway).

For either approach above, now follow the directions below

Turn southeast into the small, paved parking area with a stop-of-interest sign about the Dewdney Trail. When you pull off the highway, go straight onto the dirt track, not toward the marker. Drive in about 30 meters and you'll find a fire ring marking the sites.

~

MARSHALL (PROVIDENCE) LAKE RECREATION SITE #31
Overnight / Easy
A few tables on the far side, numerous campsites

Marshall is a pretty lake with grassy edges, surrounded by trees. A lot of people come here. The campground isn't really as far out of the way as it might look on a map, because you can use the good gravel access road to reach Hwy 3 on the other end.

If you're heading east

0 km / 0 mi
In Greenwood turn east on Green Street, going past the historic post office. The road is paved to the Cenotaph (WWI memorial).

5.3 km / 3.3 mi
Phoenix Cemetery is on the right. It has interesting fences around the plots. Pass the Driving Tour #7 stop-of-interest sign.

7.7 km / 4.8 mi
See a white sign on a pole: Marshall Lake Road.

8.2 km / 5.1 mi
Arrive at Marshall Lake. The road around the lakeside can be impassable for 2WD when the water level is high.

10.6 km / 6.6 mi
Come to a fork where you can go left to Marshall Lake.

11.1 km / 6.9 mi
Come to a fork at the Cenotaph. There's a sign pointing the way to Grand Forks. It's a wide, well-graded dirt road from here out to Hwy 3.

14.2 km / 8.8 mi
Pass the Phoenix Ski Area road.

19.8 km / 12.3 mi
Pass a misspelled sign: Phonenix Rd, and you've arrived at Hwy 3.

If you're heading west

0 km / 0 mi
At the junction of Highways 3 & 41, southwest of Grand Forks, continue northwest on Hwy 3.

15.1 km / 9.4 mi
Turn left (west) onto Phoenix Road.

20.1 km / 12.5 mi
Pass the Phoenix Ski Area road.

23.2 km / 14.4 mi
Stay straight, passing the fork by the Cenotaph. Don't turn left onto Lind Creek Road.

23.7 km / 14.7 mi
At the junction, turn right to Marshall Lake.

~

SHUSWAP RIVER & MABEL LAKE

Traveling the Shuswap River Valley is a joy. Mabel Lake is impressively long, surrounded by forested mountains. The vegetation here is lusher than in the nearby Okanagan, with thicker undergrowth and a mixture of hemlock, cedar and deciduous trees.

Noisy Creek campground on Mabel Lake

If you're in the Okanagan, drive to Enderby — north of Vernon on Hwy 97. If you're driving the Trans-Canada you can reach Enderby by turning south on Hwy 97B at Salmon Arm, or Hwy 97A at Sicamous.

0 km / 0 mi
In Enderby, at the junction of Hwy 97 and Cliff Avenue, turn east at the green highway sign: North Mabel Lake. City Hall is on the northeast corner of this junction. The paved road immediately crosses the Shuswap River. You'll soon see a green highway sign: Mabel Lake 37 km.

22.9 km / 14.2 mi
Cross Fall Creek. Continue beneath hillsides logged about twenty years ago.

26.1 km / 16.2 mi
Turn right at a visible sign facing west, to go to the Shuswap River

campground, or continue on for Mabel Lake. The Cooke Creek FS Road is across the highway.

Continue 4 kms / 2.5 miles to a brown sign at a fork. Go right or left to the Cooke Creek campgrounds on the Shuswap River.

COOKE CREEK RECREATION SITE #92
Weekend / Easy
5 tables, boat launch

On the bank of the Shuswap River is a lovely, tranquil, shaded campground. The slow-moving water here is great for canoeing, or watching salmon surge upstream in mid-October.

Continuing on the main, paved road to the north Mabel Lake campground

30.6 km / 19 mi
Turn left off the main highway. A sign on a telephone pole points toward Noisy Creek. Set your tripometer to 0 here. The main highway to the right continues to the shore of Mabel Lake, but that's not where the campground is.

0 km / 0 mi
You'll see a sign: Three Valley - Mabel FS Road. It's a good road through nicely regrown forest. Deciduous trees make it especially pleasant in fall.

11.9 km / 7.4 mi
Stay straight (right) and immediately cross a little bridge.

13.7 km / 8.5 mi
Go right at the fork, which might still be marked by a ribbon on a tree. Continue through a more recently logged area. Watch for roaming cattle.

20 km / 12.4 mi
Cross another small bridge. Beware of potholes.

21 km / 13 mi
Turn right at a fork. Look for the sign on a tall tree to your right. Drive down this small, rough road. Be patient, it's a long way down.

26.1 km / 16.2 mi
Arrive at Mabel Lake. The right branch has about 24 campsites with tables — about half along the lake. The left branch has 7 tables, 4 overlooking the water.

NOISY CREEK RECREATION SITE #100
Destination / Difficult (because it's a long way and has
a steep descent at the end)
30+ tables, cement boat launch, hiking trail

This site is a gem. The scenery is grand and the campground itself is as
well-maintained and organized as any provincial park. All it lacks are
showers and washrooms, but then it doesn't have a whopping fee
either. If you dislike crowds, we suggest you come in the off-season.
Although the campsites are well defined and comfortably spaced, this
place is packed in summer.

The creek, a 2-km-loop trail, broad beaches, and lots of forest to explore
make this a great place for ambling. Between the two camping areas is a
small peninsula: walk out for a view all the way up the lake. Obviously,
fishing is popular here. The water is warm enough for swimming in
summer. There's only one drawback: cow shit. Don't be surprised if you
bump into beachcombing bovines.

~

MABLE LAKE EAST

If you want to explore the eastern shore of beautiful Mabel Lake, there
are two recreation campgrounds there. You have to drive a long way on
gravel, but if you're camping for two nights or more, it's worthwhile.
From the end of pavement, there are tent-camping sites on the beach in
14.5 km / 9 miles. If you drive 12.5 km / 7.8 miles farther, you'll reach
the turnoff to a large campground on Cottonwood Bay that'll please
every member of the family. The road to the east side of Mable Lake
starts in Lumby. From the junction of Hwys 6 and 97 at Vernon's
eastern edge, drive just over 24 km / 15 miles to Lumby.

0 km / 0 mi
In Lumby, at the four-way stop. Take the paved road north, following signs to Mabel Lake and the provincial park.

17 km / 10.5 mi
Stay on the main paved road, going past Shuswap Falls.

28 km / 17.4 mi
The gravel FS road begins.

35 km / 21.7 mi
You get your first view of Mabel Lake.

38 km / 23.6 mi
Pass Mabel Lake Provincial Park.

42.5 km / 26.4 mi
If you'd like to pitch your tent on the beach, be looking near a sharp bend in the road for a ribbon on a tree. It marks the trail to Cascade South campground. There's no sign. Park your car on the road.

CASCADE SOUTH RECREATION SITE #3
Weekend / Moderate
3 beautiful tent sites on the beach

The first (southerly) tent site is only two minutes in, others are a bit farther. Park your car on the road and walk down to the shore.

43.2 km / 26.8 mi
There's a sign on a tree marking the trail to Cascades Waterfall. It's only a 300-meter walk. There's a pit toilet here.

43.5 km / 27 mi
Look for a ribbon here, and a trail down to the beach for another campsite.

55 km / 34 mi
Near this point, you can take the left fork down to a campground at Cottonwood Bay. You'll find it where there's a road to the left along the bottom of a cutblock. There's no sign.

COTTONWOOD BAY RECREATION SITE #1
Destination / Difficult (because it's so far)
20 campsites with tables, sandy beach for swimming, boat launch

80.5 kms / 50 mi
You'll get a view down to the north end of Mabel Lake. If you're this far up, you might want to drive 29 kms / 18 miles farther to Three Valley Gap on the Trans-Canada Hwy. 4.2 kms / 2.6 miles before reaching the highway, there's a FS campground at Frog Falls. It's described in the Arrow and Kootenay Lakes region.

~

SHUSWAP RIVER AND SUGAR LAKE

At some campgrounds you feel you have to go searching for what's beautiful about the area. Not here. At these lovely, forested sites, you can enjoy water activities in the spring, summer and fall. You can relax under big shade trees and dip in the Shuswap River. At Sugar Lake, you can set up camp and relax at a picturesque lake, with views of distant mountains and a lush forest. Logged decades ago, the land now supports a pleasing mixture of hemlock, cedar, Douglas fir and deciduous trees.

If you do want to venture beyond the lake for some rigorous activity, the turnoff to Monashee Provincial Park is 11 kms / 6.8 miles past the last Sugar Lake campground. The Monashees are for experienced, prepared hikers only.

Low-tech inter-camper communication system

If you're heading east from Vernon

From the junction of Hwys 6 and 97, at Vernon's eastern edge, drive just over 24 km / 15 miles to Lumby.

0 km / 0 mi
In Lumby, at the four-way stop.

24.4 km / 15.1 mi
You'll see a sign: MONASHEE TURNOFF 2 KM. Slow down and watch for the turn.

26.4 km / 16.4 mi
Turn left off Hwy 6, onto signed Sugar Lake Road. There's a gas station and general store at this turn (shown as the community of Cherryville on BC road maps). A green highway sign states: NAKUSP 145, FAUQUIER 87, VERNON 50, LUMBY 22.

If you're heading west from the Needles ferry on Arrow Lake

Drive 83.6 km / 51.8 miles on Hwy 6 to the gas station and general store in Cherryville, and turn right.

For either approach above, now follow the directions below

0 km / 0 mi
In Cherryville, at the turn onto Sugar Lake Road. You'll now be traveling northeast along the Shuswap River.

0.5 km / 0.3 mi
Come to an overnight pullout on the left, beside the Shuswap River, and another at 0.6 km / 0.4 mile, just before Ferry Creek bridge.

2.6 km / 1.6 mi
Cross Cherry Creek.

3.2 km / 2 mi
Look closely for a turn-in on the left, across from the gravel pit. There's an overnight pullout beside the river, enclosed by trees on two sides, but still open to the highway.

5.5 km / 3.4 mi
Turn left toward the river and drive 0.5 km / 0.3 mile to the Cherryville campground.

CHERRYVILLE RECREATION SITE #15
Weekend / Easy
Room for 3 or 4 vehicles

This is a beautiful, quiet spot on the Shuswap River. Too bad so many jerks have trashed it. We packed away two full garbage bags. Let's hope it's clean when you visit. You can pitch your tent and romp in the meadows. There's one table in trees by the river, about 30 meters from a turn-around area, reached via the right road at the site.

Continue on the Sugar Lake Road to reach the lake.

13.2 km / 8.2 mi
The road turns to dirt.

16.3 km / 10.1 mi
Stay left on the main road at the junction with Kate Creek FS Road.
Continue along the west side of the lake.

16.8 km / 10.4 mi
Go left, following the sign to Monashee Park, which also states: Radio
controlled logging road. The private South Lake Fishing Camp will be
on your right.

17.4 km / 10.8 mi
Go right at the unmarked junction.

18.2 km / 11.3 mi
Arrive at a nice **overnight pullout** with a table and enough room for
one vehicle. It's possible to launch a boat here. This spot gets good
morning sun and has a view across the lake to a mountainside.

20.1 km / 12.5 mi
Enter right to the major Sugar Lake campground. There's no sign on
the road, but it's obvious where to go.

SUGAR LAKE TWO-MILE RECREATION SITE #9
Destination / Easy
21 campsites with tables, 7+ with lake views, boat launch,
garbage cans, 3 great tent sites on grass at the water's edge

This campground is often busy, but there's enough room so you can
usually find privacy. At the entrance there's a large map of the campground, showing you the possibilities. Expect to see lots of fisherpeople
with motor boats. Beautiful trees march down the hillside to an inviting
pebble beach ideal for sunning and swimming. Daisies are profuse in June.

21.7 km / 13.5 mi
Arrive at **Sugar Lake Three-Mile Recreation Site #8**. You'll find
one table next to a creeklet — a great private spot if you're lucky to get
here first.

For the next site, continue straight. Pass the private road that turns off to the left.

22.5 km / 14 mi
Arrive at **Sugar Lake 3 1/2-Mile Recreation Site #7**. There's a
private, one-table spot here on a creeklet.

If you're heading to Monashee Provincial Park, drive 25 kms /
15.5 miles farther to the turnoff. Then go 3 kms / 2 miles. You can
camp at the trailhead parking lot, but it's just a big dirt area. Spectrum
Lake is a 6-km hike one way.

Sugar Lake, east of Vernon

~

MONASHEE MOUNTAINS

These mountains, between the Okanagan and the Kootenays, are not stunning. They're high, but gently rounded. The forest isn't special either. But you definitely get a feeling of wildness as you drive serpentine Hwy 6, from Vernon to Arrow Lake. It's a breathtaking sight looking east, down to the Arrow Lake Valley and the Selkirk Mountains on the horizon. So if you're wondering which direction to travel, we recommend leaving the Okanagan in the west and traveling east across the Monashees to Arrow Lake and the Needles - Fauquier ferry. The scenery climaxes in that direction.

Remember: you are in bear country here, so be alert. We've seen black bears and grizzlies near the highway. When camping, don't leave food out during the day. At night, don't even leave your cooler out.

If you're heading southeast on Hwy 6 to Arrow Lake

Skip below this section for directions heading northwest.

0 km / 0 mi
In Lumby, 24 km / 15 miles from the junction of Hwys 6 and 97, at Vernon's eastern edge.

26.4 km / 16.4 mi
Continue southeast toward the ferry at Needles, or turn left here at
the 3-way junction in Cherryville to go to the Shuswap River and
Sugar Lake campgrounds (described in previous pages).

52.9 km / 32.8 mi
Drive along McInytre Lake. If you'd like to camp at its east end,
slow down and watch for the turnoff.

54.1 km / 33.5 mi
For the **McIntyre Lake overnight pullout**, turn left onto the
roadside pullout. Then follow the small, old road going off left. It's
200 meters to the lake's end and a private campsite for one vehicle.

62.5 km / 38.8 mi
Arrive at an unofficial campground on your right, just before the
highway bridge over the Kettle River. There's a white sign: KM 5.0.

OLD MONASHEE HIGHWAY CAMPGROUND
Overnight / Easy
No tables, room for 6 vehicles

This exceptional overnight pullout is more like a campground,
because you can get well off the highway and there's room for
campers to spread apart. It's on the Kettle River, which here in its
upper reaches is really just a boisterous stream—audible from a distance, but not overwhelming. There are trees for shade, but not so
many they block all the sun if you want warmth. Though the highway is close, there's not enough traffic to be bothersome. Nights are
especially quiet, and passing headlights won't shine in your eyes.

64.4 km / 40.0 mi
Arrive at Monashee Summit—1241 meters elevation. **Lost Lake
Rest Area** is on the right, across from the Keefer Lake Road. It's
labeled Round Lake on the FS map. You can probably spend the
night here. We looked for a No Camping sign, but didn't see one.
There are tables in tightly grouped trees above this marshy lake
where somebody is usually fishing.

At the summit, turn left (north) onto Keefer Lake Road to find the
official Kettle River campground. The turn is marked by a
white highway sign. You'll also see a sign for the Keefer Wilderness
Resort. You reach the campground by driving in just a kilometer or
so. It's on the left.

MONASHEE KETTLE RIVER RECREATION SITE #17
Overnight / Easy
1 table, grass for tents, room for 2 groups without crowding, on the river

This is just a pleasant retreat from the highway. There's not much to do here but relax in the trees. There are no distant views to stretch your eyes.

Continuing on Hwy 6

110.0 km / 68.2 mi
Arrive at the ferry in Needles, on the west side of Arrow Lake.

If you're heading northwest from the Fauquier - Needles ferry

The campgrounds below are described in the Heading Southeast section above.

0 km / 0 mi
In Needles, at the ferry.

45.6 km / 28.3 mi
Arrive at Monashee Summit. The Lost Lake Rest Area is on your left. Turn right onto the Keefer Lake Road for **Monashee - Kettle River Recreation Site #17.**

47.5 km / 29.5 mi
Just after crossing the Kettle River, you'll arrive at the **Old Monashee Highway unofficial campground** on the left.

55.9 km / 34.7 mi
Turn right into the pullout and follow the small, dirt road going off right for 200 meters to an **overnight pullout** beside McIntyre Lake.

83.6 km / 51.8 mi
Arrive at a 3-way junction at Cherryville. A road on the right heads northeast to the **Shuswap River and Sugar Lake campgrounds.**

110.0 km / 68.2 mi
Arrive in Lumby. You can turn north here to Mabel Lake. Vernon is 24 km / 15 miles farther.

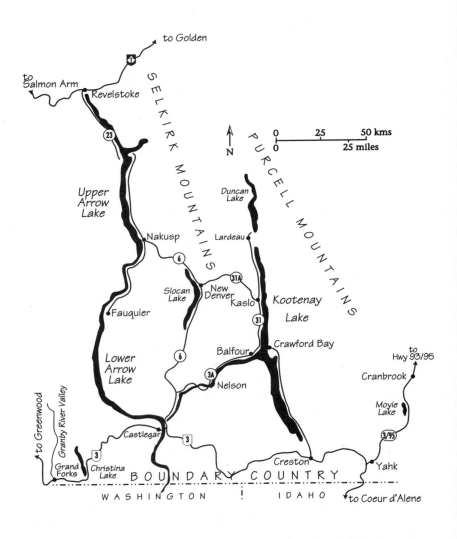

Arrow and Kootenay Lakes, Selkirk
Mountains, Boundary Country

Arrow and Kootenay Lakes, Selkirk Mountains, Boundary Country

HWY 1: NEAR REVELSTOKE

FROG FALLS RECREATION SITE #24
Overnight / Easy

These 4 campsites amid cedar and hemlock trees are unattractive, but convenient. From the tiny power station nearby, you can walk a .5-km trail east along the creek to Frog Falls.

If you're heading west

0 km / 0 mi
On Hwy 1, at the west side of Revelstoke, in the middle of the Columbia River bridge.

19.0 km / 11.8 mi
Pass the big, red buildings (Three Valley Gap), at the east end of Three Valley Lake.

21.2 km / 13.1 mi
Pass the rest area beside Three Valley Lake.

22.0 km / 13.6 mi
Across from a large, paved pullout, turn left (south). You'll see an orange sign on the right: Wap-Mabel.

If you're heading east

From Sicamous on Hwy 1, drive northeast 49 kms / 30.4 miles, then start slowing down. You'll be coming to Three Valley Lake. From the middle of the bridge at the northwest end of the lake, drive 1.3 kms / .8 mile southeast. Across from a large, paved pullout at the height of the land, turn right (south) onto a dirt road.

For either approach above, now follow the directions below

0 km / 0 mi
Just off Hwy 1, as you turn south onto Three Valley-Mabel Lake FS Road, which is signed .9 km / .6 mile in. At 2.7 kms / 1.7 miles stay right where a road forks left.

4.2 km / 2.6 mi
A signpost marks 4 kms. In .2 km more, a spur road on the left leads to Frog Falls campground. For Wap Lake campsites, continue on the main road.

4.7 km / 2.9 mi
South of the bridge over the creek, stay straight at the fork. Continue southwest about 4.25 kms / 2.6 miles to the east end of Wap Lake. The recreation site with a few campsites and some overnight pullouts is on the southwest side of the lake, beside the road.

Mabel Lake's north end is in another 17 kms / 10.5 miles.

~

TANGIER RIVER RECREATION SITE #6
Weekend / Easy
12 tables, garbage cans, covered wood storage

This campground, much better than the cramped pay campground across the highway, is a good base for exploring Revelstoke National Park, only 5 kms / 3 miles away. The campsites, set in rich hemlocks, are above the creek. The roaring river muffles highway and train noise.

If you're heading east

From Revelstoke, drive 34 kms / 21 miles on Hwy 1 to Canyon Hot Springs. Then slow down and be looking for the turnoff to Tangier River. The small FS road is on your left, just after crossing the bridge over Tangier River. Drive in .6 km / .4 mile to the campground.

If you're heading west

0 km / 0 mi
At Rogers Pass in Glacier National Park, by the Petro Canada station and Park Info Centre.

35.4 km / 22 mi
Be looking for a turn on your right just before an unobtrusive bridge.

36.2 km / 22.5 mi
Turn right onto a small dirt road before the highway crosses Tangier River. Drive in .6 km / .4 mile to a sign at the beginning of the FS campground.

36.9 km / 22.9 mi
If you get to the Canyon Hot Springs entrance on the left, you've gone too far.

~

LAKE REVELSTOKE & KINBASKET LAKE
Weekend / Easy

These campgrounds are reached via Hwy 23, which heads north from Revelstoke along the east side of the Columbia River. The river has been dammed to form 130-km long Lake Revelstoke. The road is paved all the way to Mica Dam. It's about two hours to the end. Lots of people drive it, so expect company. This road is the farthest north you can drive along the Columbia River toward its source. On the map, it looks lonely and wild. It's not. Intense logging has left this area decidedly unwild. And the once roaring river is now dammed. Of course, many of the side canyons still look untamed, especially across the lake.

You'll see mostly gentle mountains, not rugged peaks. It is thrilling to look across the expanse of Kinbasket Lake at road's end, even if you don't have a boat to venture out in. But if you're vacationing, don't spend your precious time driving way up here. It's better to spend it on the other side of the Rocky Mountains in Jasper National Park. Fisherpeople, however, seem to love these campgrounds, so fishing must be good at least some of the time.

If you're heading west

Turn north off Hwy 1 onto Hwy 23, before you get all the way down into Revelstoke.

If you're heading east

Pass through Revelstoke and turn north onto Hwy 23, just as Hwy 1 starts ascending.

For either approach above, now follow the directions below

Follow Hwy 23 north to its end. You'll come to the town of Mica Creek in 134 kms / 83 miles. **Pitt Creek Recreation Site #16** is just before Mica Creek. It can get unpleasantly crowded in summer.

The final campground, **Potlatch Creek Recreation Site #18**, is several kilometers past the Mica dam. It's a large, open parking-area above the lake, with space for four parties pleasantly apart. There's a boat launch.

~

Obstacle course provided at Octopus Creek, Lower Arrow Lake

Octopus Creek suntanning bed. Protective eyewear supplied free of charge.

ARROW LAKES

These spectacular lakes are about 200 kilometers long, in a narrow valley clutched by mountains. It's definitely an area you should get to if you live in B.C. or Alberta. The two car ferries, one on Upper Arrow and one on Lower Arrow, give you a magnificent view of the scenery. And both ferries are free, provided by B.C. Highways, which, of course, is funded by our taxes. There aren't many free campgrounds along the lakes, but here are a few.

SOUTH OF FAUQUIER

The logging road heading south from Fauquier isn't just gravel, it's jostley and rocky. You'd think a road paralleling a lakeshore would be fairly flat, but this one climbs. You'll need patience in a 2WD vehicle. Don't drive it at night when you're tired and irritable, only when you're awake and tenacious.

If you're heading east from the Okanagan

Travel on Hwy 6 and take the ferry from Needles to the east side. Drive up .5 km / .3 mile from the ferry into Fauquier.

If you're heading south from Revelstoke

Travel on Hwy 23 south along Upper Arrow Lake. Take the ferry from Shelter Bay to Galena Bay. Then continue south on Hwy 23 to Nakusp. Take Hwy 6 south to Fauquier.

If you're heading west from Kootenay Lake

Take Hwy 31A or 3A west to Hwy 6, which travels along Slocan Lake. Go north to Nakusp. Then turn south along Arrow Lake's eastern shore. Continue to Fauquier.

For either approach above, now follow the directions below

0 km / 0 mi
In Fauquier, turn south off the main road at the blue sign with white letters: Gas - Lodging. This is Applegrove Road, paved at first, passing in front of the Arrow Lake Motel. When it joins Lower Fauquier Road in about a kilometer, it turns to dirt.

3 km / 1.8 mi
The road levels and runs parallel to the power lines.

10.1 km / 6.3 mi
Turn right for the first campground. (If you come to a wooden bridge over Taite Creek on the main logging road, you've gone too far.) A narrow road enclosed by trees descends to the lake in .8 km / .5 mile. Fallen trees could make it difficult for motorhomes.

TAITE CREEK RECREATION SITE #51
Weekend / Moderate
3 tables, boat launch, beach at low water, shade

This is a good spot for fishing, canoeing, and enjoying views of the lake.

Continue on the main logging road for the second campground.

17.2 km / 10.7 mi
Arrive at Octopus campground. There's one table right beside the creek and a second one within sight and sound of it.

OCTOPUS RECREATION SITE #52
Weekend / Difficult
2 tables, boat launch, little shade

This campground features the same recreation possibilities as Taite Creek, with the added attractions of rockhopping through an obstacle course, testing your skills on a balance beam, and, on a clear day, suntanning — special beds and protective eyewear provided free of charge. Our photos will explain.

Even though it's right beside the road, we like Octopus better than Taite because the creek is boisterous and amusing.

~

NEAR NAKUSP

These campgrounds are just outside Nakusp, which is at the junction of Hwys 6 and 23, on the southern end of Upper Arrow Lake.

WILSON LAKE WEST RECREATION SITE #41
Weekend / Moderate
1 table, maybe 1 Ogopogo

This unusual campground has a remarkable feeling of seclusion, which might give some people the creeps. At the end of a narrow, steep-sided lake, this site is dark much of the day, because the mountainside blocks the morning and afternoon sun. The lake looks deep. You wouldn't be surprised if Ogopogo emerged here. The old settler's cabin nearby could easily evoke ghost tales about a backwoods trapper or hermit.

Wilson Lake road is steep and fairly rough. Even so, you can get to Wilson Lake in 23 minutes going slowly and reasonably. You'll need a strong, or at least steady, engine to ascend the last .5 km / .3 mile coming out from the lake. So don't proceed if you're in doubt.

Definitely don't drive a motorhome or pull a trailer here. The worst section of the road along the Wilson and Fitzstubbs Creeks is from the west entrance until you get to the bottom of the mountainside at the east end of Wilson Lake — about 10 kms / 6.2 miles. Then it's mostly level back out to Hwy 6, at which point you're 5 kms / 3 miles from New Denver.

Nakusp beach on Upper Arrow Lake, a short drive from the Box Lake and Wilson Lake campgrounds

If you're heading southeast from Nakusp

From the junction of Hwys 6 East and 6 West, follow Hwy 6 East for 6.6 kms / 4.1 miles to the signed Wilson Lake Road. The turnoff will be on your left, before arriving at Box Lake. Set your tripometer to 0.

If you're heading northwest toward Nakusp

From New Denver, drive 39 kms / 24 miles. Then look for a dirt road on your right, immediately after passing Box Lake. A white sign marks the beginning: Wilson Lake Road. Set your tripometer to 0.

For either approach above, now follow the directions below

0 km / 0 mi
At the turn onto Wilson Lake Road.

3.2 km / 2 mi
Go straight (right) at the junction. A red sign in the middle of the fork points right: Wilson Lake.

4.5 km / 2.8 mi
This is the highest point on the climb to the west end of Wilson Lake.

5.3 km / 3.3 mi
Go right at the junction with a Kimbol sign (white letters on red-orange). The left route is for trucks or 4WD vehicles.

6.6 km / 4.1 mi
Go straight at the junction. See a sign on the right: Wilson Creek FS Road and Beaver Lake. You can go right if you want to bounce around more, or if you're out for a joy ride in your high-clearance vehicle. The right road goes to a campground at Wilson Lake East, then parallels Fitzstubbs Creek to arrive at a large **campground on Beaver Lake**. It then continues through to Hwy 6, five kilometers north of New Denver.

7.2 km / 4.5 mi
A brown sign marks your arrival at the Wilson Lake turn-in. Go right at the junction. Or turn around. This is your last chance to do so before heading down a particularly rough, narrow stretch. It's one of those backroads where it's the grit of the driver, not the car, that determines if it's doable. Descend steeply another .5 km / .3 mile to the lake.

If you have 4WD you can go to Horseshoe Lake, a short distance away via the left road.

If you want to drive the Wilson - Fitzstubbs Creek Road
from its southeastern end near New Denver

Use this entrance if you want to explore a backroad valley off the paved highway, or you want to fish at Beaver Lake. You can travel all the way through to Wilson Lake, but if you simply want a free campsite close to pavement, it's better to take Hwy 6 to the northwestern end of Wilson Lake Road.

0 km / 0 mi
Start in New Denver and go north on Hwy 6 toward Nakusp.

5.5 km / 3.4 mi
Turn right just before the bridge over Wilson Creek, to reach Beaver and Wilson Lake campgrounds.

11 km / 6.8 mi
Don't miss seeing Wilson Falls. There's a sign on the road, just before you cross the creek. Drive up 1 km. It's about a half-hour walk to the falls.

21 km / 13 mi
Arrive at **Beaver Lake Recreation Site #38**. It's a large campground set in trees.

~

BOX LAKE RECREATION SITE #43
Overnight / Easy
7 tables, fishing dock, creeklet at one end

This is a beautiful spot, in a rich hemlock-and-spruce forest. Baby's breath and thick ferns add to the gentle beauty. The campground is on the side of the lake that gets afternoon shade. If it weren't for the road noise across the lake, you could easily imagine being deep in the wilds. We wish we'd known about this one years ago. We've driven right by this turnoff many times when we needed a place to camp. We just hope you leave room for us.

If you're heading southeast from Nakusp

0 km / 0 mi
In Nakusp, at the junction of Hwys 6 East & 6 West, head southeast toward New Denver.

7.1 km / 4.4 mi
You'll see Box Lake on your right, just past the Wilson Lake Road. At the end of the lake, be looking for a road on the right.

10.3 km / 6.4 mi
There's a brown sign on the right, where a road curves down: Box Lake. Make a hairpin turn to your right.

12.2 km / 7.6 mi
Arrive at Box Lake campground.

If you're heading northwest to Nakusp

From New Denver, drive 39 kms / 24 miles on Hwy 6. Then look for a dirt road on your left, immediately before Box Lake. A brown sign marks the road leading down off the highway. Drive 1.9 kms / 1.2 miles in to the campground.

~

Superb camping at Wragge Beach, Slocan Lake, near New Denver

WRAGGE BEACH RECREATION SITE #37
Destination / Moderate
5 tables on the lakeshore, 3 tables off in the trees, day-use area, 5 walk-in tent sites with tables in the trees just off the beach

This amazingly lovely spot on Slocan Lake has a white, pebbly, almost sandy beach. The water is clear and deep. The looming Selkirk Mountains surround you. The beautiful forest of hemlocks and cedars adds to the magic. A good road the whole way passes through a regrown area of skinny trees. It's a surprise to drive in all this way, and still hear distant road noise across the lake — especially trucks during the day. It quiets down after 10 p.m.

When we entered the logging road, we took a wrong turn onto a smaller road and saw a black bear, then a second bear, probably a grizzly. WOW! That was exciting. Take proper bear-country precautions.

When we approached the campground around 8:30 at night, we got another surprise — the place was packed with nine groups of campers. We expected to see only a few people here, since there are beautiful campgrounds in and around New Denver. The turnoff to Wragge Beach isn't marked on the highway, but word gets around about these special places.

If you're heading northwest toward Nakusp

From the junction of Hwys 6 and 31A in New Denver, drive northwest 14.8 kms / 9.2 miles. Just past the end of Slocan Lake, look for Bonanza Road on your left. Turn there and set your tripometer to 0.

If you're heading southeast toward New Denver

From the east end of Summit Lake on Hwy 6, drive about 13 kms / 8 miles. Just before you reach the north end of Slocan Lake, look for Bonanza Road on your right and turn onto it.

For either approach above, now follow the directions below

0 km / 0 mi
At the turnoff from Hwy 6 onto Bonanza Road.

1 km / .6 mi
After the bridge, the road turns to gravel. Go right on Shannon Creek FS Road. The left road is paved, probably to private homes.

3.2 km / 2 mi
Stay right on the main road at the unmarked junction.

3.9 km / 2.4 mi
Go left (straight) on the main road at the junction. There's a brown sign on the left: Wragge Beach Road.

5 km / 3.1 mi
Cross a creek. At the next junction continue straight (left). The road going uphill to the right is closed.

6.5 km / 4 mi
Go straight (left) at the junction. A sign high on a tree points the way to Wragge Beach.

8.7 km / 5.4 mi
Go straight where a fork makes a sharp turn back to the left.

9.7 km / 6 mi
After you cross a creek, the road steepens.

10.5 km / 6.5 mi
Arrive at Wragge Beach.

~

HWY 31A: NEW DENVER TO KASLO

IDAHO LOOKOUT RECREATION SITE #36
Weekend (although the Kootenays are a Destination) / Difficult
1 table, room for 3 to park in a compact area

It's amazing to see how this narrow road threads up the mountainside, and even more amazing that 2WD vehicles can manage it. Drive carefully so there are no surprise head-ons with other vehicles. There are few places to pass on this precipitous road, so always note where the last wider stretch was. It's about a half-hour drive up from the mining town of Sandon.

From up top you look down on Slocan Lake and the villages of Silverton and New Denver. The vistas of the Kokanee, Valhalla, Slocan and Goat Mountains are superb. Here you realize how much country there is to explore in the Kootenays. You'll be jubilant you're alive to witness this glory.

The small, alpine campground is in Wildgoose Basin, almost at the end of the road. It's not a good place for a spread-out camp, or more than a night or two. Even if you're not camping there, plan on driving up and hiking the 1.4 km-trail to the lookout. You'll have to hike about 1.5 kms farther until the end of July when the snow clears completely to the end of the road. The Forest Service keeps tabs on the snow-melt progress, and they post how far up you can drive.

If you're heading east toward Kaslo

From New Denver, at the junction of Hwys 6 and 31A (by the Petro Canada station) drive 7.5 kms / 4.7 miles east to the signed turnoff for Sandon. Turn right (south). Set your tripometer to 0 there.

If you're heading west toward New Denver

The turnoff is about 39.5 kms / 24.5 miles northwest of Kaslo. You'll see a sign for Sandon on the left (south) side. Set your tripometer to 0 there.

Looking down on Slocan Lake from Idaho Lookout

For either approach above, now follow the directions below

0 km / 0 mi
At the turnoff from Hwy 31A. You can cruise at 60 kph on pavement to Sandon.

5.7 km / 3.5 mi
Arrive in Sandon, where the road turns to dirt. Follow the white sign to Idaho Peak. Go over a bridge, then turn left on Slocan Star Road. There's a brown FS sign: Idaho Lookout 12 km.

6 km / 3.8 mi
Turn right at the old train car. You'll begin the ascent at this brown sign: ID LO FS Rd.

8.4 km / 5.2 mi
Go straight (right) at the junction.

10 km / 6.3 mi
Stay left at the junction.

14.2 km / 8.8 mi
We parked at a large pullout on a tight switchback. The road was getting too steep for our car and we enjoyed walking anyway.

15.6 km / 9.7 mi
Arrive at Wildgoose Basin campground. In late June, there was still too much snow on the road to continue driving. Later in summer, you can drive 2.5 kms / 1.5 miles farther.

~

BEAR LAKE OVERNIGHT PULLOUT
Overnight / Easy
No tables, just a pleasant spot to sleep

Bear Lake is ringed by forested mountains and snowy peaks, near the summit between Kaslo and New Denver. The pullouts beside this small, pretty lake are right across from the highway, so they don't warrant anything more than an overnight stay. The sunburned people we saw, however, looked like they'd been there all day trying to catch fish.

If you're heading east toward Kaslo

0 km / 0 mi
In New Denver, at the junction of Hwys 6 and 31A, by the Petro Canada station.

7.5 km / 4.7 mi
Pass the turnoff to Sandon and the Idaho Lookout Recreation Area described above.

12.6 km / 7.8 mi
Pass the Beaver Pond pullout.

14.5 km / 9.0 mi
Go left on the gravel road just before Bear Lake and a sign on the highway: Welcome to Kootenay Lake Forest District. There are very narrow overnight pullouts at .5 km / .3 mile and a bit farther. The road makes

a loop back to the highway, but it might be swamped by snow runoff. If you want to check the second entrance for another overnight pullout, it's 1.1 kms / .7 mile farther down the highway, just past the end of the lake.

If you're heading west to New Denver

From Washington Street and 'A' Avenue in Kaslo, drive 31.6 kms / 19.6 miles. Immediately after passing Bear Lake, turn right onto a dirt road for **overnight pullouts.**

The turnoff to Sandon and the Idaho Lookout Recreation Site is 7 kms / 4.3 miles beyond Bear Lake.

~

KOOTENAY LAKE

This is an incredibly beautiful area with steep, wild mountains and long, deep lakes. You can spend many vacations here, even a lifetime — as increasingly more people are deciding to do. The possibilities for outdoor recreation are endless. The village of Kaslo on Kootenay Lake at the junction of Hwys 31A and 31 is a charming haven. As in the Arrow Lake area, there aren't many free campgrounds.

MILFORD LAKE RECREATION SITE #5
Overnight / Moderate
2 tables

This pleasant sub-alpine lake on a mountainside north of Kaslo can't compare to the grand magnificence of Kootenay Lake. But Milford offers more peace and intimacy and could be nice for a night. The lake is in the middle of a cutblock that was logged in the '60's, but there's a strip of tall trees around the lake.

Though the road is accessible by all 2WD vehicles, it's not suitable for motorhomes since it has tight turns and steep grades.

0 km / 0 mi
Start in Kaslo. Take Hwy 31, going north on the west side of Kootenay Lake, toward Lardeau.

9.4 km / 5.8 mi
Turn left onto Milford Lake Road, which slices diagonally from the highway and starts switchbacking up the hill.

18.2 km / 11.3 mi
Arrive at Milford Lake.

Glacier Creek, Duncan Lake, Kootenays

GLACIER CREEK RECREATION SITE #3
Destination / Moderate

Just north of Kootenay Lake is long Duncan Lake. When it's drawn down, you can see much of the muddy, stump-studded bottom. But the area is otherwise quite beautiful. The well-spaced campsites are shaded in pretty forest on a small point next to energetic Glacier Creek.

For an excursion, drive south along the east side of Kootenay Lake, to Johnsons Landing. From there, hike the trail into Fry Creek canyon. Early summer is a good time to see all the waterfalls cascading into the narrow valley.

Heading north from Kaslo

From the junction of Hwy 31 and 31A, drive north 28.3 kms / 17.5 miles to Lardeau, near the end of Kootenay Lake.

0 km / 0 mi
In Lardeau, continue north. A BC Parks sign ahead warns of the turn you'll be taking toward the Purcell Mountains and Fry Canyon.

6.1 km / 3.8 mi
At the junction go right onto Argenta Road. In .6 km / .4 mile cross Duncan River bridge and continue on dirt road just after.

7.4 km / 4.6 mi

At the junction go straight, heading north up the east side of Duncan Lake, and in .2 km cross Hamill Creek. A right turn leads south to Argenta and Fry Creek canyon.

17.9 km / 11.1 mi

Glacier Creek campground, with twelve sites, is on the left.

~

GARLAND BAY RECREATION SITE #9
Destination / Moderate
12 tables, boat launch, wharf, shade, sandy beach

This campground is very popular in summer. No wonder. It's on stunning, fiord-like Kootenay Lake. There's a lot to occupy you for a weekend or an entire week: sightseeing, fishing, boating, and invigorating swimming.

From Creston drive northwest on Hwy 3A to Kootenay Bay. Or from Balfour (between Nelson and Kaslo, on Hwy 3A/31), take the car ferry northeast across Kootenay Lake to Kootenay Bay.

For either approach above, now follow the directions below

0 km / 0 mi

From the Kootenay Bay ferry-landing, on the east side of the lake, drive north 1.1 km / .7 mile and turn left (north) toward Riondel.

9.8 km / 6.1 mi

Arrive in Riondel. After curving left onto Fowler, turn right on Eastman and follow signs to Riondel Beach Campground, which is not free.

11.0 km / 6.8 mi

From the campground entrance, continue straight on Riondel North Road.

14.2 km / 8.8 mi

Cross Tom O'Shanter Creek bridge and continue north. You're now on Kootenay Lake East FS Road.

17.0 km / 10.5 mi

Trailhead parking for Pebble Beach Recreation Site #12 is on the left. Tenting sites at the lake are 2 kms down the path.

17.7 km / 11.0 mi

Stay left at the fork. Look for a waterfall in the gorge 1 km farther.

23.6 km / 14.6 mi

After passing Driftwood Cove Resort and crossing a creek, turn left at the sign: Garland Bay. A steep, rough road leads .3 km down to the lakeside.

GRANBY RIVER VALLEY, NORTH OF GRAND FORKS

This is a beautiful river valley that travelers on Hwy 3 usually don't visit. It's worth exploring, even if an afternoon is all you can give it. Some hillsides are covered in green meadows, some sprinkled with trees, others decorated by rock faces. The wide valley is good cycling country with a paved road all the way to the first campground. You can spend your time bicycling, fishing, swimming, or relaxing.

0 km / 0 mi
From Grand Forks on Hwy 3, start from the east side of the Granby River bridge and head north on Granby Road.

16.1 km / 10 mi
Come to a junction with the west side road. Go right (straight) up the valley.

44 km / 27.3 mi
Arrive at the first Granby River campground and a junction with a road leading up the west side of Burrell Creek.

GRANBY - BURRELL RECREATION SITE #35
Weekend / Easy
2 tables, grass for tents

At the confluence of the Granby River and Burrell Creek, is a pretty, relaxing campground. It's a good base to explore the valley. The view of Bunch Grass Hill, a rocky bluff, gives the site character. There's a deep swimming hole at the wooden bridge.

At the confluence of the Granby River and Burrell Creek, north of Grand Forks

If you want to visit another campground in the area, go left at the junction, just after the Granby - Burrell campground. Signs warn you to use caution Monday through Friday, because it's an active logging road. The wide road heading to Gable Creek is bumpy and sometimes steep. You'll pass Burns Creek Road.

49.3 km / 30.6 mi
Go left at the signed fork to Gable Creek. Wind down a hill to the campsite.

51 km / 31.5 mi
Arrive at a clearing in trees by the creek.

GABLE CREEK RECREATION SITE #34
Weekend / Moderate
1 table, room for 1 vehicle

You could pretend this private spot is your homestead. If you like to sit and read or fish, you might want to stay a few days. But there's not much else to do here. The hill blocks the sun by 4 or 5 p.m. even in summer.

If you head straight (right) at the 49.3 km / 30.6 mile fork described above, the road continues north along the Granby River. That way you'll come upon two more small campgrounds on the west bank of the Granby River: **Howe Creek #33** and **Eight Mile Flats #49**. There's a hiking trail along the Granby River from the end of the logging road.

From the 44 km / 27.3 mile junction, next to the Granby - Burrell campground, take the right fork to continue north along Burrell Creek to two more campgrounds.

BLUEJOINT - BURRELL CREEK RECREATION SITE #31
Overnight / Moderate
2 tables, nothing more than a place to sleep

This closed-in campground amid scrappy, dog-haired lodgepole pines is not attractive. Kids might enjoy running around in all the grass — if the mosquitoes don't get 'em. Only come here if you're already in the area and the other campgrounds are full. **St. Annes Creek Recreation Site #48** is a few kilometers beyond this one.

0 km / 0 mi
On the bridge over Burrell Creek.

1 km / .6 mi
Pavement ends.

8 km / 5 mi
Stay left. Don't cross the river. There might still be a green sign here: Franklin Bridge closed. But that's just about at road's end anyway. The narrow road hugs the rocky hillside on your left.

12.4 km / 7.7 mi
Arrive at Bluejoint - Burrell Creek campground.

~

HWY 3: GRAND FORKS EAST TO CRANBROOK

TROUT CREEK RECREATION SITE #44
Overnight / Moderate

If you're in the area, it's probably better to stay down at one of the campgrounds on Christina Lake than to come here. Some people, however, might want this alternative to camping at crowded Christina Lake. You could camp in the quiet pines at night and spend the day at the lake. It's a fairly long drive up to the site, which is huddled next to a tiny creek in a dark forest at a hairpin turn in the road.

0 km / 0 mi
In the town of Christina Lake, where Santa Rosa Road leaves Hwy 3. This is across from the BC Travel Info Centre and marked by a sign: Maintained for 22 km, no thru road.

1.5 km / .9 mi
The pavement ends. The road climbs up the hillside, affording a nice view of Christina Lake.

10 km / 6 mi
Stay right at the fork. A private road goes left.

14 km / 8.7 mi
Arrive at Trout Creek.

~

CASTLEGAR CITY PARK
Overnight / Easy
Tables, large parking lot for many vehicles, garbage cans

Castlegar sits in a pretty valley where the Kootenay and Columbia Rivers meet. The city provides this convenient campground. Thanks for your generosity, Castlegar. Campers: please be respectful of the campground, the city, and its residents. Let's not give them any reason to revoke our camping privileges.

Go to Castelgar, which is at the junction of Hwys 6, 3, and 22, between Nelson and Grand Forks. From downtown Castlegar, take Columbia Avenue heading toward Trail. Turn left on 20th Street. Follow the sign to the Community Recreation Complex and BC Travel Info Centre. The City Park is just past the Info Centre. If you need any more directions, ask someone how to get to the Aquatic Recreation Complex.

To the right of the Aquatic Recreation Complex, there's a dirt parking lot by pine trees and a big playing field. That's where you can park for the night. The grass in the shade makes a good place for tents. There are toilets in the grey brick building close to the tennis courts. No fires are allowed. You can go swimming or get a shower at the indoor pool.

~

Campfire Questions

Add spark to your evening powwow by asking your campfire mates unusual questions. Go around in a circle. Limit answers to a few minutes, to keep everyone involved. No judging allowed. The person who asks is the last person to answer. Here are suggestions. If you had time to learn and money to hire the best instructors, what would you like to master? What character in what movie would you most like to be? What was your most embarrassing moment? If you could experience the outcome of a path you didn't take, what juncture in life would you return to? Of anyone in the world, past or present, who would you most like to be friends with? What personal trait would you like to improve? When did you feel most proud of yourself?

BOUNDARY LAKE RECREATION SITE #25
Weekend / Moderate
North shore has 11 tables, 3 wharves, a small beach,
south shore has 3 tables

The lower extension of the Selkirk Mountains has surprisingly deep valleys and high passes. This medium-size lake is in a mountain basin. It's great for fishing or canoeing, and swimming on a hot day. It's busy here on weekends. It can get buggy, so bring repellent and a tent with good mosquito netting.

If you're heading west from Creston

From the junction of Hwys 3 & 3A in Creston, drive 29 kms / 17.8 miles to the turnoff. Set your tripometer to 0.

If you're heading east from Salmo

From the Bridal Lake picnic area in Stagleap Provincial Park, drive 14.6 km / 9 miles to the turnoff. Set your tripometer to 0.

For either approach above, now follow the directions below

0 km / 0 mi
Turn south on Maryland Creek Road, which drops below the highway. There's an old log cabin (Jordan's) across the highway. Within a kilometer you'll cross Summit Creek.

3.2 km / 2.0 mi
Go right at a small signed junction. It's a narrow, bumpy road, but not bad. You'll travel up the hill, level off, go through meadows, then down a long hill. Stay right at all junctions until the 14-km point.

14.0 km / 8.7 mi
Go left at the Y-intersection and continue on the main road.

17.3 km / 10.7 mi
Stay left at the fork.

Almost 19 km /12 mi
Take a sharp right turn down to the campground at Boundary Lake.

~

GOAT RIVER CANYON RECREATION SITE #16
5 tables, room for more, firewood

This is a beautiful campground on a creek between Creston and Yahk. Though it has an open feeling, it also has a cozy atmosphere in the trees. You can explore a trail along the creek. Deep pools by the bridge make for great swimming.

If you're heading east on Hwy 3

From the junction of Hwys 3 & 3A in Creston, drive 21 km / 13 miles to Kitchner. Set your tripometer to 0.

If you're heading west on Hwy 3

From the junction of Hwys 3 & 95, west of Yahk, drive 19.7 km / 12.2 miles to Kitchner. Set your tripometer to 0.

For either approach above, now follow the directions below

0 km / 0 mi
In Kitchner, at the red-roofed Kitchner Cafe, drive Leadville Road north. Travel on the east side of the river.

8.1 km / 5 mi
At the junction with Leadville Creek stay left on the main road.

11 km / 6.8 mi
Cross a wooden bridge and go left at the signed entrance for the Goat River campground.

~

OUTSIDE YAHK

The town of Yahk is on Hwy 3, east of Creston and south of Moyie Lake. The campgrounds along Hawkins Creek and at Mineral Lake are quite handy for cross-province travelers, whether camping overnight or just picnicking. The access is easy.

HAWKINS CREEK
Weekend / Easy

These sites are in a pretty valley, situated on the creekside. They're heavily used on weekends and during hunting season.

If you're heading northeast

One kilometer / 0.6 mile northeast of Yahk Provincial Park, immediately after crossing the Moyie River, turn right (southeast) onto Yahk Meadow Creek Road. Set your tripometer to 0.

If you're heading west

From the community of Moyie, be looking in 32.5 km / 20 miles for Yahk Meadow Creek Road. It's on your left, just before the Moyie River bridge, on the east side of Yahk. Turn left (southeast) and set your tripometer to 0.

For either approach above, now follow the directions below

0 km / 0 mi
At the turn onto Yahk Meadow Creek Road. In 100 meters, pass River Avenue and continue straight. Pavement ends in 0.8 km / 0.5 mile, but the gravel road is good.

3.8 km / 2.4 mi
Arrive at **Hawkins Creek Rec Site #51 (or #17).** It has 4 tables. The best campsite is the first one, alone on the creek. The logging road is now labeled HAWKINS-CANUCK CREEK FS ROAD. To reach other campgrounds, proceed straight. Don't cross the bridge.

7.2 km / 4.5 mi
Canuck Creek Recreation Site is on the right. Drive 200 meters

through a meadow to the campsites. Four sites are separate from each other, jutting into the creek.

9.0 km / 5.6 mi
Arrive at **America Creek Recreation Site #52 (or #18)**. It has 5 tables along the creek.

20 km / 12.4 mi
Arrive at **Cold Creek Recreation Site #53** (or #19), with two tables along the creek.

~

MINERAL LAKE RECREATION SITE # 49
Overnight / Easy

This is a convenient campground because it's not far off Hwy 3/95, the main route between the Rockies and the Kootenays. It's quite primitive and rough, however. There are no tables and the area itself is unattractive, so you probably won't want to stay more than a night.

If you're heading south from Cranbrook

Drive 17.0 km / 10.5 miles from the Visitor Info Centre on the southeast edge of town. Turn right at the sign MOYIE LAKE PROVINCIAL PARK. You'll also see a green sign: 4 MINERAL LAKE. Set your tripometer to 0.

If you're heading northeast from Yahk

Drive 12.5 km / 7.8 miles from the community of Moyie. Turn left at the sign MOYIE LAKE PROVINCIAL PARK. You'll also see a green sign: 4 MINERAL LAKE. Set your tripometer to 0.

For either approach above, now follow the directions below

0 km / 0 mi
Turning off Hwy 3/95, onto paved Monroe Lake Road.

0.7 km / 0.4 mi
Go right, toward Mineral Lake.

2.3 km / 1.4 mi
At the 3-way junction, continue straight on dirt Lamb Creek road. The small left fork is private. A paved road on the right leads to Monroe Lake and private cottages.

3.8 km / 2.4 mi
Arrive at pullouts on the left, on Mineral Lake's north shore. Proceed another 50 meters then go left to another campsite on the lake. A narrow road continues along the west side of the lake.

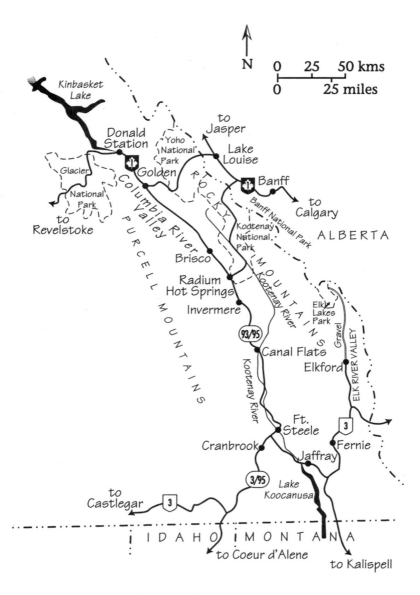

Purcell and Rocky Mountains,
Columbia and Kootenay River Valleys

Purcell and Rocky Mountains, Columbia and Kootenay River Valleys

NORTHWEST OF GOLDEN: DONALD STATION ROAD & KINBASKET LAKE

The first two campgrounds are not far off the highway, so they're excellent for an overnight stop when you're traveling Trans-Canada Hwy 1. They're also a good base for exploring more of this spectacular mountain country.

Past the first couple sites off the Donald road, the mountains you see from the road are unremarkable. Heavy logging, which still continues, has made them even less attractive. The land looks exhausted. These are the busiest industrial logging roads we've traveled. And the campgrounds, except the one way up the end of Bush Arm at Valenciennes Canyon, aren't really worth going to. Another drawback is that the magnificent Columbia River has been dammed, so instead of ripsnorting rapids and riparian flora and fauna, all you see are the muddy, stump-studded banks of an unnatural lake.

Of course, not liking what you see doesn't mean an exploratory trip has been a waste. Getting to know any patch of countryside is worth-while. And who knows, maybe you'll like it even if we don't. If you just want to see what's up there, go for it. If you're a fisherperson, maybe you'll love it.

If you're heading west

Drive 24 kms / 15 miles northwest from Golden and turn right (north) onto Donald Road. This turn is .8 km / .5 mile before the highway crosses the Columbia River.

If you're heading east

From the northern boundary of Glacier National Park, continue driving northeast to the Columbia River Valley. You'll see the long, narrow Columbia Reach (the lower arm of Kinbasket Lake) on your left as you're descending a mountainside. After dropping into the valley and just .8 km / .5 mile after crossing the Columbia River, turn left (north) onto Donald Road.

For either approach above, now follow the directions below

0 km / 0 mi
At the beginning of Donald Road.

1 km / .6 mi
Go left at the junction. You'll see Big Bend Road at a stop sign. There's also another sign: No Thru Road.

2 km / 1.3 mi
Turn left below the main road, across from a gravel pit, to arrive at Waitabit Creek. Or continue on the main road, for the next turn to Bluewater Creek campground.

WAITABIT CREEK RECREATION SITE #12
Overnight / Easy
4 tables, tent sites, well spaced

4.3 km / 2.7 mi
Come to a fork. Turn left onto an unmarked road and drive 2 kms / 1.3 miles to Bluewater Creek. The road is rutted — easy enough when dry, but could be bad when wet. The bridge straight ahead is out, so be careful driving in. You'll see a brown sign: Recreation Site.

BLUEWATER RECREATION SITE #31
Weekend / Easy
A couple campsites, 1 table

The beauty of the mountains and the rush of the river are stimulating and relaxing.

Continuing beyond the turnoffs to the first two campgrounds on the Donald hauling road

7.6 km / 4.7 mi
Pass bad clearcuts.

8.5 km / 5.3 mi
Drive over a bridge and come to a terrible campground at Bluewater Creek crossing. It's just an **overnight pullout** with one table.

12 km / 7.4 mi
Stay straight on the main road at the junction with Bush-Bluewater Road.

13 km / 8 mi
Pass an unsigned road. Stay straight.

24.3 km / 15.1 mi
Arrive at Blackwater Lake.

BLACKWATER LAKE RECREATION SITE #17
Weekend / Moderate (because it's a long way)
4 tables, no shade, wheelchair-accessible fishing ramp and toilet

This campground on a frolicky creek is useful if you're heading farther up the Columbia Reach and Kinbasket Lake, but otherwise we don't recommend it. It's a depressing area, surrounded by clearcut hillsides with only young trees at the edge of the site. All the ancient giants have been felled. To our surprise, lots of people were enjoying this small lake.

29.6 km / 18.4 mi
Turn left at a lone tree, where there's a sign: **Recreation Site**. Drive in toward the hillside. Don't go straight — the road falls into a ditch that way. You'll find a cozy, grassy campground with two tables amid the cedars.

35 km / 21.7 mi
Arrive at Giant Cedars Interpretation Trails, with one table for day use.

39 km / 24.2 mi
Turn left near the bottom of a big hill, to go to the FS campground on Esplanade Bay. This side road winds 6.5 kms / 4 miles down to the lake. Cross a small bridge over Succor Creek. The map doesn't even hint at all the switchbacks, but it's a good road.

45.4 km / 28.2 mi
Come to a high, brown sign: Public - Camping - Private. Go left, then left again to arrive at Esplanade Bay Campground.

ESPLANADE BAY RECREATION SITE #19
Weekend / Moderate (because it's a long way)
A few campsites overlooking the lake, a few in low trees

From this campground, you get a commanding view over the Columbia Reach of Kinbasket Lake. The drawback is that the lake's water level could be low. Giant lakes like this one aren't always as magnificent as they look on the map. If it's still there, you might enjoy using the deluxe barbecue left by a previous camper.

To reach **Bush Arm Recreation Site #29**, continue past the 39 km / 24.2 mile turnoff to Esplanade Bay. In 5.3 kms / 3.3 miles, turn right at another junction. From here, it's 5 kms / 3 miles to a small campground with a boat launch.

If you're willing to brave more logging trucks, bouncy roads and billowing dust, follow the Kinbasket - Bush Arm Road along the southeast side of the lake, to the end of the arm. Don't cross over at Goodfellow Creek. About 24 kms / 15 miles after the last campground, you'll be rewarded with **Valenciennes River Recreation Site #20**. It's pleasantly situated in trees, at the junction of the Bush and Valenciennes Rivers, and offers a 2-km hiking trail to a spectacular canyon.

The farther you go up the Bush River road from here, the better the scenery. Eventually you'll see the glacier-topped peaks of the Rocky Mountains.

Barbecue left by a neighborly camper, Esplanade Bay, Columbia Reach

~

BEAVERMOUTH RECREATION SITE #21
Overnight / Moderate
About 6 campsites

This campground is on the west side of the southern arm of the Columbia Reach, where the Beaver River empties into it. Maybe they should call it Rabbitmouth. We saw lots of rabbits, but no beavers. Much of the camping season the lake is surrounded by a mud flat, so most people will probably only want to stay here overnight. Too bad. The setting would otherwise be magnificent. The FS camp has more attractive campsites and more privacy than the pay campground nearby. You just don't get showers or a lawn. You get pine needles instead.

If you're heading west from Golden

Drive just west of Donald Station, to the bridge over the Columbia River. It's about 25 kms / 15 miles from Golden. Set your tripometer to 0 on the bridge. Drive 26.7 kms / 16.6 miles to the turnoff for Beavermouth campground.

If you're heading east from Glacier National Park

From the large national-park sign, when leaving Glacier National Park's eastern side, drive 8.4 kms / 5.2 miles northeast. It's mostly uphill to the turnoff. When you can peer down the long, narrow arm of Kinbasket Lake, as the highway begins descending, look for the turnoff.

For either approach above, now follow the directions below

0 km / 0 mi
Turning north off Hwy 1. You'll see a large, commercial sign: Big Lake Resort — boat rentals, RV Park. After you turn, there are two signs: Columbia West FS Rd, and Camping 4.9 km.

5.3 km / 3.3 miles
The Beavermouth campground is just past the resort. Cross the Beaver River on a high bridge. There's a sign on the right bluff. Take the second entrance.

~

NEAR GOLDEN

WISEMAN CREEK RECREATION SITE #11
Overnight / Easy
1 table, a grassy tent site

The scenery at this quiet campground is nothing special to make you want to stay long. In summer, the mosquitoes are horrific, because it's next to a big, shallow, marshy pond. Fishing? We're not sure. Looked more like a place to go frog gigging.

From the Trans-Canada Hwy bridge over the Columbia River, near Donald Station (about 25 kms / 15 miles northwest from Golden), drive northwest 6 kms / 3.7 miles and turn south onto Donald FS Road. It's off the end of a fairly tight bend in the highway pointing south. (The first bend west of Donald Station points north.) 8.4 kms / 5.2 miles from the turnoff, you'll arrive at Wiseman Creek.

~

HUNTER CREEK RECREATION SITE #43
Destination / Difficult
1 table, grassy tent sites, a big pullout with grassy mounds

This hard-to-find campground is on the shore of the rip-roaring Kicking Horse River. It's east of Golden and just west of the Yoho National Park boundary. The sandy riverbank is used by rafting companies for a group lunch spot. But just above is the FS campground. Please respect other groups using the area and don't disturb the tarps and tables left for the next raft trip coming through. It gives you the feeling of snooping through somebody's chest of drawers.

Once you leave the highway, it's a very steep road down, with myriad forks. It's confusing, but your goal is a simple one: get 1.3 kms / .8 mile down to the river. Don't be too concerned about any unclear forks. The roads all lead to the river. There's no sign at the top. It's not for motorhomes or timid drivers, but 2WD is okay. Once you start in, you're committed because you can't turn around until the bottom.

If you're heading northwest on Hwy 1

The turnoff is 6.4 kms / 4 miles past the western boundary of Yoho National Park. Set your tripometer at that boundary. Turn left onto a small, rough road, immediately after crossing the highway bridge over Hunter Creek — that's just west of the bridge.

If you're heading southeast from Golden on Hwy 1

0 km / 0 mi
On Hwy 1, at the turnoff into Golden, as the Trans-Canada begins up the steep hill.

14.3 km / 8.9 mi
Drive across Park Bridge. It's the second large highway bridge over the Kicking Horse River, out of Golden. The turnoff for Hunter Creek is 5.3 kms / 3.3 miles southeast (upstream) of this bridge. You're halfway there when you pass the truck brake-check pullout.

17 km / 10.6 mi
Pass a truck brake-check pullout on your left.

19.6 km / 12.2 mi
Turn right, immediately before the highway bridge over Hunter Creek. This narrow, rough road is at a small pullout. You'll see a yellow & black warning sign on a small concrete bridge. It looks like the beginning of this road was paved; now it's all broken up. Drive 1.3 kms / .8 mile down to the river.

~

CEDAR LAKE RECREATION SITE #41
Weekend / Moderate
1 table almost in the lake, 3 campsites without tables in the trees

We were told this lake is popular with jet skiers, so it might not be quiet. It's a very small lake with some mountain views.

Start in Golden at the junction of Hwys 1 & 95. At the 7-11 Store, on the main street passing through town near the Trans-Canada, go north on 10th Avenue. Take the road to White Tooth Ski Area.

0 km / 0 mi
A green highway sign on 7th Street North points the way to White Tooth Ski Area.

2.6 km / 1.6 mi
Go left, onto Dogtooth Canyon FS Road. You'll get good views of the surrounding mountains. Ignore all side roads.

8.9 km / 5.5 mi
Go left to Cedar Lake at the junction. The ski area is to the right.

10.8 km / 6.7 mi
Go left at the junction and take an immediate right at the fork.

11.3 km / 7 mi
Arrive at Cedar Lake campground.

~

HWY 95: GOLDEN TO INVERMERE

MITTEN LAKE RECREATION SITE #33
Weekend / Moderate
About 12 campsites with tables, boat launch

Good views of the Purcell Mountains await you at this popular, medium-size lake.Wild roses sprinkle the site in June. The water is warm enough in summer for pleasant swimming. Many campsites have at least partial views of the lake.

On Hwy 95, drive 34 kms / 21 miles south of Golden, or 40.5 kms / 25 miles north of Brisco, to the town of Parson.

Mitten Lake and the Purcell Mountains, Columbia River Valley

0 km / 0 mi
In Parson, turn off Hwy 95, onto the signed Spillamacheen FS Road. Stay straight on the main road. Steel yourself for a long drive through scruffy forest without views; the destination is worth it.

7 km / 4.4 mi
Make a sharp hairpin turn left and see the sign: Mitten L Rd.

7.2 km / 4.5 mi
Go left. Right leads to Mountain Mineral Mining. Travel on a fairly smooth surface, through a logged area. This road could be slick in rain.

15 km / 9.4 mi
Go left for Mitten Lake at the junction.

If you go right here, before the marshy area, you'll come to **Bittern Lake Recreation Site #34** in about 1 km / .6 mile. Ideal for a small group, it offers a tiny lake, shade trees, a dock, and one table.

18 km / 11.2 mi
Drive past a marshy area.

18.2 km / 11.3 mi
An **overnight pullout** on your right faces the lake and mountains.

18.3 km / 11.4 mi
Arrive at the first Mitten Lake campsite, with one table. Go just past it to find two tables in trees.

18.8 km / 11.7 mi
Stay right at this junction to go around the side of the lake.

19.5 km / 12.1 mi
Come to two tables, a dock, and an easy boat launch. Most of the campsites are a bit farther around the lake.

~

PURCELL MOUNTAINS

BUGABOO CREEK RECREATION SITE #28
Destination / Difficult (because it's a long way)
4 campsites by a creek, near a trailhead to the
spectacular Bugaboo Mountains

The sky-piercing spires of the Bugaboo Mountains are part of the Purcells — a much older range than the Rockies. For the best views, be sure to hike to the Conrad Kain Hut from the trailhead parking lot, or to Cobalt Lake from near the C.M.H. Lodge. Both hikes are about 5 kms one way. You're in grizzly country here. Don't invite bears into your camp. Take all the necessary precautions.

Just beyond the campground is a trailhead for Chalis Creek. You can hike 5 km one-way up to the alpine and views of the Bugs. For details, pick up a brochure at the FS office in Invermere. Continue up the road and see a minor junction flagged. You'll be on the southeast side of the creek. It's wrong on the brochure. You don't have to cross the creek, as the map shows.

The logging road has a very steep, rough section at about 5 kms going in. Then it levels out and isn't bad. It's just a long drive: 45 kms one way.

The first two times we visited the park to hike, we didn't know there was a campground nearby. We slept in our car at the trailhead parking lot, where climbers often pitch their tents. If you park here to go on an overnight hike, remember that marauding porcupines have been known to munch car tires, engine hoses and fan belts. To prevent this, look for the chicken wire that might still be left in the lot and use it to make a fence around your car. We've also heard scattering moth balls under and around your car might keep the rascals away.

If you're heading south from Golden

From the junction of Hwys 1 & 95, drive south on Hwy 95 for 77.3 kms / 48 miles to the town of Brisco. Set your tripometer to 0.

If you're heading north from Radium

From the junction of Hwys 93 & 95, drive north on Hwy 95 for 28 kms / 17.4 miles to the town of Brisco. Set your tripometer to 0.

For either approach above, now follow the directions below

0 km / 0 mi
Turn west off Hwy 95, following the sign to Bugaboo Provincial Park. Drive toward the mill, then turn right along the railroad tracks.

3.5 km / 2.2 mi
Turn right, at the junction that has a brown sign: Bugaboo 45 km.

5 km / 3.1 mi
Go left at the junction where there's a trail information sign. The road is very rough for 1.5 kms / .9 mile and has a steep, narrow ascent. Take it easy. Where the road tops out, you'll see a sign: 42 km Bugaboos. Then the road is much better.

6.5 km / 4 mi
At this junction, take the Bugaboos main road, to the right.

41 km / 25.5 mi
Near the Recreation Area boundary, instead of turning right to the parking lot for the Conrad Kain Hut trailhead, turn left and drive across Bugaboo Creek. Drive one kilometer farther, to a brown post indicating a left turn. Go another few hundred meters. Then go left again to the Bugaboo Creek FS campground.

~

STOCKDALE CREEK RECREATION SITE #12
Weekend / Difficult (because it's a long way)
A little-used campground on the creek, split into two parts

This pleasant campground can be used as a base camp to get an early start hiking into the incredible Lake of the Hanging Glacier — a premier sight in the Purcell Mountains. Wait until mid-July for avalanche danger to subside. The road's end trailhead is 45 km / 28 miles from Invermere; 39 km / 24 miles from Radium Hot Springs. Allow 1.5 hours for the drive.

If you're near Invermere

Turn off Hwy 93/95 at the signs for Invermere. Proceed 3.0 km / 1.8 miles into town.

0 km / 0 mi
On the north side of town, at the bridge over the Columbia River, go northwest on the road signed Panorama-Wilmer.

2.0 km / 1.2 mi
Immediately after crossing Toby Creek, turn right, toward Wilmer. You're now on Westside Road, which at this point is paved. It becomes Water Street near Wilmer.

4.7 km / 3.0 mi
Go right, onto Main Avenue.

5.2 km / 3.2 mi
Bear left onto the dirt FS Road.

16.0 km / 10.0 mi
At the four-way junction, turn left (west) onto Horsethief Creek FS Road. Right leads 10.5 km / 6.5 miles northeast to Radium. Straight leads to several **FS campgrounds at the Cartwright Lakes**, near KM 51.

20.3 km / 12.6 mi
Stay left, passing Forster FS Road forking right. Continue west on Horsethief Road. At **30.0 km / 18.0 miles** cross to the south side of the creek.

Near 42 km / 26 mi
Stay right, passing a side road going left (south) up McDonald Creek.

Near 45 km / 28 mi
Look for Stockdale Creek campground, on your right, near the KM 38 signpost.

If you're near Radium Hot Springs

0 km / 0 mile
From the junction of Hwys 93 & 95, near the entrance to Kootenay National Park, drive west onto Forsters Landing Road.

1.4 km / 0.9 mi
Reach a junction just before the Slocan Group mill. Set your tripometer

to 0 again here, so it will be in sync with the KM signposts.

0 km / 0 mi
At the turn left (west) onto Horsethief Creek FS Road. Soon cross railroad tracks, then the Columbia River.

3.0 km / 1.8 mi
Stay left on the main road, at the junction with Steamboat Mountain Road. Ignore all forks until the next major junction.

9.2 km / 5.7 mi
Reach a well-signed, major junction and a KM 9 signpost. Continue straight on Horsethief Creek Road, signed for Hanging Glacier. Left goes southeast to Invermere, on the Westside Road. Right leads northwest to several **FS campgrounds at the Cartwright Lakes,** near KM 51.

23 km / 14 mi
Cross to the south side of the creek. **Near 35 km / 22 miles**, stay right, passing a side road going left (south) up McDonald Creek.

Near 38 km / 23.5 mi
Look for Stockdale campground, near the KM 38 signpost.

~

ROCKY MOUNTAINS & KOOTENAY RIVER

These campgrounds, on the rushing, glacial waters of the Kootenay River, are just south of Kootenay National Park. The water's energetic play provides dramatic, musical entertainment. The Kootenay is a favorite with rafters and tour companies. It's the best canoeing river in the region for a multi-day trip. There are Class II and III rapids.

You're in grizzly country here. Don't invite bears into your camp. Take all the necessary precautions.

We don't include specific directions for long backroads east toward the Rockies. The access is usually too rough and tedious, and the clearcuts too plentiful. It's better to spend your time in the national parks. Of course, if you live near the parks, you might want to find new terrain to play in. In the Kootenay River area, we offer general directions to get you started.

It's worth paying to camp in the Rocky Mountain National Parks, even if you have to be with more people. Here you're in the heart of a mighty mountain range, as awesome as any in the world. Your contribution will help preserve these great sanctuaries. It's like an offering to support your place of worship. We find the Rockies more spiritually powerful than any man-made structure. If you want to see them at their best, get off the highway, get out of your car, and hike. Buy a copy of our book, *Don't Waste Your Time in the Canadian Rockies*. It's an opinionated hiking guide to help you make the most of this magnificent wilderness. In addition to giving full route descriptions, it rates and reviews over 90 hikes in Banff, Jasper, Yoho, Kootenay and Waterton national parks. If you can't find it in a store, send $16 CDN ($14 US) to Voice in the Wilderness Press, P.O. Box 71, Riondel, B.C. V0B 2B0 Canada.

Just outside Kootenay National Park, at Radium Hot Springs

If you're heading south through Kootenay National Park

At the south end of the park, near where Hwy 93 starts turning southwest, look for McLeod Meadows Campground on your left. Drive 8 km / 5 miles past McLeod, then turn left (southeast) onto signed Settlers Road, which is dirt. It's before the highway starts ascending. Set your tripometer to 0.

If you're heading northeast from Radium Hot Springs

From Kootenay National Park's south-entrance toll booth and office, drive 19 km / 11.8 miles northeast through the park on Hwy 93. At the bottom of the hill, turn right (southeast) onto signed Settlers Road, which is dirt. Set your tripometer to 0.

For either approach above, now follow the directions below

0 km / 0 mi

Turning onto Settlers Road. Though dirt, the road is smooth, broad, flat. Easy to drive even at night. It's an active logging road, however, so be cautious. You won't see the surrounding mountains while driving through this tunnel of trees.

12.0 km / 7.4 mi

Leave Kootenay National Park.

12.6 km / 7.8 mi

At the junction, stay straight (right) on the Kootenay-Settlers Road to continue south to the Horseshoe Rapids campground.

Horseshoe Rapids on the Kootenay River, Rocky Mountains

You can also go left at this junction, onto the Kootenay—Palliser Road, to reach Riverbend campground and the Palliser and Albert River roads. For directions, skip below the Horseshoe Rapids description.

18.0 km / 11.0 mi

Drive through meadows and a stand of aspen.

19.3 km / 12.0 mi

Pass a spur road on the left. It leads into a big meadow — a possible overnight pullout. Keep it in mind in case your vehicle is unable to negotiate the final descent to Horseshoe Rapids or the tiny campground there is full.

19.6 km / 12.2 mi
Turn left and descend on a small, rough road signed for Horseshoe
Rapids. It's immediately after a gully with a creek (in a culvert under the
road), and just before Bear Creek road ascends right. Dropping to
Horseshoe, beware of a long, deep depression at 0.5 km / 0.3 mile. If it's
filled with water, check it out before proceeding the final 0.3 km / 0.2
mile down to the river.

HORSESHOE RAPIDS RECREATION SITE #50
Destination / Moderate
2 tables, flat space for a tent on the point

This campground is on the Kootenay River, at the rapids for which it's
named. It has a lonely, isolated feeling. Kayakers and rafters sometimes
use it for a put-in or take-out.

*The following directions describe the Kootenay—Palliser Road, on the west side of
the river, from the 12.6 km / 7.8 mile junction mentioned above.*

0 km / 0 mi
Turning onto Kootenay—Palliser Road. Stay left on the main road in
100 meters.

1.5 km / 0.9 mi
After crossing the Kootenay River on a wooden bridge, turn left to
Riverbend Campground. It's on private property. As of this writing
there's no fee, but free camping privileges could be revoked at any time.
Be sure to keep the area clean and put your campfire totally out. Though
the site is near the road, there's usually little traffic. Kayakers and rafters
sometimes use it for a put-in or take-out.

2.2 km / 1.5 mi
From the signed fork, the Cross River FS Road leads left to the Natural
Bridge Cross-Country Ski area and hiking trails. Go right (south) if you're
heading to the Palliser River.

If you continue along the east side of the Kootenay River, south to the
Palliser River, you can explore more deep mountain valleys. Drive south
on the Palliser Road for about 15 km / 9.3 miles. It's rough compared to
the west side road. You'll reach a bridge leading to the south side of the
Palliser River. Then turn left (east). In about 3 km / 2 miles, you'll arrive
at the large, open **Albert-Palliser Recreation Site #52**. There's
another junction soon after. If you go left (north) here, you'll cross to the
north side of the Palliser, where a road parallels the Albert River.

You can follow the Albert River road northeast, beneath the Royal Group
mountains, to a trailhead at road's end. Here you can walk a few kilo-

meters to exquisite Leman Lake. If you've ever hiked to Burstall Pass from the Alberta side, you've looked way down at Leman Lake. Clearcuts along the road have regrown nicely.

~

HWY 93: FAIRMONT HOT SPRINGS TO ELKO

These campgrounds are in dry country. The Purcells catch most of the moisture passing through. So expect hot temperatures in summer, and a good chance for clear skies.

FINDLAY CREEK RECREATION SITE #6
and WHITETAIL LAKE RECREATION SITE #8
Weekend / Moderate
Findlay Creek really isn't worth the drive, but you might think Whitetail Lake is. The road is terribly rocky and bumpy.

From the Kootenay River bridge at **Canal Flats**, drive 5 km / 3 miles northwest on Hwy 93/95. Or, from the big sign at the entrance to **Fairmount Hot Springs**, drive south just over 21 km / 13 miles. From either approach, turn west off Hwy 93, at the sign BLUE LAKE FOREST CENTRE.

0 km / 0 mi
Turning west off Hwy 93. After 0.8 km / 0.5 mile on pavement, proceed on Findlay Creek FS Road.

2.2 km / 1.4 mi
Continue straight, passing a left fork.

4.8 km / 3.0 mi
The short trail to Findlay Falls is on your left. It's possible to camp in this **overnight pullout** overlooking the creek.

5.7 km / 3.5 mi
Stay straight, toward Whitetail Lake. (Skookumchuck FS Road is on the left.)

11.4 km / 7 mi
For Whitetail Lake, continue 1.6 km / 1 mile on the main road from this junction. Then turn right, heading northwest for about 10 km / 6.2 miles. **For Findlay Creek**, go left at this junction. In 400 meters, the camp-ground is visible across the creek. **Near 13.3 km / 8.2 miles**, cross the bridge and go left. Drive the smaller, rough road about 1.5 km / 1 mile back to the sites.

~

JOHNSON LAKE RECREATION SITE #2
Overnight / Easy
2 campgrounds on a pretty lake, warm-water swimming in summer

If you're heading south on Hwy 93

From the Kootenay River bridge at Canal Flats, drive nearly 23 km / 14 miles to the signposted turnoff. Turn right (west).

If you're heading north on Hwy 93

From the Kootenay River bridge just south of Skookumchuck, between Canal Flats and Wasa, drive 5.7 km / 3.5 miles to the signposted turnoff. Turn left (west).

For either approach above, now follow the directions below

Drive in 50 meters to a signpost. The south end of the lake is left; the north end right. It's 0.5 km / 0.3 mile to the south-end campground. For the reedier (but less popular) north end campground, continue right 0.8 km / 0.5 mile, then turn sharply left and drive 100 meters down to a couple campsites.

~

TAMARACK RECREATION SITE #1
AND LARCHWOOD LAKES RECREATION SITE #3
Weekend / Easy

Both sites are pretty, but the mountain view at Tamarack is better. The twisty road to Tamarack gets tedious, but it's an easy, rolly ride—good for mountain biking.

If you're heading south on Hwy 93/95

From the Kootenay River bridge just south of Skookumchuck, between Canal Flats and Wasa, drive 1.1 km / 0.7 mile to the turnoff. Turn right (west) onto Farstad Way. The pulp mill is also this way.

If you're heading north on Hwy 93/95

From the junction of Hwys 95A and 93/95, northeast of Kimberley, drive 11.4 km / 7 miles. Turn left (west) onto Farstad Way.

Horseshoe Lake and the Rocky Mountains

For either approach above, now follow the directions below

0 km / 0 mile
At the turnoff. The road is initially paved. Near the 2 KM signpost, turn left on Torrent Road for Tamarack and Larchwood lakes.

2.6 km / 1.6 mi
Bear right on the main road and cross railroad tracks. At 3 km / 1.8 miles, cross the creek again and recross the tracks. The road becomes smooth gravel.

4.6 km / 2.9 mi
Reach a junction. Go left for Tamarack. *The directions for the right turn to Larchwood are described below.*

4.9 km / 3.0 mi
Bear left. At **7.4 km / 4.6 miles**, fork right at the sign.

8.4 km / 5.2 mi
Arrive at Tamarack Lake. It has 2 tables, 3 sites.

Back at the 4.6-km / 2.9-mi junction, head right for Larchwood Lake.
8.0 km / 5.0 mi from the highway, bear left and go uphill on the main road.

9.0 km / 5.5 mi
Arrive at Larchwood. The campsites are spaced well apart. The lake is 200 meters beyond.

~

HORSESHOE LAKE RECREATION SITE #45
Destination / Easy
12 tables

This campground has a lot to offer. The lake is in a spectacular setting at the base of the steeply rising Rocky Mountains. The dirt roads around the lake make a great mountain biking course. The pleasant, aspen-and-pine forest creates a relaxing atmosphere. There's a rigorous trail heading up into the Steeples, and several other less ambitious trails in the area. Contact the Cranbrook Forest Office for a *Steeples Area Trails Map*. The Steeples trailhead is about 2 kms south of Horseshoe Lake.

Drive this backroad beside the Steeples, as an alternative to the main Hwy 3/93. You can make an excellent road-cycling loop by using this eastside road in combination with Hwy 3/ 93.

Remember, you're in grizzly country. Don't invite bears into your camp. Take all the necessary precautions.

If you're heading south from the junction of Hwys 93/95 and 3/93

Look for the turn one kilometer north of Fort Steele. Follow the sign toward Norbury Lake Provincial Park.

0 km / 0 mi
Turn left (southeast) on Wardner—Ft. Steele Road to travel the east side of the Kootenay River.

0.6 km / 0.4 mi
Pass an **overnight pullout** on the west side of the Wildhorse River. It's about 20 meters in on the dirt road. Back on the main road at **1.4 km / 0.9 mile**, there's an **overnight pullout** beside the Kootenay River.

11.5 km / 7.1 mi
Look closely on your left for a small sign marking the turnoff to Horseshoe Lake.

If you're heading north toward Fort Steele

Drive Hwy 3/93 about 11 km / 7 miles northwest of Jaffray. Just before crossing the bridge over the Kootenay River, turn right onto the signed Wardner—Ft Steele Road. Set your tripometer to 0.

0 km / 0 mi
At the turn onto the Wardner—Ft Steele Road. There's a sign here for Norbury Lake Provincial Park. You'll pass the park in 15 km / 9 miles. Continue on pavement along the east side of the river.

19 km / 11.8 mi
Look closely on your right for a small sign marking the turnoff to Horseshoe Lake.

For either approach above, now follow the directions below

In 300 meters, reach a fork. Campsites are 0.5 km / 0.3 mile in either direction. Right leads around the far (east) side of Horseshoe Lake. Turning left, you'll be able to see the rugged Rockies from across the lake. If you go left, stay left on the upper road to proceed around the lake. High water floods the lower road.

~

WAPITI RECREATION SITE #25
Weekend / Easy
A big, grassy meadow, 5 tables on the east side of the lake

The scenery isn't dramatic, but it's a peaceful, pastoral spot. If you're looking for quiet, away from the busy Rocky Mountain National Park campgrounds, here it is. And if you've explored the national parks a lot, this is a good destination for a few days. Roam the hills. Play music under the trees. Count water lilies. Nap in the shade.

If you're heading east on Hwy 3/93

From the junction of Hwys 95/93 and 3/93 between Cranbrook and Ft. Steele, it's 26 km / 16 miles to the Kootenay River bridge, just southeast of Wardner. From there, go uphill, continue south for 5.6 km / 3.5 miles, then turn right (south) onto paved Rosicky Road.

Wapiti Lake, southeast of Cranbrook

If you're heading west

From the junction of Hwy 3/93 and the Jaffray-Baynes Lake Road (in Jaffray), continue 6 km / 3.7 miles on Hwy 3/93, then turn left (south) onto paved Rosicky Road.

For either approach above, now follow the directions below

0 km / 0 mi
At the turn onto Rosicky Road.

0.4 km / 0.25 mi
Turn sharply left at the ranch, onto dirt Shelbourne Road.

1.5 km / 0.9 mi
Turn right at the signpost. In another 100 meters, stay left and continue downhill.

2.2 km / 1.4 mi
Arrive at Wapiti Lake. **At 2.8 km / 1.7 miles**, you reach the campground.

NORTH STAR LAKE RECREATION SITE #26
Weekend / Easy
9 tables

Summer heat, horseflies and dust diminish the pleasure of sitting beneath ponderosa pines and gazing at distant mountains. The campsites are a bit too close together.

From the community of Jaffray (on Hwy 3/93, between Ft. Steele and Cranbrook) drive paved Jaffray-Baynes Lake Road south.

0 km / 0 mi
Turning onto Jaffray-Baynes Lake Road.

4.7 km / 2.9 mi
Turn left onto the signposted dirt road.

6.5 km / 4 mi
Arrive at North Star Lake campground.

KIKOMUN CREEK RECREATION SITE #30
Weekend / Easy
5 well-spaced tables

This campground, surrounded by meadows and sparse forest, stretches along a healthy creek.

On Hwy 3/93, between Ft. Steele and Fernie

The turnoff is 2 km / 1.2 miles west of the junction of Hwys 3 & 93, near Elko. Turn southwest onto Kikomun-Newgate Road and set your tripometer to 0.

0 km / 0 mi
Turning onto Kikomun-Newgate Road.

5.0 km / 3.0 mi
Turn right onto the signposted dirt road. Bear left at the two forks.

7.0 km / 4.3 mi
Arrive at the campground.

~

ROCK CREEK RECREATION SITE #29
Weekend / Easy
Large campground in an open meadow beside a creek

Space for 3 campsites on the edge of a meadow ringed by trees. The approach road is probably too narrow and overgrown for motorhomes.

If you're heading east between Cranbrook and Fernie

From the lumber mill at Galloway, just southeast of Jaffray, drive 7 km / 4.2 miles to the turnoff.

If you're heading west between Fernie and Cranbrook

From the junction of Hwys 3 & 93, just west of Elko, drive 5.5 km / 3.4 miles to the turnoff.

For either approach above, follow the directions below

0 km / 0 mi
Turn west off Hwy 3/93 onto Rock Lake Road. The surface is good gravel. Rock Lake Camp, which you'll see signs for, is not the free FS campground.

1.6 km / 1 mi
Where the main road curves right to the pay campground, bear left onto—of course—the narrow, rough, potholed road.

3.7 km / 2.3 mi
At the 4-way junction, turn right. Soon pass through beautiful meadows.

4.2 km / 2.6 mi
Pass roads forking right and left. Proceed straight, downhill through forest.

4.6 km / 2.9 mi
Turn left on the unsigned spur road. The campground is 100 meters ahead, on a slow creek.

4.9 km / 3.0 mi
Reach an **overnight pullout** in a meadow. The area offers other possible campsites as well.

~

ELK VALLEY

6 campgrounds and many overnight pullouts,
along a 70-km stretch from Elkford to Elk Lakes Park

Drive on Hwy 3 to the town of Sparwood, near the Alberta border. Take Hwy 43 north to Elkford, where a smooth, gravel road leads you through a pretty Rocky Mountain valley to spectacular Elk Lakes Park. It's near the provincial border, just south of Peter Lougheed Park and the Kananaskis Lakes in Alberta. The hike into Petain Glacier is wonderful. Allow a full day to explore the valley and cirque. Even if you only hike along the lakes, you'll get great views of peaks and alpine slopes.

The many FS campgrounds in this beautiful valley are along the Elk River. Three are close together, at the north end. The farthest up is **Upper Elk River Recreation Site #1**, in an open area on the river, 3.5 kms / 2.2 miles from the provincial park. At **Tobermorey Creek Recreation Site #2**, also at the upper end, there's a cabin beside the road that's available for camping: first come, first served. It'll be hard to get after September 1, when hunting season starts. You can camp at the parking lot at road's end, but it's not developed as a campground. The lot is under power lines. If you walk an easy, level, twenty minutes into the park, you'll find tent sites.

You're in grizzly country. Don't invite bears into your camp. Take all the necessary precautions. If you walk in to pitch your tent, be sure to hang your food in a tree.

Home

Universe is home for earth.
Air is home for wind.
Tree is home for bird.
Meadow is home for flower.
Dirt is home for seed.
Water is home for whale.
Mind is home for idea.
Fire is home for warmth.
Tent is home for camper.
Earth is home for all.

Forest District Office Addresses and Phone Numbers

Direct your questions about camping to the Recreation Specialist, unless you're simply requesting a district map. If you're calling from Vancouver, dial the local Inquiry B.C. number: 660-2421. For other areas in B.C., dial 1-800-663-7867. State the forest district office you want them to connect you with and give them the number. That way there's no charge to you.

VANCOUVER FOREST REGION
ph: (250) 751-7001
2100 Labieux Road
Nanaimo, BC V9T 6E9

Campbell River Forest District
ph: (250) 286-9300
370 Dogwood Street South
Campbell River, BC V9W 6Y7

Chilliwack Forest District
ph: (604) 794-2100
Box 159, 9850 S. McGrath Road
Rosedale, BC V0X 1X0

Duncan Forest District
ph: (250) 746-2700
5785 Duncan Street
Duncan, BC V9L 5G2

Port Alberni Forest District
ph: (250) 724-9205
4227 6th Avenue
Port Alberni, BC V9Y 4N1

Port McNeill Forest District
ph: (250) 956-5000
Box 7000, 2291 Mine Road Place
Port McNeill, BC V0N 2R0

Squamish Forest District
ph: (604) 898-2100
42000 Loggers Lane
Squamish, BC V0N 3G0

Sunshine Coast Forest District
ph: (604) 485-0700
7077 Duncan Street
Powell River, BC V8A 1W1

KAMLOOPS FOREST REGION
ph: (250) 828-4131
515 Columbia Street
Kamloops, BC V2C 2T7

Kamloops Forest District
ph: (250) 371-6500
1255 Dalhousie Drive
Kamloops, BC V2C 5Z5

Lillooet Forest District
ph: (250) 256-1200
650 Industrial Place, Bag 700
Lillooet, BC V0K 1V0

Merritt Forest District
ph: (250) 378-8400
Bag 4400, Hwy 5A Airport Rd
Merritt, BC V0K 2B0

Penticton Forest District
ph: (250) 490-2200
Bag 700, 102 Industrial Place
Penticton, BC V2A 7C8

Salmon Arm Forest District
ph: (250) 832-1401
Bag 100, 2780 10th Avenue NE
Salmon Arm, BC V1E 4S4

Vernon Forest District
ph: (250) 558-1700
2501 14th Avenue
Vernon, BC V1T 8Z1

NELSON FOREST REGION
ph: (250) 354-6200
518 Lake Street
Nelson, BC V1L 4C6

Arrow Forest District
ph: (250) 365-8600
845 Columbia Avenue
Castlegar, BC V1N 1H3

Boundary Forest District
ph: (250) 442-5411
Box 2650, 136 Sagamore Avenue
Grand Forks, BC V0H 1H0

Cranbrook Forest District
ph: (250) 426-1700
1902 Theatre Road
Cranbrook, BC V1C 4H4

Golden Forest District
ph: (250) 344-7500
Box 1380, 600 - 9th Street North
Golden, BC V0A 1H0

Invermere Forest District
ph: (250) 342-4200
Box 189, 625 4th Street
Invermere, BC V0A 1K0

Kootenay Lake Forest District
ph: (250) 825-1100
R.R. #1 Ridgewood Road
Nelson, BC V1L 5P4

Revelstoke Forest District
ph: (250) 837-7611
Box 9158, RPO #3
1761 Big Eddy Road
Revelstoke, BC V0E 2S0

BC Parks

BC Parks has produced superb regional maps, which show many of the major gravel roads and all the provincial park campgrounds. The following maps can be useful in conjunction with this book: Vancouver Island, Lower Mainland, Cariboo-Shuswap-Okanagan, Kootenays.

These maps are available free-of-charge at most Tourist Info Centres, in towns and cities throughout B.C. If you want to get one before you travel, contact BC Parks. For the Vancouver District, call (604) 924-2200, or write 1610 Mount Seymour Road, North Vancouver, B.C. V7G 1L3. For the headquarters office, call (250) 387-5002, fax (250) 387-5757, or write 2nd Floor - 800 Johnson Street, Victoria B.C. V8V 1X4. Remember to ask Inquiry B.C. to connect you: in Vancouver, 660-2421; for other areas in B.C., 1-800-663-7867.

If BC Parks discontinues printing regional maps, use the British Columbia Road Map and Parks Guide for general orientation. BC Parks will mail you one. So will Discover BC: (604) 663-6000 within Vancouver, 1-800-663-6000 throughout North America, (604) 387-1642 from overseas.

Born to Camp

Kathy and Craig have free-camped all their lives. While she was still a baby in diapers, Kathy's parents took her camping most weekends. Her earliest memories are of her mother cooking dinner under a tarp draped from the back of the family's pickup while her father listened to the rain. As a boy, Craig was obsessed with fly fishing. He backpacked to remote trout streams, until he realized the joy of hiking and camping is an end in itself and all that fishing gear was just slowing him down. Together, Kathy and Craig have perfected the art of free-camping. Their camping adventures have taken them throughout North America, Europe, Australia and New Zealand. They've driven all kinds of vehicles to all kinds of places in all kinds of weather. It hasn't always been idyllic.

One time, they pitched their tent at midnight on the grounds of an English country manor. They were hitchhiking. Unable to afford a hotel, they had only two choices. A fenced, tussocky paddock crowded with cattle? Or the manor lawn? They knocked at the imposing door to ask permission, but nobody appeared. So they set their travel alarm for 5:30 a.m. The next morning, they packed quickly, left unseen, and walked three kilometers to Stonehenge. They watched it emerge from the fog at sunrise, before anyone else arrived.

Asleep under the stars beside a creek near Payson, Arizona, they were startled by a gang of Hell's Angels in the middle of the night. The bikers roared in, only a few feet from the Copelands' heads, but otherwise weren't a problem. Until morning. After the bikers took off, Craig discovered they'd dumped one of their buddies. He was bleeding and out cold.

Again in Europe, they were exploring the Cairngorm Mountains of northern Scotland. This time they were driving Freida — a rusty, old, Bedford Beagle they'd bought for $93 US. As always, they wanted to camp free. A sign on a dirt road caught their eye: Forestry Personnel Only. They risked it, but couldn't find even a tiny pullout. So they started turning around, backed into a ditch and became hopelessly mired. "Guess this is where we say goodbye to Freida," Craig said. But before they could load their backpacks and start hiking, a forestry official drove up in his truck. After a light rebuke, he towed them out. Feeling lucky, the Copelands splurged that night and paid for a campsite at the national park.

On the Oregon side of the Columbia River Gorge is the Eagle Creek Trail, which the Copelands had just finished hiking. It was so late they decided to camp in their car at the trailhead, but later wished they hadn't. A light directly over their heads woke them up. Another hiker? A policeman? A thief? A murderer? They laid there wondering, zipped into their sleeping bags, stuffed into the back of their car, their hearts pounding with adrenalin. "He's going to break into the car," Kathy whispered. Craig roared like a bear. They saw the flashlight bob away into the night. It was probably a teenage burglar, but they didn't wait to find out. They raced onto the highway and, still dazed, approached the bridge over the Columbia. With Kathy still in her bag and Craig in his underwear, they presented an interesting site to the matron in the toll booth. They eventually fell asleep, parked on a residential street in North Bonneville, Washington.

Now you can understand why Kathy and Craig are thrilled to live in British Columbia. They say it offers the easiest, most enjoyable, most abundant free camping of anyplace they've ever traveled.

Other books from Voice in the Wilderness Press

Look for these and other guidebooks by the Copelands in outdoor shops and book stores. You can also order them by sending a cheque to Voice in the Wilderness Press, P.O. Box 71, Riondel, B.C. V0B 2B0 Canada. If you order more than one book, deduct the following amount from the total cost: $3 CDN for shipments within Canada, $4 US to the States. Allow 2-3 weeks for delivery in Canada, 3-4 weeks in the U.S.

The Don't Waste Your Time® *hiking guidebook series rates and reviews trails to help people get the most from these magnificent wilderness areas. Includes shoulder-season trips for more hiking opportunities.*

Don't Waste Your Time®
   in the BC Coast Mountains......................................$17 CDN $15 US
      ISBN 0-9698016-3-7   1997 edition, 288 pages
72 hikes in southwest BC. Includes Vancouver's North Shore mountains, Garibaldi Provincial Park, and the Whistler-Pemberton region.

Don't Waste Your Time®
   in the Canadian Rockies..$16 CDN $14 US
      ISBN 0-9698016-0-2   1998 edition, 224 pages
Over 90 hikes in Banff, Jasper, Kootenay, Yoho and Waterton national parks, plus Mt. Robson and Mt. Assiniboine provincial parks.

Don't Waste Your Time®
   in the North Cascades.. $20 CDN $17 US
      ISBN 0-89997-182-2   1996 edition, 364 pages
110 hikes in southern BC and northern Washington. Includes North Cascades National Park, and Mt. Baker and Glacier Peak wilderness areas, plus BC's Manning and Cathedral parks.